"Those who forget the past
are destined to reelect it."

Brent Nelson Ph. D.

CAPITOL HILLARY

SEX, MONEY, POWER.

THE CLINTON-IZATION OF AMERICAN POLITICS

IN
THE 1992 PRESIDENTIAL CAMPAIGN

BRENT NELSON PH. D.

HH

Heather Hill

Table of Contents

Chapter 4

Chapter 5

Chapter 6

Chapter 7

Chapter 8

Chapter 9

Chapter 10

Chapter 11

Chapter 12

.

Preface

The 1992 campaign could be called a tale of two campaigns. It was the best of campaigns, it was the worst of campaigns.

This was arguably the most significant presidential election campaign in modern history. The purpose of this book is to examine how an obscure governor from a small, politically negligible state with no national experience or notoriety defeated the most popular incumbent in history.

What the Clintons accomplished was quite remarkable. They did not have politically notable names and did not come from wealth, a political family, or a politically powerful state like the Roosevelts, the Bushes, or the Kennedys.

This book explains not only the process by which the election was won and lost, but also how and why this process works. It is a process that can be utilized by practically any candidate running for virtually any office in order to win.

This campaign exemplifies what to do and what not to do. It has had an important affect on election campaigns to this day. So, candidates and their campaign staff could use this case study as a playbook for success.

This book chronicles what transpired as the 1992 presidential election campaign unfolded, and its implications for the nation.

Since then, a lot has happened.

The world has undergone turmoil and transformation. Terrorism, globalization, climate change, and the proliferation of the internet to name just a few. The world has changed, technology has changed, times have changed, people have changed, and the country has changed.

So, why does this campaign matter now?

It matters because of the divisiveness and gridlock that are so prevalent in American politics today.

It matters because our nation is facing a high degree of uncertainty about the future.

It matters because the never ending campaign has replaced governing, keeping the level of uncertainty and tension high inhibiting growth and prosperity.

It matters because the economy remains for many mired in recession with declining incomes, increasing costs, the loss of personal net worth, and the lack of well paying jobs.

It matters because the US economy is very likely to slip from the largest, most dynamic in the world to become number two.

It matters because increasing government involvement in people's lives is eroding our freedoms at an alarming rate.

It matters because we face unprecedented threats from abroad and there is a very high likelihood of the US fighting another war.

It matters because this campaign gets at the core of what we might expect from future presidential campaigns and what to expect from future presidents.

It matters because we have become fixated on labels. We want to elect a conservative, liberal, Democrat, Republican, minority, woman, and so on as president. Shouldn't we be more concerned with electing someone competent? Someone who can solve the problems the nation is facing.

It matters because those who forget the past are destined to reelect it. And people all too often get the government they deserve.

The first time we heard all of this it was new, so there was no way of knowing how things would turn out. Now, we can benefit from the passage of time. We know what happened after Election Day. The good and bad. The successes and scandals. So, lets go back to 1992 to look at what the Clintons said and did. Then we can ask, did they do what they said they would do?

Will anyone remember what happened in the 1992 presidential campaign? There is a new generation of voters who were not even born, let alone know what happened back then.

Over twenty years after we were first introduced to Bill and Hillary, we are facing the prospect of history repeating itself. This book recalls their introduction to national politics to remind us.

Because, how quickly we forget.

Chapter 1
The Revolution Begins

A new day was about to dawn.

The revolution was at hand.

It would be the beginning of a new era. An era that would shape the destiny of a nation and in doing so would change the world forever.

As the sun began to break through the warm overcast day, on the west steps of a great nation's capitol, a new leader looked out to the future and took the first step to a new tomorrow. In his Inaugural Address, Ronald Wilson Reagan sought to return the nation to the values set forth by its founders and set a new course for a nation that would come to be known as the Reagan Revolution.

In his address, Reagan set the tone for his eight years in office and defined the nature of the revolution he would begin that day in Washington. Calling for a new beginning to renew ourselves and the nation, people must be put back to work, the economy must be restored, taxes must be made fair, and we must stop mortgaging our children's future.

The solution to the nation's problems rested on the foundation of this revolution that was based on the idea that, "Government was not the solution to our problem, government is the problem." The solution rested with every day heroes like farmers, factory workers, and doctors all of whom embodied the ideals of the American Dream, "To begin an era of national renewal."

Reagan had succeeded to do what the last two presidential administrations failed to do, he had restored the notion of the transcendence of the spirit back into the American Dream and created out of those images a unity in rhetoric, if not in reality. It is this ideal that epitomized a transcendence of the national spirit that lay in its people, not institutions. As Reagan told the assembled crowd, "We must realize that no arsenal or no weapon in the arsenals of the world is so formidable as the will and moral courage of free men and women."

Looking out over the magnificent vistas from the west side of the Capitol, Reagan saw the memorials to Washington, Jefferson, and Lincoln. Reagan bound everyday heroes into the history of the American saga by evoking the memories of the Founding Fathers who established an ideal of government that we must strive to restore for all the people.

In order to legitimize his transcendence from candidate to president, Reagan completed the circle of the American saga by invoking both Washington and Lincoln, the two most admired presidents in the political pantheon. In a most dramatic manner, Reagan recalled the sacrifices of those who served their country calling for the nation to work together and for people to believe in themselves as united together we could do great deeds in order to solve the problems we faced.

As decisive as Reagan's victory may have been, months before Election Day it had not seemed to be nearly as certain. Early in the campaign former President Gerald Ford, rumored to enter the race, was preferred by half the Republicans and Reagan held only about a quarter of the potential votes. Incumbent President Carter faced strong opposition from within his own party from Senator Ted Kennedy. And they all faced a third party challenge from John Anderson, a Republican Congressman from Illinois who ran with former Democratic Wisconsin Governor Patrick Lucey, for the Unity Party.

Having lost the Republican nomination twice, once in 1968, again in 1976, and at this, his third try in 1980, Reagan lost his first primary contest in Iowa to George Bush prompting speculation that Reagan was unable to make a comeback. Reagan had not run in any election in a decade and his age and health became a concern because at 69 years old he would be the oldest president ever elected.

Ultimately, the Reagan victory was called a landslide, cutting into traditional Democratic strongholds such as in the South leading to the coining of a new term, "Reagan Democrats." The change carried into Congress where the Senate turned Republican and the House became more conservative causing a change in the leadership of key committees.

It was the beginning of a new era. Reagan's landslide victory and sweeping Republican gains in Congress would produce a new conservatism in American politics that would come to mark a change in the political ideology of the nation for over a decade. It would come to be called the Reagan Revolution.

Eight years later.

For the first time since Martin Van Buren, a sitting vice president was about to be inaugurated as a newly elected president. In 1988, the newly elected president was faced with the problem of following a popular and charismatic member of his own party into the White House. Having served as Ronald Reagan's vice president for the last eight years, George Bush was left with the duty, at least in part, to continue the Reagan Revolution.

Given the ideological distance between Reagan's campaign and the Carter Presidency, Reagan could easily and skillfully define his administration as leading the vanguard to reclaim the government from its own bureaucracy and return it to the people. Bush, on the other hand, was obliged to stay the course.

As George Bush took the oath of office, the ghosts of the Reagan years hung deeply around the occasion. One of the nagging questions hanging over Bush was whether or not the nation would see a new George Bush or an imitation of the Reagan Administration. Bush inaugurated a gentle rebellion, bringing a softer, more humanitarian face to the revolution by calling for the people, "to make kinder the face of the nation and gentler the face of the world."

By the time of the 1988 GOP convention, Bush was already beginning to move towards establishing a different agenda and set of policies than the Reagan administration. In his acceptance speech at the convention, Bush ventured as far as saying, "I do not hate government," although he qualified the statement with, "A government that remembers that the people are its masters is a good and needed thing." This view stood in contrast to Reagan's assertion in his first inaugural address that, "Government is not the solution to our problem, government is the problem." Bush's background of eastern moderate views and a long tradition of family involvement in government service stood in sharp contrast to the conservative rugged western outsider persona of Reagan.

In his desire to associate himself with the legacy of the Reagan administration, while simultaneously forging a separate identity, Bush occasionally contradicted his own vision. He was striving to highlight the government's success, but he also showed where it had fallen short. He alluded to a new era where the United States has been perfected, yet still falls short of perfection with problems that had yet to be solved. These two voices clash in Bush's Inaugural Address. On the one hand, Bush spoke of a restored America, a refreshed nation ready to push on. Yet, on the other hand, he evoked those elements that prevented a full restoration from taking place.

Despite eight years of Republican administration and a long period of economic growth, the Republicans were a minority party in both the Senate and House. Despite earlier successes that characterized the first Reagan administration, when Republicans held control of the Senate and a landslide victory in 1984, Reagan had experienced increasing opposition from Congress. So, as president, Bush would now find it necessary to make concessions, but the question was what concessions would need to be made and how would they happen? This quandary was indicative of the position Bush's administration ultimately found itself in, remaining committed to the past administration, but having to deal with the same problems.

So, on Inauguration Day, on the front steps of the United States Capitol, George Bush characterized himself as standing on "democracy's front porch" in an effort to convey his vision of a good, just, and kind government. The success of the past served as a foundation for the future a "nation refreshed by freedom" standing ready to push on where a "new breeze is blowing." It was a kinder, gentler revolution. And yet...

The revolution saw monumental change take place in unprecedented events. Double digit inflation was reduced to a memory. The Berlin Wall would fall, giving way to German unification. People all over Eastern Europe would reject Communism and free themselves from the shackles of tyranny in populist revolts. As the biggest threat to world stability and security quietly vanished into the history books, the Soviet Union, who we once called the evil empire, we would now call, our friends. The Cold War was over, and people the world over who yearned for freedom had won.

The United States would lead a coalition of nations from around the globe to defeat the world's fourth largest army to stop blatant aggression and a euphoric nation would make George Bush the most popular president in history. Once again the revolution was there, refreshed and renewed. But something was wrong. Events would soon change dramatically. A new breeze would again blow.

The revolution was about to come crashing down, marking its end.

As in all revolutions, especially ones of a political nature, there are those who ride the tide of victory and those who suffer in the shallows of defeat. The stunning success of the Reagan Revolution in 1980 was blamed for the defeat of a promising political star in The South.

A thousand miles away, the promise of youth suffered an untimely demise. A career of public service, that held the future prospect of national office, which had barely begun, was abruptly cut short in a staggering defeat that attracted little notice. As a new president was inaugurated ushering in a new era full of promise, an obscure governor in Arkansas suffered an untimely defeat after serving only one term in office. As one door had opened, another had closed.

In a twist of irony that never could have been imagined this man from Arkansas, who had suffered such a crushing defeat, would win back his office and rise to topple the revolution. A dozen years later, it would be that very man who had been swept out of the governor's office by the Reagan Revolution that would bring it to an abrupt end.

A new day was about to dawn bringing with it a new beginning. The old order would pass and the world would once again be changed. A man of little national note or experience in foreign affairs, plagued by scandal leaving his campaign for dead, would push forward against inestimable odds,

To defeat the most dynamic presidential legacy in modern history.

Chapter 2
Legitimizing The Right To Govern

One of the most challenging problems in any governmental system is establishing the right to rule. In ancient times, rulers claimed descendancy from the gods or ruled by divine right. Over time, the method of establishing the right to rule has changed, however, the need for leaders and governments to prove their ability to lead has changed little.

As kings and courts gave way to presidents and parliaments, the people had a more direct influence in the choice of their government through the elective process. This established the notion of a government's claim to rule by popular mandate as being conferred directly by the people.

As civilization developed and changed, so did the nature of government rule. Few governments today refer to supernatural forces to support the political order, however, the fundamental principle remains the same. There is a process of legitimating political power in which a government and its leaders are invested with the right to rule, or govern society. The absence of a clear mandate to lead can create confusion or even anarchy.

The consequence of this problem can be manifested in the overthrow of political regimes through military coups or populist movements. No less significant are the gains and losses of political influence by leaders in democratic governments that can affect their ability to govern. In this respect, the problem of political legitimation is more one of persuasive negotiation than a test of power or military might.

Legitimation of Political Power.

The 1992 presidential election left Republicans wondering what went wrong and Democrats wondering what went right. An obscure, little known governor of a small state defeated the most popular president in history. Examining traditional defining elements of elections such as a candidate's character, fitness for office, experience, campaign issues, approval ratings, and scandals seemed to add little insight into what transpired.

However, these elements may not determine a candidate's electoral viability, but instead the result may be due to the underlying persuasive characterization of these elements. The key factor in explaining what turned the 1992 presidential election may lie in how these characterizations were shared with the public to create a larger social reality.

This book examines the campaigns of the three major candidates for president; Republican incumbent President George H. W. Bush, Democratic challenger Arkansas Governor Bill Clinton, and independent candidate Texas businessman H. Ross Perot. It examines the campaign from their announcement to run for office through the primaries, the conventions, the debates, to Election Day.

This book examines the issues raised by the candidates and how they characterized them to the public. It utilizes scholarly research for the purpose of reporting, commentary, analysis, and criticism to create new insights into public discourse. The material utilized herein came from the candidates, their campaign organizations, polls, and the media including speeches, advance texts, transcripts, press releases, campaign literature, books, television, news conferences, and appearances. This material was selected for its representativeness of the campaign.

The legitimation of political power to establish an administration's right to govern can be characterized as the process by which a government and its leaders are invested with power by the members of a society. The relationship between a society and its leaders is constantly changing. These changes are based on the rules that are agreed upon by all concerned. Since governments are not entities unto themselves, but rather are joint ventures comprised of individuals, both the government and individual leaders can be subject to this process gaining or losing legitimacy concurrently or separately.

A leader or administration is rarely perceived as having an absolute right to govern or having no right to govern at all. Instead, there is some intermediate degree of rightness and support inherent in each institution. For instance, Congress can suffer the loss of esteem while that of individual members can remain high. The degree to which a leader is deemed to be legitimate to govern is determined by the number of citizens who accept the rule of the government. Even after winning election to office, a president can suffer a loss of legitimacy that hampers their ability to govern or move legislation through Congress.

A government and its leaders have the ability, through use of political rhetoric to convince, condition, or alter the perceptions of the people as to their appropriateness to govern. The degree of legitimacy in a government and its leaders can be seen as a function of their ability to foster the people's faith in a regime. The ability of a government to gain the people's support involves ongoing communication between a government's leaders and the people regarding the validation of mutual goals and needs based on reaffirming a shared set of values.

In the United States, two political parties vie for the right to govern through popular election. In such a system this regular change of power, while having become routine, presents subtle problems in the establishment of a candidate's legitimate right to govern. The adversarial nature of the American political system is likely to express itself in the subsequent loss of influence of the party that loses power and a significant increase in influence of the party that gains power.

In the democratic context, the process of legitimation is not the claim of divine right nor is it an exercise in coercive force by those in power. Accordingly, determinants of political legitimacy in a democracy are accomplished rhetorically. An election campaign can be seen as a series of persuasive rhetorical attempts by both sides to undermine their opponent's legitimacy and their right to govern while bolstering their own. In order to make their claim for office, candidates often draw upon forces recognized by the electorate. These forces can include traditions, values, beliefs, and mandates from the people.

Creating a Public Persona.

Before entering the race for office, a candidate often gives extensive thought to the creation of their public persona. This is a process in which candidates may reflect on the past while planning for the future, occasionally bordering on soul searching. The development of this persona can include their justifications as to why they want to run, what they want to accomplish, and what programs they would enact once in office. This process can include developing messages that they will communicate to the public in order to explain who they are and what they stand for as a candidate. This persona is developed for public consumption even if it diverges from the private personality of the candidate and who they are.

Candidates and their advisors may spend months or years developing a candidate's public persona in preparation for a campaign, as was likely the case with Clinton's campaign. A candidate's persona can be developed in the public eye, shaped by public opinion, and shared in the media over years of public service, as was the case with Bush. A candidate's persona may develop spontaneously in public while being honed behind the scenes, evolving during the unfolding of the campaign, as seems to have been the case with Perot.

Whatever the case, a candidate will spend much time forging their public persona to be better able to share meaning with the public to motivate the voters to elect them to office. A candidate's public persona may differ or overlap their own actual personality. During this development period, a candidate's campaign team will likely discuss strategy, evaluate issues, analyze poll data, and study current events, while also anticipating future developments. So, a candidate's campaign team develops a public persona for their candidate that reflects their own dramatic narratives. Their characterization of the candidate is one that a campaign team develops to engage the voting public to share their version of social reality.

During these meetings they may share their own meanings within the group developing their own group culture, which can become a part of the candidate's overall campaign. At this time, a specialized version of social reality may develop within the campaign team. In this process, their public version of social reality may emerge. It is the development of a specialized social reality that can tell people who the candidate is, what the candidate stands for, and where the candidate fits into the course of history.

Since most candidates have a public persona created by their campaign organizations, the rhetoric of the candidates is recognized to consist not only of their personal positions and ideas, but also those generated by their campaign staff. As the degree of authorship of material referenced herein may not be known, and because much of the campaign planning and implementation is a group effort, the sources of material often come from a candidate's campaign team.

In some cases, sources other than the candidates are employed to make or support statements generated by the campaign team in the creation of a public persona. During a campaign, the campaign team utilizes a number of people to deliver their message. In some cases, other speakers are deemed a better source of information than the candidate themselves. These other sources include the vice presidential candidates, the candidates' wives, members of the candidates' party, members of the candidates' family, friends, acquaintances, and ordinary people.

The Nature of Uncertainty.

Life is chaotic. Things can happen unexpectedly or for no apparent reason. We want to know why things happen to us, so we look for explanations. We want to know what to expect from other people, so we try to understand their motivations. We want to know what will happen in the future, so we can make plans. All these things create uncertainty.

Politics and government can be a source of public uncertainty. We want to know what to expect from our leaders. We want to know how the government will affect our lives, now and in the future. We want to know so that we can make plans for the future. When there is a low degree of uncertainty it creates stability, which gives us a feeling of security. When we don't know what to expect, there can be a high degree of uncertainty creating apprehension and tension.

It can be beneficial to measure the degree of public uncertainty in many areas, such as with an uncertainty index, because it has the power to motivate people's behavior. When people experience something unfamiliar to them it can create tension making them uncomfortable, which can motivate them to take action to reduce it. This tension is often resolved through the construction of a social reality driven by the characterizations of real life events and experiences. For instance, people want to know why the economy is bad and when it will improve, so they look for explanations. And they often look to politicians for those answers.

Many presidents and political leaders reduce uncertainty about themselves and their policies by creating their own specialized version of social reality that not only explains their programs, but also includes a vision of what society should become. For instance, Franklin Roosevelt had the New Deal, which created a vision of a renewed America being led out of the depression. These visions can be composed of dramatic narratives that also includes heroes and villains, along with their actions that can be characterized as good or bad.

The Nature of Shared Meaning.

When people communicate, they talk about themselves often telling stories about their past experiences. When they do, they might edit these stories to make them more interesting and exciting to the listener. When people understand and can relate to these stories they share meaning. They have the same understanding of what they mean and possibly share their own stories about similar experiences. This can create a connection, so they feel that they have something in common. This can make people seem more likable, even creating feelings of empathy. Candidates create stories about themselves and their experiences to share meaning with the voters in a similar way. They do this to make themselves appear more personable and likeable to motivate people to vote for them.

The process of sharing meaning deals with the human tendency to want to understand the motivation for people's behavior to reduce uncertainty about them. Shared meaning is how a person makes a connection with other people, so that they see things in a similar way. This is how a candidate gains and maintains people's support. Shared meaning can help to recall familiar stories for those who share them. If a specific story has not been shared, it would not make sense and the entire story would have to be explained. So, when Clinton used the shared meaning of 'read my lips' in the campaign, he did not have to retell the entire story of Bush raising taxes. Similarly, Bush's shared meaning of 'tax and spend' was designed to trigger negative characterizations about Clinton and the Democrats.

In this book, poll data was utilized in new and creative ways to determine the effectiveness of how the candidates had shared meaning with the voters. In evaluating shared meanings, several poll measures were utilized throughout the campaign. One measure was the president's approval rating, which measured the percentage of the people who approved or disapproved of how Bush was doing his job as president. Other poll measures consisted of each candidate's favorability and unfavorability ratings. Potential voters were asked if they had a favorable or unfavorable opinion of Bush, Clinton, and Perot, resulting in a percentage of the people who viewed each candidate as favorable and unfavorable. This poll data can also be used as a measure of a candidate's legitimacy and public perception of their right to govern.

In another poll measure, the public was asked if the election was held to-day, which candidate; Bush, Clinton, or Perot, would they most likely vote for as president. Voters were then asked if their support was either strong or weak. Specific issues were also measured to determine how important the public viewed them as well as how well the public felt each of the candidates would handle them. The extent that public opinion reflects a candidate's characterization of their persona or events would provide an indication of how well the voters were sharing meaning with their dramatic narratives and a particular version of social reality. How the media reported and interpreted events was also examined to see how each candidate's view of social reality was being shared by them and the general public.

The Nature of Dramatic Narratives.

When people come together they often tell stories, but instead of giving an accounting of events, they may characterize and embellish what transpired. When people tell stories that have meaning to other people, they may join in and share their own similar experiences. These stories can be emotional and might motivate people to take action. This process can take place in a group as well as through mediated messages such as a public speech or television program.

People share meaning by using dramatic narratives. When people share dramatic narratives, they have the same understanding of events and common ground is created. Much of how we frame our experiences and understand reality is communicated through dramatic narratives. Dramatic narratives consist of a story or the retelling of certain events. They often have an emotional quality to make them more interesting or exciting. They are usually created to have a desired effect on people like informing, entertaining, or persuading them.

Dramatic narratives characterize events from a particular point of view. They are invested with meaning by the people who create and share them. Dramatic narratives can characterize an event or person by investing them with meaning to make sense out of previously confusing or chaotic circumstances. Dramatic narratives can characterize people and their behaviors as acceptable or not. This can create the perception of heroes and villains who exhibit behaviors that are good or evil, which tells people how to act and what values are important.

Examining dramatic narratives provides a way to understand the shared meanings embedded in what a person says, as well as their underlying motives. Shared meanings tell us about our culture, what we value, what we believe, and who we are. Political campaigns are a persuasive form of communication that can be considered analogous to drama because they focus on actors who play roles and act out scenes, which includes casting specific individuals as heroes and villains. So, dramatic narratives could be considered a specialized form of communication.

It could be said that literary forms fall into two basic categories, fact and fiction. So, there is the inherent assumption that if someone is not telling the truth, they are lying. If fact comprises those things that are verifiably true and fiction is an imaginative creation developed through invention that does not represent actual reality, then political candidates may do neither. Instead, they may take an inherent reality, like the economy or health care, choose a few pertinent items and then present their own version that carries an emotional and persuasive quality. This persuasive strategy falls between fact and fiction into the realm of dramatic narratives. This approach serves to explain real world events by giving them a shared meaning that makes a connection with the public to create and maintain their version of social reality. Much of how social reality is constructed happens through dramatic narratives.

The Nature of Social Reality.

Over time, many dramatic narratives can form a recognizable and meaningful view of society that creates social reality. The power of social reality lies in its ability to explain our experiences and the world around us. It can be used to explain the motivation for people's behavior. The sharing of social reality is a way of creating a common understanding of the world and how it works. The shared meaning imbedded in dramatic narratives can create a social reality for people. Even though it may or may not accurately reflect actual physical reality, it may be no less real for them.

Social reality is created because people want to reduce uncertainty. They want to know about the world around them and social reality can be used to explain and predict physical reality. People want to know why the economy is bad and when things will get better. In election campaigns, people want to know what they can expect from their government and what the government expects from them. These issues are often explained through social reality. This means that social reality can be as important to society as physical reality because much of human interaction and social institutions are socially constructed.

Social reality is attractive because it can explain seemingly chaotic events by telling people what is happening to them and how they fit into the grand scheme of things. The use of social reality derives from the human need to reduce uncertainty by explaining events to make sense of them. It can also facilitate public confidence in a government by reducing uncertainty about it. People often prefer a reality they have created themselves because it is more comfortable when made up of familiar elements of their own design.

Social reality can be powerful because it tells people how to interpret physical reality. It tells them how to communicate with other people. It tells them what behaviors are accepted and which ones are not. It is a comprehensive explanation of how things work in society. As people begin to exchange ideas they share dramatic narratives and a collective social reality begins to form that communicates who they are and what they are about.

When people begin to recognize themselves as part of a group, a more specialized version of social reality with its own boundaries is developed that serves to define the group and its members. These boundaries set out who are members and who are not, how one becomes a member, and establishes group traditions or rituals. There are many examples of specialized forms of social reality, such as those found in politics, religion, and culture. These specialized versions of social reality often fit into a larger societal social reality. Social reality can be restrictive as it can be a means of social control by influencing or motivating people's behavior, however, it also serves to provide stability without which society could not function.

A specialized version of social reality provides a way for those who share it to interpret actual physical reality to determine what it means for them. This meaning may be interpreted differently by different groups depending on their past experiences and previously shared meanings. In the political realm, there are many of these groups such as conservatives, liberals, Democrats, Republicans, Independents, and moderates. This book is not intended to advance a particular type of political discourse, policy, or ideology. It is intended as scholarly research for educational and critical analysis of the effectiveness of the use of dramatic narratives to share meaning to create and sustain social reality.

Groups seek not only to establish their own identity, but they also seek to gain new members to convert to their movement and to share their specialized version of social reality. The use of public speeches and the media can communicate a group's particular view of social reality to large audiences. This can create a larger community and motivate people to take action.

Many political, religious, and social groups have sought to further their causes by moving larger groups of people to action through the creation of shared meaning. Through the use of dramatic narratives, these meanings can be shared by larger groups. Many of these persuasive techniques are firmly embedded in a larger societal social reality. They have been handed down over many generations and so are often recalled and employed by politicians. Candidates develop their own specialized version of social reality in order to share meaning with the voters. This shared meaning can be developed by the candidate and their campaign team over time or it can be created spontaneously in the media and with the public.

The campaign team, as well as the candidate, will share their own meanings when they communicate dramatic narratives about themselves, the opposition, the voters, and the campaign. This creates a group culture that can determine their electoral success or failure. They might create a culture that is open to new information and ideas, including listening to the people. Conversely, they can become closed off, even becoming arrogant having an attitude that they know what they are doing. People who have different ideas or try to help them might be castigated as a nuisance and ignored or met with hostility. This type of culture is likely to end in defeat because it reduces the ability to bring in new ideas that can serve to share meaning with the voters.

In order to share their version of social reality, politicians must attract people to share them. Some people are predisposed to them, however, others share a different version of social reality. When people have a different social reality, they must first be separated from their attachments to the version they currently share. Their current shared meanings are often attacked as repugnant, bigoted, or outdated, so that they can be shown how wrong or misguided they really are. When their old social reality is attacked, a person may feel lost, angry, disturbed, or upset. They may also feel a sense of uncertainty about their beliefs or an attraction to new ones as they are now looking for a new version of social reality.

Once people are persuaded that their old beliefs are wrong, they may experience a period of self searching or struggle between the old and new realities. After a period of time, they may come to a new awareness when the new social reality falls into place, so they now see things in a new way. When the conversion process ends, they may feel relieved that their conflict is resolved. They may be asked to show their commitment to the new social reality with some kind of public action such as voting, giving money, or volunteering for a candidate.

Once a political version of social reality has emerged and attracted followers, there is the problem of maintaining their commitment. Some groups are able to keep their social reality stable over long periods of time, while others suffer from decline and decay, or may abruptly come to an end. The process of keeping a group together is accomplished through ongoing shared meaning. This serves to keep the people who share the vision committed by maintaining their adherence to it as well as to bring back those who have fallen away.

People who have fallen away might be criticized and pressured to conform to the new social reality. This can be accomplished by comparing an individual's undesirable behavior and bad character to the ideals contained in the new social reality. The objective is to encourage recognition of their shortcomings, followed by repentance and a renewed commitment to the new social reality. This process can help to bring those who lose the vision back in line to conform to the demands of the new version of social reality.

How widely a candidate's social reality is shared can be reflected in their own dramatic narratives. One method of observing how well they are shared is though repetition of a particular story. During the course of a campaign, candidates try to reflect on how their messages are being received by the voters. When one catches on with the public, it tends to be repeated and when they do not catch on with the public, they are more likely to be dropped. No single speech or television ad is likely to sway the outcome of a campaign. It is the consistent weaving together of many forms of political discourse utilizing familiar dramatic narratives that share meaning with the voters that determines electoral success.

Social reality has a larger, more important function, it can affect who we are as an individual and what kind of person we want to be. It can determine who we are as a people and what kind of nation we want to be. It can inspire people to fight for a cause and for what they feel is right. Our government and social institutions were at one time only an idea shared by people sometime in the past. It was their vision of what society should be that shaped the world we live in today. It is the shared meanings we have today that will determine what kind of world future generations will live in tomorrow.

Social reality is important because no one ever carried a banner for a balance sheet. No one ever marched for a government report. No one ever died for a survey.

Chapter 3
The Campaign Gets Underway

This chapter examines how each of the three major candidates developed their respective versions of social reality at the onset of the 1992 presidential campaign. It serves to illustrate the development and structure of each candidate's social reality in comparison to how it changed as the campaign progressed.

As the election season drew near, the candidates began to develop their public persona and the dramatic narratives they would employ. Each of the three candidates approached their campaign in different ways to establish their political legitimacy, with varying degrees of success.

Clinton Takes On Washington.

The political challenges that faced Clinton at the beginning of the election were legion. As the governor of a small state, he had little or no national name recognition. He would be facing an incumbent president who had amassed the highest approval rating of a postwar president. In announcing his candidacy, he entered what would become a pack of Democratic contenders that the media referred to as the B squad, as there appeared to be a general unwillingness on the part of leading Democrats to enter the race. If the Democratic Party lost the election with unseasoned candidates because more experienced candidates were reluctant to enter the race, the party could be seriously weakened. (Washington Post, January 2, 1992)

Therefore, Clinton needed to forge his own mandate and create a national identity by distinguishing himself from the other candidates in his party and from the current president. With Clinton being relatively unknown nationally at the beginning of the campaign, he had the advantage of not having a well known national persona to influence the public's perception of him. This gave him wide leeway to craft a new public persona of himself that would appeal to as wide an audience as possible. So, Clinton needed to create a message that would not only hold traditional Democratic supporters, but one that would also convert enough voters to defeat the Republican version of social reality that had won the last three presidential elections.

Clinton's version of social reality must be as broad and attractive as possible in order to gain enough votes to win. He must craft several dramatic narratives to support his version of social reality and then communicate them clearly to the people. These narratives describe familiar villains and heroes, and the qualities that make their actions good or bad. The people must know their role in these narratives and what is expected of them. In this process, Clinton needed not only to decide how he should characterize himself, but also how, in what situations, and how often he would deliver these messages. He also needed to decide what media to use for additional messages, what form those messages would take, and who would deliver them.

Early in the campaign, Clinton communicated a unified version of social reality consisting of various dramatic narratives. These dramatic narratives served as the basis for the messages that were targeted to various segments of the electorate. His dramatic narratives appealed to those who were dissatisfied with present circumstances and wanted change. Also targeted were those who shared the older traditional Democratic social reality to provide him a base of support. This strategy alone would not be enough to win as demonstrated in past elections, so he would have to attack and replace Republican dramatic narratives with new Clinton narratives in order to draw in moderate, independent, and Republican voters.

In order to attract converts, Clinton employed the process of shared meaning with voters who might be open to Clinton's version of social reality by castigating familiar Republican dramatic narratives as repugnant. After shaking loose familiar Republican narratives, he searched for ways to get his new dramatic narratives to share meaning with the public. In order to do this, Clinton would need to attack Bush's high foreign policy ratings while exploiting Bush's declining approval ratings and the public's growing concerns over the state of the economy.

The Clinton Version of Social Reality.

To meet the challenges of the election, Clinton created a unified social reality over the course of the campaign that shared meaning with the voting public. Various portions of this social reality would be utilized at different times for specific audiences. This analysis provides an overview of how Clinton created his version of social reality comprised of dramatic narratives that were shared with the public at the beginning of the campaign and as it unfolded.

Clinton's version of social reality characterized the nation as being devastated by the present government in Washington. He characterized it as coming apart at the seams, deteriorating, and in serious decline. The people were hurting and the government was mired in gridlock. A great nation, once respected abroad, had become the laughing stock of the world. Present conditions were characterized as intolerable and the people were suffering. These problems were presented as the legacy of twelve years of neglect and failed economic policies of trickle down that did not trickle.

The scene in Washington was characterized as villainous by Clinton. This situation had been caused by an administration that was out of touch with the people and unable to solve their problems. Many opportunities had emerged that were missed and not acted upon by the current president. The government was characterized as full of elected officials who had forgotten the people who had sent them there. The people in Washington were characterized as privileged, out of touch, self serving, and morally repugnant to the commonly shared values of the people. The American Dream, which was built on hard work, had been destroyed by a government that made people work harder for less while rewarding speculation, privilege, and special interests.

Clinton's version of social reality connected Bush to the problems in Washington and characterized him as having no program to solve the people's problems because he did not even understand what the problems were himself. Bush was dishonest because he broke his no new taxes pledge and raised taxes without telling the people. Clinton characterized Bush as having no plan for the country because he lacked leadership ability.

The country needed a new leader with a new approach to solve its economic problems because Bush's past policies had failed. Clinton characterized a nation with a deteriorated industrial base, a poor educational system, and a sluggish economy. We could not compete in a global market without an industrial base and skilled workers. Clinton connected foreign policy to domestic policy because in order to succeed abroad the country must be strong at home.

In contrast to the negative characterization of Washington, Clinton presented a positive and hopeful image of Arkansas under his leadership. Arkansas was characterized as an island of hope and a laboratory of democracy that was now under siege, having to hold out against the evils of Washington. Clinton cast himself as the hero who would bring hope to America because he was born in Hope, Arkansas and grew up in a working class neighborhood in a small town. Hope was a special place, an idyllic community, and the embodiment of small town Americana. Clinton used Hope as a model for his vision of an America full of the kind, honest, and hard working people that he was in the race to help.

Growing up in humble beginnings in a small town had made Clinton the personification of the American Dream. As part of his dramatic narrative, he sought to support and protect the American Dream to give it back to the people. He would not stand by and let the next generation be the first to be worse off than their parents. As a young man he met then President John F. Kennedy at the White House. After that experience he wanted to help the people of Arkansas and knew that he would enter a life in government. This meeting with Kennedy was documented in a photograph of them together. During the campaign, this photo was characterized as a symbolic passing of the torch between generations anointing Clinton as the heir of the Kennedy legacy. For Clinton, this was the defining moment in his life, when his future destiny in public service was forged.

Clinton said that by restoring the values of the past, the future could be better. He characterized a scene of a future with a country united, with new opportunity where people took pride and responsibility in their family, schools, and communities. Clinton could provide the leadership needed to solve problems and inspire the hope of achieving a better tomorrow.

As a new breed of politician and an agent of change, Clinton distanced himself from typical Democratic policies of tax and spend by characterizing himself as a new type of Democrat. According to Clinton, change was not only to alter the direction of the country through a new administration, it was also a change in ideology. He was a hard working and thoughtful leader who was concerned about the people and could get things done. Being endorsed by Nobel Prize winners, economists, business leaders, and Republicans helped him to make the case that he could help the nation.

The people and Clinton must act together to reclaim their government by restoring the bond between the people and their government. He would return the government to the people based on the traditions and values that comprised the foundation of society. This created a version of social reality Clinton called "The New Covenant." He would use this term to define the role of government, while restoring a sense of commitment to the future and to future generations. According to Clinton, The New Covenant was a solemn agreement between him and the people founded on the sacred principles that had been lost and that he would restore. In order to restore this bond, there must be a change in government as the present state of affairs was unacceptable.

Clinton was cast as the hero who when elected would make the people his priority. In this dramatic narrative good, decent, and hard working people had been abandoned by their government. Clinton would restore fairness and economic equality to reward people who worked hard and played by the rules. It was not right that people had been forced to keep less for themselves under the Bush Presidency. He was a leader who knew their troubles and problems first hand because he shared their hopes and dreams. Clinton characterized his campaign as a crusade to put people first and restore the forgotten middle class, in order to build a new economic order of empowerment and opportunity.

Clinton Announces His Candidacy.

On October 3, 1991, in front of the Old State House in Little Rock, Arkansas the standing governor announced to a gathered crowd of supporters his intention to run for president of the United States of America. He made his announcement in a place of significance that illustrated who he was and what he stood for. By announcing his candidacy well before the primary elections, he would start his campaign early to give him time to gain much needed name recognition.

In his announcement speech, Clinton began to outline the dramatic narratives of his campaign that were designed to cause widespread sharing of his new social reality with the public. His version of social reality, referred to as The New Covenant, was about facilitating change to fix the problems in Washington and to restore the American Dream to the people. His announcement speech was significant because it began the transformation of a governor into a presidential candidate and set the tone for his campaign.

In his announcement, Clinton was cast as the hero of the people. He characterized himself as a public servant who was now going to, "step beyond a life and a job I love, to make a commitment to a larger cause." (Clinton, Announcement) In this dramatic narrative Clinton, who was cast as the hero, was following a path of public service by sacrificing his welfare for the greater good of the people. He often referred to his many years of public service as governor, which implied popular support and the continued approval of his constituency, who were the people that knew him best.

Referring to the work accomplished in Arkansas, he bound himself and the people together as one to move forward and make things better for all. He alluded to the traditional values of "work, faith, family, individual responsibility, and community," which they had preserved. These were values that he claimed were presently under attack from all around him. (Clinton, Announcement)

In order to motivate the people to take action, Clinton characterized himself as sharing the people's values and beliefs that were being threatened by the Bush administration that was afraid to change with the rest of the world. Clinton described the people as experiencing the loss of the American Dream. He predicted the next generation would be the first one to be worse off than the previous one. He said, we now find "everything we believe in, everything we've fought for, is threatened by an administration that refuses to take care of our own, has turned its back on the middle class, and is afraid to change while the world is changing." (Clinton, Announcement)

Clinton contrasted how the ideal state of Arkansas had prospered under his leadership as an island of hope surrounded by a nation in despair. Employing military metaphors he set up a battle like dramatic narrative with the idealistic community of Arkansas characterized as being under siege by the evil federal government, with the current administration as the villain.

Clinton's speech sought to undermine Bush's legitimacy when he referred to Republicans who had tried to divide the country by telling people that America's problems weren't the Republican's problems. While the other party had avoided taking any responsibility, Clinton would be the one to provide the solutions.

The government had abandoned its own people, so now the people, with Clinton's leadership, must move to reclaim their government if the nation was to move forward and solve the problems it faced. He then moved beyond the inclusion of the people of Arkansas and included all Americans, referring to them as 'us' and the Republicans in Washington as 'them.'

Clinton went further towards describing present conditions in which the country had lost its way and was rapidly headed in the wrong direction. He described the paralysis in Washington. The government had no plan or vision for the future. There was only neglect, selfishness, and division. In his characterization of

Washington he described those who grew rich through speculation and exploited the government at the workers' and taxpayers' expense.

These people who exploited others were another set of villains in Clinton's speech. They had been sanctioned by the Republicans in Washington who turned a blind eye to these events because they no longer cared for the people who elected them. According to Clinton, those at the top had sold out the people by supporting an ethic of "get it while you can and the heck with everybody else." Clinton tried to counter a widely shared Bush dramatic narrative when he said, a thousand points of light leaves a lot of darkness. (Clinton, Announcement)

Clinton's announcement sought to establish his legitimacy on the national scene when he equated his administration in Arkansas with popular past Presidents Truman, Roosevelt, and Kennedy because they had stood up for what was right, so he would too. Clinton would protect America from greed in a way that the Bush administration had failed to do.

Clinton characterized the foreign policy of the Bush Administration in a less direct way. He equated the death of communism with the loss of the American Dream. The Soviet Union was a great nation that fell not from outside forces, but rather from trouble within. The implication was that events around the world were unimportant when we did not look after our own people at home. To undermine one of Bush's strengths, Clinton claimed that a safe and secure world could not be obtained unless America could first be strong at home.

Another way Clinton characterized the differences between himself and Bush was to describe a classroom where children were afraid of gangs beating them up, afraid of being shot, and were facing problems from drugs. He contrasted these current conditions with his own childhood, growing up in Hope where he was "raised to believe in the American dream, in family values, in individual responsibility, and in the obligation of government to help people who were doing the best they could." (Clinton, Announcement)

This contrast represented the difference between his values of the American Dream and the consequences of Bush and the Republican leadership. It was a choice between a present situation that was the result of twelve years of neglect and a future in which government supported hardworking middle class families by restoring the values of the past.

In presenting his initial version of social reality, Clinton utilized many dramatic narratives to reach the voters. As an unknown candidate, he needed to build a following through the use of shared meaning to make a connection with the voters. So, he created a version of social reality casting Bush and the Republicans in the role of villains who had hurt the people and the country, This approach was designed to share meaning with the public to gain their support by convincing Bush supporters to vote for him.

Clinton's task was to create a new version of social reality with himself as the person who, with the people's help, would change government to restore the American Dream. This was necessary if he was to gain converts to his candidacy. Clinton sought to share meaning with the people by using the words 'us' or 'we,' to bind him with the people so they would take action.

From the beginning, Clinton sought to undermine Bush's legitimacy by characterizing Bush as the people's opponent. His purpose was to firmly establish his own candidacy as a superior alternative to Bush. Of all the candidates, Clinton started out with the strongest message suggesting it was developed months, perhaps years before his announcement. He came the closest to creating a unified version of social reality that connected with the people through shared meanings by using dramatic narratives about himself and Bush.

Shortly after his announcement, Clinton moved quickly to begin campaigning to gain support for his candidacy. He connected himself with the people who elected him in Arkansas to establish his legitimacy and create a dramatic narrative of prosperity with himself as the hero. This dramatic narrative was essential to Clinton's legitimacy because it degraded the audience's perception of present reality by attacking the government and economic conditions in the country, with the exception of himself and his state.

During the campaign, Clinton would deploy a wide repertoire of dramatic narratives about unemployment, the economy, and the people in Washington. If he could create the widespread perception that almost everyone was suffering, except those in Arkansas, he could undermine Bush's legitimacy while depicting himself as a more competent and caring leader.

Clinton utilized a version of social reality that was well developed in advance of his announcement to run. His initial message consisted of several dramatic narratives that tied into familiar traditions and communal values. They were remarkably consistent and wavered little as the campaign progressed. This helped him to gain converts by using repetition of these initial campaign narratives to create a feeling of stability and familiarity as the campaign wore on.

Bush Creates Uncertainty.

In contrast to Clinton, the dramatic narratives disseminated by the Bush campaign lacked direction and coherence. He did not characterize a clear and attractive version of social reality. Even Bush himself was conspicuous by his absence in the campaign. This lack of a unified social reality is explained to some extent because Bush had a tendency of avoiding the use of dramatic narratives to inspire or even inform the public.

Rather than embracing the Reagan version of social reality, Bush seemed reluctant to utilize familiar dramatic narratives needed to maintain it. As president,

Bush seemed to distance himself from the inherited legacy of Reagan by redefining the Republican ideology for America from a strong defense and a less governmental approach, to a kinder, gentler view of America. In doing so, Bush did not maintain the Reagan version of social reality and many of the dramatic narratives used so successfully by Reagan, while failing to replace them with any meaningful ones of his own. Perhaps, people voted for Bush in 1988 expecting a third Reagan term, but by the time Bush ran for reelection in 1992 they realized this was not what they got.

As president, Bush rarely explained what he did or why he did it. There were very good reasons for going back on his infamous read my lips statement, but he never bothered to explain them in any coherent manner. The tax compromise helped the economy and only took effect during his last few months in office. It would be Clinton who would be the beneficiary of the deal and get the credit for the economic growth that followed.

In his initial campaign messages, Bush characterized recent world events such as successes in foreign policy rather than any bold domestic programs. Successes abroad had helped to make the world safer, so he could concentrate on the domestic agenda. However, he said that there were still dangers and new challenges around the world that we must be ready to meet. Calls for isolationism and claims that foreign policy was not important must be resisted. The nation must stay engaged and strong abroad, while meeting changing demands at home.

Bush recalled the accomplishments of the past in order to confront the challenges of the future that faced the nation. Bush described an inseparable link between foreign and domestic policy, in which engagement abroad created growth and stability at home. The experiences and resources gained from foreign policy successes abroad could now be used to solve domestic problems. Bush characterized America as being well positioned to open free markets and create jobs, while fighting off the villains of special interests and protectionists.

The villains in Bush's dramatic narratives were members of Congress who did not operate in a fiscally responsible way. They had an incentive to tax and spend because it gave them power and influence. Bush characterized the opposition as looking only at America's problems and exploiting the people by telling them America was a nation in decline with its best days past. The American Dream was under attack by a villainous government that destroyed individual freedoms. Fundamental American values were being eroded by big government and tax and spend liberals like Clinton who destroyed individual freedom and raised taxes.

Bush characterized the difference between the two parties as a cultural divide between fighting for what was right and refusing to see what was wrong. He also created a dramatic narrative of America's future in which decisions would be made by the people, not government. For Bush, the election would be a turning point by entering a new era with a new Congress that would be elected that year.

Alluding to dramatic narratives of restoration, he wanted to get back to the work he started twelve years ago. Bush characterized himself as the agent of real change, the kind of change that mattered with a return to traditional values. His agenda was a plan for transition from the old ways to the future through shared values and renewal at home by empowering people instead of government.

Bush Announces His Candidacy.

On February 12, 1992, the anniversary of Abraham Lincoln's birthday, in the ballroom of the J. R. Marriott Hotel in Washington, DC, Bush officially announced that he would seek a second term as president. Bush was in a unique position with the strongest claim for a popular mandate from the people because he was the elected president and had previously been elected vice president for two terms. Only a few months before, he had registered in the polls as the most popular president in history.

Bush's announcement was made in a place of no real significance to him or what he stood for, so it had no inherent shared meaning. Where candidates announce their candidacy has great significance because it shares meaning with the public and sets the tone for their campaign. Bush called his announcement speech a simple message to serve as the basis of his campaign. He said, "I believe government is too big and costs too much." We need "a government really worthy of the people." (Bush, Announcement) However, in his speech Bush was not the central hero nor did he present any clear vision for the next four years.

In his announcement speech, Bush recalled basic American values. He referred to the revolution, which began in 1980 to free America from malaise and to achieve its destiny, but this dramatic narrative was incomplete because he did not claim having a hand in the progress of the past. He only mentioned the reason for seeking a second term was to finish the important work that he had begun. Bush made no mention of a popular mandate or self sacrifice by serving the public as other candidates often did.

Bush described the status quo as sound, so he could not cast himself as the hero who would save the country from the evil it faced in the current economic conditions. When he discussed foreign affairs, Bush did characterize several positive dramatic narratives, however, he did not say that he was responsible for them. He neither mentioned himself or the American people, leaving his dramatic narratives without any heroes or clear course of action.

In his speech, Bush did not lay the groundwork to establish himself as the people's chosen leader in the past or in the future. Neither did he bind himself with them into a collective 'we' or 'us' as other candidates had done to create any shared meaning. He did not choose a location for his announcement speech that visually symbolized his campaign or that represented familiar traditions such as a return to his roots or shared values that he wanted to restore.

Instead, Bush communicated a trackless set of dramatic narratives that lacked a coherent social reality. Bush's announcement speech gave the appearance of being hastily put together in response to outside pressure. The impression of his campaign being in disarray was furthered because he left immediately after his announcement to go to New Hampshire to defend himself against his opponents' attacks.

The best known candidate with the highest name recognition at the onset of the election campaign was incumbent President Bush. He had a well known public persona developed during his twelve years as president and vice president. As a popular incumbent, Bush seemed virtually assured reelection throughout 1991. Following the Gulf War, he had obtained the highest approval ratings of any post-war president with an 89% approval rating and a disapproval rating of only 8%. In 1991, Bush was named the most admired man and was ranked the seventh greatest president in history. (Gallup Poll, December 11, 28 1991, February 28, March 3, 1992)

As the campaign season approached, the challenge for Bush was to main-tain this wave of popularity and build upon it up to the election. The main task of his campaign was to keep those who shared his version of social reality and voted for him in the last election committed to him. It would take some effort to keep his supporters and bring back those who no longer shared his version of social reality. In the intervening months between the Gulf War and his announcement to run, Bush's foreign policy victories gave way to difficulties at home with the economy. By January, the past year's euphoria over the Gulf War was steadily eroding, being replaced with domestic concerns at home.

By the beginning of 1992 the economy was the issue that was the public's top concern (93%) followed by education (87%), unemployment (84%), health care policy (80%), and the federal budget deficit (79%). The national defense (43%) and foreign affairs (37%) ranked at the bottom of the list as the least impor-tant issues of concern to voters. Eight out of ten people felt that the economy was in bad shape and 67% felt that Bush was spending too much time on foreign affairs and not enough on domestic problems. (Gallup Poll, January 19, 1992)

The media reported stories of the declining economy and it grew to be the single most important issue with the public. Reports about the failing economy (CBS Evening News, January 3, 1992) and the economy being dead in the water (Washington Week, January 3, 1992) represented media characterizations of recent events. These interpretations were even confirmed by Bush when he apologized for the state of the economy (New York Times, January 24, 1992), acknowledging that it was in decline and that he needed to take stronger leadership to improve it. (Washington Post, January 16, 1992)

As the nation's attention changed, so did their impression of Bush. By the first week of 1992, the president's approval ratings had dropped from a record high of 89% to below 50% (46%) for the first time in his term. It was also the first time his disapproval ratings (47%) were higher than his approval ratings (46%). (Gallup Poll, January 19, 1992) These ratings were not seen at the time as significant in light of historical perspectives, which kept several prominent Democrats from challenging Bush.

Approval ratings for Reagan and Nixon averaged 44% and 50%, respectively in their third year in office and they handily won a second term. However, this time more people disapproved than approved of Bush's performance as president. This change in public support was most likely due to the effectiveness of his oppositions' version of social reality being shared by the public, compounded by the lack of an effective version of social reality of his own to counter them.

In January, Bush began campaigning in New Hampshire to fend off attacks from Democrats who asserted that he was insensitive to the plight of people hurt by the recession. Fellow Republican Pat Buchanan ran the first negative television ads attacking Bush as being dishonest, showing him saying "Read my lips, no new taxes," which was later effectively exploited by Clinton. The Buchanan ad stated, "Bush betrayed our trust," promising to cut spending, provide jobs, and not raise taxes. It then asked the voters, "Can we afford four more years of broken promises?" Buchanan later produced a controversial ad showing men partially dressed in leather, accusing the Bush Administration of "investing our tax dollars" in "art too shocking to show." (Buchanan, Television Ads)

Instead of creating and sharing his version of social reality, Bush had been forced to defend himself against growing allegations that he had ignored the people's problems here at home making him appear out of touch. (World News Tonight, January 15, 1992) This reactionary approach led to the perception that Bush had to be forced to jump awkwardly into the race to defend himself and his record before any official announcement of his candidacy. His actions were interpreted by the media as a sign of weakness that resulted in Bush being characterized as being on the run. (CNN Newsmaker, January 18, 1992)

These changes for Bush may have been due to shifting public opinion, changing media attention, or the exploitation of these issues by Clinton and Buchanan. Since the most significant drop in Bush's approval rating occurred after Clinton's announcement, from 65% in October 1991 to 46% in January 1992, (Gallup Poll, January 12, 1992) it seems likely that the Clinton and Buchanan dramatic narratives, shared in the media and by the public were effective in eroding Bush's legitimacy. With the campaign in full swing and after a month of campaigning had passed, Bush waited until February 12, 1992 to finally announce his candidacy for reelection.

During the initial stages of the election, the Bush campaign was in disarray. He was unable to clearly articulate what he stood for or how a second term would be defined. Bush seemed to concentrate on details rather than creating any form of shared meaning with the public to communicate his version of social reality and what he wanted for the next four years. This set a lackluster tone that was carried throughout the campaign.

The Bush Version of Social Reality.

The initial Bush version of social reality was convoluted and not well developed. It appeared to consist of poorly thought out dramatic narratives that failed to share meaning with the public. Bush needed to hold supporters to his version of social reality, which he found difficult to accomplish with growing opposition. Bush maintained an initial strategy of campaigning by governing, by being the president and conducting the nation's business.

However, relentless attacks from challengers of both parties forced him into a defensive posture. He only began campaigning to defend himself against attacks from his own party making him appear weak and without a plan. The nature of his announcement to run for reelection raises the question of his intent to run, as it appeared to be hastily conceived and the campaign had been in full swing for over a month before he announced his candidacy.

In announcing his candidacy, Bush did not utilize any clear, imaginative, or exciting dramatic narratives that had the potential to create a version of social reality that would engage the imagination to encourage the support of large numbers of voters. Indeed this failure invited criticism that would plague Bush throughout the campaign. Bush was not only indistinct in articulating any clear reasons for voters to support his candidacy, he was also unable to develop any strong reasons to undermine his opponent's legitimacy. He was at a disadvantage at this time because his Democratic opponent had not yet been determined, so instead he chose to attack the opposition party.

Bush was under attack from several opponents, but he failed to respond directly to them, instead he chose to attack the Democrats in Congress. Bush's dramatic narratives were undefined, only referring to the entrenched opposition clinging to the old ways and subverting progress in solving the nation's problems. This nondescript group was characterized as having blocked progress to fight crime, improve education, cut regulation, and encourage growth. Eventually, this vaguely described group was associated with the Democrats in Congress, which Bush would confront more directly later in the campaign.

Bush called for an end to this obstruction of progress, extolling those who impeded it to get out of the way. Bush offered no attractive and detailed dramatic narrative to explain how things would get moving. Instead he relied on the general assertion that together he and the people would restore the government and decency. He did not say how this restoration would be accomplished nor did he offer a vision of a future America restored under his leadership. While the dramatic narrative of restoration was alluded to, it was not well developed.

Bush appeared vulnerable in his own party following Buchanan receiving 37% of the vote and demonstrated by his dropping approval ratings as president. The media shared dramatic narratives that Bush was weak and that his reelection could now be threatened. A Gallup Poll (February 9, 1992) reported that 74% of Buchanan supporters defined themselves as an anti-Bush protest vote rather than supporting their candidate.

The same poll reported that 48% of Democrats were not satisfied with the current candidates and wanted to see another candidate enter the race. There was growing public dissent reflected in the media's dramatic narratives creating the opportunity for an independent candidate to emerge. To the extent that Perot shared that view, the upcoming New Hampshire primary presented a good time and a good reason for him to enter the race.

Perot On Television.

Ross Perot was the last of the three major candidates to enter the presidential campaign. On February 20, 1992, appearing on the Live with Larry King Show on CNN, Perot alluded to his interest in running for president, but only if drafted by the people. This announcement would turn out to be the beginning of one of the most bizarre political campaigns in American history. His offer came shortly after the New Hampshire primary results were in. Clinton, who had been named by the media as the Democratic front runner since January, came in second to Paul Tsongas. This came on the heels of Clinton being damaged by allegations of infidelity and draft dodging, raising questions about his ability to be elected.

Perot faced a unique challenge in his quest for the presidency. It was a challenge he could not readily overcome, which may explain his slow entry into the race despite the opportunities presented by recent trends. As he had never served in an elected office, Perot could not employ many of the traditional approaches normally utilized by politicians to legitimize their candidacy. Typically, candidates characterize their record of service in political positions or their record of populist support in winning past elections.

Perot could claim neither as he had no experience in political office to support his candidacy. So, his approach in claiming a popular mandate was essential to his political legitimacy. Perot had been in the national spotlight several times during his confrontations with General Motors executives. He was famous for the daring rescue of his employees who had been held captive in Iran. This rescue was made into a best selling book and movie. His public persona was of a person who worked hard to become very successful because he could get things done.

So, Perot took a very different approach to announcing his candidacy. Instead of the traditional announcement speech given on the capitol steps, in a hotel ballroom, or in a farmer's field, he called for the people to support him from a television studio.

The Perot Version of Social Reality.

In order to develop his version of social reality, Perot created a scene of an America in trouble caused by an intolerable situation in Washington. Across the nation people were out of work and families were hurt by failed economic policies. The future of our children and grandchildren was being mortgaged by the national debt, which the government would not address. The nation's industrial base was deteriorating with good jobs going abroad. So, the nation was in danger of losing the American Dream.

The administration in Washington was doing nothing to help the people or to create jobs because they had no idea what to do to help. Neither Bush nor Clinton had ever run a business or created jobs, like Perot had done. They had spent most of their lives in government, which was the problem not the solution. Perot created a scene of Washington full of people who came to serve, but instead ended up cashing in. Elected officials listened to special interests and foreign lobbyists rather than representing the people.

The people in Washington did not know how to work together, all they knew was how to fight each other. Perot characterized this situation in Washington as a mess and blamed Bush because he was out of touch with the people. Perot, like Clinton, promised that if elected he would rid the country of the mess in Washington and the people would once again realize the American Dream. Perot attacked Clinton's record of creating jobs and economic progress in Arkansas. He questioned Clinton's experience and assertions of having the management skills to run the nation on the basis of being the governor of Arkansas. Perot criticized Clinton's claim of economic growth, characterizing Arkansas as ranking near or at the bottom of the nation in areas important to running the country. After years of Clinton's leadership, Arkansas had made little progress to solve even the most basic problems.

Perot presented a scene of America in which it was the people's role to correct the problems the nation faced by restoring the government without harming what was good. He used the dramatic narrative of restoration to characterize himself as returning the government to the people. Perot asserted that his political principles were drawn from traditional social values coming from the people themselves. So, he created a dramatic narrative of himself as the representative of the people drawing upon popular support as his sanctioning agent.

Perot would run if the people wanted him to because volunteer organizations had placed him on the ballot. He claimed that he would address the issues they felt were important to restore the American Dream for all Americans. Claiming that the people had spoken, Perot would remain in the election for them as the servant of the people. He did not want to be president out of personal ambition because he was busy with his business and family, but he would do this because he loved the people.

In his version of social reality, Perot presented himself as a personification of the American Dream. He was a man who had worked hard and had come from humble beginnings to achieve great success. He was in this for love of country and love of its people. He wanted to pass on the American Dream that he had experienced to our children and grandchildren. Perot was willing to put his wallet on the table in order to finance his own campaign. He was his own man who did not accept contributions from special interests or have foreign lobbyists on his staff. Claiming a populist mandate based on tradition and communal values, Perot personified these values that came from the people themselves.

Perot included his audience as an integral part of his version of social reality by using communal values and linking them with his own. Perot had spent a lifetime helping others to demonstrate a future in which, as the servant of the people, he would help the nation solve its problems. In presenting a better future of economic prosperity for everyone, Perot was preserving the American Dream for future generations.

Perot Announces A Petition Drive.

In a media age it should not be surprising to find candidates announcing their candidacy live on television, yet it was most unusual when Perot did so in 1992. When Perot publicly announced his intent to run for president live on the Larry King Show on CNN, he told the viewers that if people supported him and he was placed on the ballot in all fifty states, he would run for president. This essentially constituted his announcement to run even though he later insisted it was not a campaign, but rather a petition drive to get him on the ballot. Once on the ballot, he would then decide if he would run. He concluded that if the people found anybody better along the way, that person could run instead. This move served to insulate him from the media scrutiny that his competitors experienced.

Perot characterized a corrupt government that had lost its will to help the very people who had brought it to power in the first place. Perot spoke of a government that had lost touch with the people and was hopelessly mired in gridlock. Washington insiders were the villains who wasted the people's money and mortgaged their future. Perot, with the help of the American people, could unlock gridlock and restore the government to the people. As an example of this position, Perot championed an electronic town hall where important national issues would be debated and the people would decide their fate.

In his announcement, Perot characterized himself as a humble public servant who took his orders directly from the people and not from evil special interests. He characterized a corrupt government that had lost its way, so it needed to be restored to the people and the values of the past. He was the hero sanctioned by popular support from ordinary working people and only with their help could he do this important work. Thus, he created a complete and compelling dramatic narrative that was central to his version of social reality.

Perot needed to establish his own mandate, but was careful to couch it in terms of a grass roots movement in which the public determined the nature of his candidacy rather than his own ambition for prestige or power. He presented himself as a person who had no desire to be president, characterizing the presidency as "the toughest, dirtiest, most thankless job in the world." He stated, "Anybody intelligent enough to do this job wouldn't want it." (Perot, Larry King Live) He did not choose a direct approach to establish his campaign, but rather used a more indirect one contingent upon public approval.

Perot seemed to take advantage of a growing voter discontent with present conditions and candidates. He developed a dramatic narrative meant to undermine the Bush administration without giving specifics. At the outset of the campaign, Perot did not have a coherent version of social reality, instead he developed several dramatic narratives that criticized the political establishment and what he saw as the problems facing the nation. Perot focused on the deficit and national debt, which had ballooned under Reagan and Bush. In a direct reference to Bush calling Reagan's economic program "voodoo economics" in the 1980 primary, Perot said the country was now in "deep voodoo." This reference to Bush's failed economic policy would be one he would carry through the campaign.

Perot's version of social reality was strikingly similar to Clinton's version in many ways. Both utilized similar characterizations of the present economic situation as the worst since the Great Depression because of the mismanagement in Washington. Both characterized the people in Washington, who should be the people's servants, as being corrupt and out of touch with the people. Both called for change in Washington to save the nation from the evils of government. And both Clinton and Perot used the American Dream dramatic narrative in similar ways to legitimize their candidacy.

It would be these similarities that would play a pivotal role in the months to come.

Chapter 4
The Primaries

The primary campaign began at different times for the three major candidates. Clinton had announced his candidacy, had begun to develop his version of social reality and public persona, and had campaigned and debated other Democratic candidates before either Bush or Perot had officially announced their candidacy.

This early show of political strength may have accounted for the media sharing a dramatic narrative that characterized Clinton as the leading Democratic candidate in January (New York Times, January 14, 1992) and the Democratic front runner. (Washington Post, January 3, 1992)

During this time, the media began to share this dramatic narrative despite Jerry Brown leading Clinton in voter preference polls 21% to 17%. (Gallup Poll, January 19, 1992) In view of differences in the timing of each candidate's announcement, this analysis of Clinton's campaign includes a portion that occurred before the previously discussed Bush and Perot campaigns. This difference in timing accounts for some repetition and overlap of material.

The Democratic Primary Campaign.

After announcing his candidacy for president, Clinton was faced with a number of obstacles that he would have to overcome in his bid for the presidency. The biggest challenge of Clinton's primary campaign was to carry forward and build upon the dramatic narratives he introduced in his announcement speech. Within that framework, he needed to gain name recognition so that he would stand out in a crowded field of contenders. The ultimate objective for Clinton was to gain the needed number of delegates through the primaries to secure his party's nomination for president before their summer convention.

Early in the campaign, Clinton gave a series of three speeches at his alma mater Georgetown University in Washington DC. (He had graduated from Georgetown with a Bachelor of Science in Foreign Service in 1968.) In these speeches he drew together various dramatic narratives designed to share meaning with the voters, to develop his version of social reality. These speeches were significant because they outlined his plan for the nation, a plan he would utilize for the rest of the campaign. These speeches all focused on his dramatic narrative of The New Covenant. The three speeches were titled The New Covenant: Responsibility and Rebuilding the American Community given on October 23, 1991, A New Covenant for Economic Change given on November 20, 1991, and A New Covenant for American Security given on December 12, 1991.

Clinton and The New Covenant.

In these speeches, Clinton developed one of the core dramatic narratives of his version of social reality. Clinton chose to use The New Covenant as the name of his program, similar to how Franklin Roosevelt used The New Deal. Clinton would use The New Covenant frequently during the campaign as a way to connect his values with those of the people. More importantly, The New Covenant was used to legitimize Clinton as a national leader by characterizing him as someone steeped in history and tradition.

The term "New Covenant" has a long history in religious doctrine. It has been used to define the relationship between God and his followers. It is described in The Old Testament in Jeremiah 31:31-33, which reads, "I will make a new covenant with the people." "It will not be like the covenant I made with their ancestors when I took them by the hand to lead them out of Egypt, because they broke my covenant." "I will put my laws in their minds and write them on their hearts. I will be their God, and they will be my people." The New Covenant was consecrated at the Last Supper by Jesus, as described in the New Testament, Luke 22:20, who after supper took the cup and said to his disciples, "This cup is the new covenant in my blood, which is poured out for you."

The New Covenant replaced the Mosaic or Old Covenant that God made with Moses on Mount Sinai to deliver the Israelites from Egypt as described in the first five books of the Bible and the Torah. The New Covenant is a gracious covenant, so that those who are included are reconciled to God by grace and not by acts. Jesus redeemed his people by his death on the cross, so that all who believe shall receive forgiveness of their sins. The New Covenant is often characterized as a pact between God and his people who were chosen to be saved and once made could not be withdrawn. It was also a pact made by God with his people that required them to have faith and be obedient to his word.

Clinton reiterated The New Covenant as the core dramatic narrative of his campaign when he said, "Today we need to forge a New Covenant that will repair the damaged bond between the people and their government." Clinton defined this bond as "a solemn agreement between the people and their government." (Clinton, Responsibility and Rebuilding the American Community) This narrative placed him in a godlike position as the main actor who, by repairing the bond would restore the government to the people.

For Clinton, The New Covenant was "a new approach founded on our most sacred principles as a nation." (Clinton, Responsibility and Rebuilding the American Community) It was both old, being grounded in the sacred tradition and values at the foundation of our society, as well as new, by being a new type of politician poised to revitalize and restore the best of the traditional values shared by Clinton and the people. Thus, he tied The New Covenant to another old and revered dramatic narrative in American history, that of restoration.

In order to demonstrate that the bond between the government and the people was broken and in need of restoration, Clinton characterized the Bush administration as corrupt and self serving. In this regard, his dramatic narrative was an elaborate and detailed description of our leaders who had helped the rich and dishonest become wealthier at the expense of our own people, while things became tougher for average hardworking people.

Clinton used specific dramatic narratives in which savings and loans were run by crooks who, like defense contractors, stole from hardworking taxpayers. The government not only did nothing to change this, it promoted private gain over public obligations, special interests over the public good, and the accumulation of wealth and fame over honest work and family values. Clinton characterized himself as a man of action who was offering America a New Covenant, so that they would support him politically and in exchange he would guarantee to return government to the best American tradition.

Clinton extended his version of social reality to include a global perspective claiming that foreign policy needed to be in line with the moral values that Americans share. He chose to attack Bush by characterizing his foreign policy, commonly thought to be Bush's greatest strength, as repugnant to these mainstream values. Clinton characterized Bush as a villain who ignored moral standards and put personal relationships ahead of humanitarian values shared by all Americans.

To provide proof, Clinton told the story of Bush sending envoys to China when the repressive government permitted human rights violations, in essence implying that Bush had condoned these acts. Bush's false choice between foreign and domestic policy had hurt the economy and the country. Bush's foreign policy successes had not helped, but had hurt the average person. In a reference to Bush, Clinton reasoned that the old ways of the past no longer worked in a rapidly changing world.

Here Clinton sought to pry people loose from previously held beliefs that depicted Bush as a foreign policy expert who had achieved important successes abroad. In order to expand his original version of social reality, Clinton depicted the scene abroad by acknowledging the fall of communism, the fall of the Berlin Wall, the unification of Germany, Middle East peace, and reform in South Africa. Clinton used a mainstay of his version of social reality, the American dream to recharacterize foreign policy.

In his speech, Clinton shifted the focus to domestic issues by stating, "While the American Dream reigns supreme abroad, it is dying here at home." (Clinton, Responsibility and Rebuilding the American Community) Here Clinton characterized Bush as having no vision, leadership, or strategy. A president was needed who had a new approach, a president who could solve economic problems and restore new life to the American Dream.

The Nature of Restoration.

Restoration is an old and familiar dramatic narrative that was frequently utilized by the candidates during this election campaign. The attraction of the restoration dramatic narrative is in its ability to maintain previously shared meanings by keeping them intact, while calling for change.

The restoration dramatic narrative has both sacred and secular versions. As a part of their social reality, speakers in both the religious and political realms have utilized the restoration dramatic narrative. The sacred version is based on Jesus and his disciples establishing the values and principles for the Christian Church. The subsequent failure of the church did not result in the rejection of Christianity, but was instead seen as a falling away from the values of the church. The restoration dramatic narrative calls for a return to the original foundation of the church. Throughout history, when a society experienced a time of troubles, it was often interpreted as evidence of a divine message that it had lost its way and must return to its original values.

The secular version of the restoration dramatic narrative is based on the values and principles established by the original founders of the nation. The subsequent failure of the government and society to uphold those principles was seen not as a failure of the system of government, but rather a falling away from the true principles upon which the nation was founded.

What was required was a change from current values, but this was not a change that turned its back on the past, nor was it a change to something new or foreign. Rather, it was change that returned to traditional values and principles that had been forsaken. This dramatic narrative served as a secular depiction of the heritage of government based on the glorification of a golden age sometime in the past. All who participate in the dramatic narrative share a common social bond as well as a bond with the founders of the institution being restored.

In order to escape the negative connotations embedded in commonly shared dramatic narratives about politicians, Clinton used an old dramatic narrative that had been used by a long list of presidential candidates including Carter and Reagan. Clinton characterized himself as not being a typical politician, so he could begin to break up old ideas about the parties to cast himself in a different mold.

Clinton used a dramatic narrative of an idealistic state of Arkansas where budgets were balanced and economic growth provided good jobs. This approach was designed to establish his legitimacy and to separate him from the evils of the government he attacked. Clinton characterized the election as "a crusade to build a new economic order" and "a better future." He would restore "basic values," "the forgotten middle class," "opportunity," and "the American dream." (Clinton, The New Covenant: Responsibility and Rebuilding the American Community, Economic Change, and American Security,)

Changing Public Opinion.

Clinton began campaigning in October and by January Bush had suffered his biggest loss of public approval since becoming president, slipping from 65% to 50%. Bush's performance also rated low on issues determined to be most important to voters including 24% on the economy, 25% on the budget deficit, and 26% on health care. (Gallup Poll, January 12, 1992) Even though issues raised by Clinton remained important to voters, his name recognition was relatively low at 9% in November, rising to 17% by the first of the year. (Gallup Poll, October 31, 1991 to January 3, 1992)

By February, public opinion was changing about Bush and the state of the nation providing evidence that Clinton's dramatic narratives were taking hold with the electorate. A growing number of people now felt that they were worse off than a year ago (43%), that working hard would not get them ahead (58%), and the next generation would be worse off than the last (61%). As a reference to Clinton's dramatic narrative of the American Dream, a majority felt that the basic premise of upward mobility was no longer something to be taken for granted. The Gallup Poll noted a trend in public opinion that began in October suggesting that the ever increasing barrage of attacks from presidential hopefuls, even from Bush's own party, were being shared with the public. (Gallup Poll, February 2, 1992)

Many of the poll categories reflected Clinton's dramatic narratives, which would suggest that they were being shared by an increasingly larger audience. Perhaps, the electorate had previously shared these dramatic narratives and Clinton recognized that fact and exploited it. However, as the campaign progressed, Clinton's dramatic narratives were being shared by a steadily increasing number of people, while Bush's dramatic narratives were being shared by fewer and fewer.

The Persecuted Victim Dramatic Narrative.

Just one month before the New Hampshire primary, Clinton was hit with accusations about his draft record and reports of marital infidelity. In an attempt to defuse the sharing of these dramatic narratives, Clinton went on television with counter narratives that he characterized as the truth. Clinton may well have recognized that dramatic narratives about his draft dodging and infidelity had a powerful attraction for the media and the public. If they were widely shared, they could well end his candidacy, so more direct measures were needed to save his campaign. In past elections, other candidates had their careers cut short over less.

In January, Clinton was forced to publicly respond to tabloid newspaper reports about his alleged twelve year affair with Gennifer Flowers, a cabaret singer turned television reporter. A week later, more information emerged including the release of tape recorded conversations between Clinton and Flowers. These tapes contained derogatory remarks about New York Governor Mario Cuomo, including slurs against Italians forcing Clinton to publicly apologize to Governor Cuomo.

In response to charges of infidelity, Clinton and his wife appeared on a special edition of Sixty Minutes to refute the allegations. The program was strategically aired between the Super Bowl and Bush's State of the Union address for maximum impact. The Clintons were interviewed by CBS correspondent Steve Kroft. (Many years later, Kroft would admit to alleged marital infidelity himself.)

Clinton's strategy was to not respond directly to the accusations leveled against him. He did not answer the question of whether or not he had extramarital relations. Rather he spun out a series of dramatic narratives in which he appealed to the public to respect and preserve his family's private life.

In responding to questions surrounding his alleged infidelity, Clinton described his marriage as having had problems, but these matters were only between himself and his wife, Hillary, so they were not the public's business. Only mentioning that he had hurt his family at times, he and Hillary appealed for the media and the public to respect their "zone of privacy." He said, "I have acknowledged wrongdoing. I have acknowledged causing pain in my marriage." He characterized his accusers and the press as exploiting him and his family for their own gain. In turn, he attacked the press and blamed them for trying to get him.

In response to questions about her husband's alleged infidelity, Hillary said one of her most well known quotes of the campaign. She said, "You know, I'm not sittin' here as some little woman standin' by my man, like Tammy Wynette. I'm sittin' here because I love him, and I respect him, and I honor what he's been through and what we've been through together. And you know, if that's not enough for people, then heck, don't vote for him." (Sixty Minutes, January 26, 1992)

In responding to these scandals and accusations, Clinton shifted the focus of the dramatic narrative from a question of infidelity to reaffirming his initial version of social reality of addressing the people's business. With this shift he could characterize attacks as not only attacks on him, but on the American people as well. Clinton was in the race for the people, not to debate his private personal issues. A self serving group of villains were sensationalizing events for their own personal gain at the people's expense. He characterized a better future for the campaign in which the focus of the debate returned to the truly important issues facing the nation, issues that the people wanted addressed.

Clinton said that defending himself from these accusations distracted his energies from addressing more important issues. The people wanted their problems solved and were not interested in his personal life, which had little bearing on his ability to get things done. Past dramatic narratives were quickly employed and stressed to divert attention from his scandals.

Although he dropped 15 points in the polls, from 37% to 22%, and lost the New Hampshire primary to Paul Tsongas, the public was not sharing the media's dramatic narratives about Clinton's infidelity to any great extent. His characterization of events were being shared by a majority of the people with 73% agreeing that the issue was a private matter between him and Hillary. Additionally, 66% felt that they could vote for a candidate who had an affair. (Gallup Poll, February 16, 1992, ABC News Poll, January 28, 1992)

Bill and Hillary's Sixty Minutes appearance contributed to the viewers sharing favorable impressions about the Clintons. After viewing the broadcast more viewers believed Clinton than believed Flowers. Over half felt that Clinton was unfairly treated by the media, that marital infidelity should not be an issue in the election, and that the matter had nothing to do with his ability to do the job. Clinton had apparently succeeded in defusing a potentially dangerous sharing of negative dramatic narratives about him.

A short time later, the Clinton campaign was further rocked with scandal and Clinton was forced to respond to evidence about his favorable treatment in an Army ROTC deferment program in order to avoid the draft and military service during the Vietnam War. These dramatic narratives were being characterized in the media and as a result they were shared by the public.

In response, Clinton released a letter that he said was written at the time to his army commander thanking him for keeping him out of the draft. The letter went on to explain Clinton's reasons for why he backed out of joining. The letter detailed his objections to the war and the mental anguish he was suffering. This issue increased in intensity when it became public that Clinton had organized rallies protesting the war and criticizing the US military while he was studying at Oxford University in England. In order to control the damage from accusations of draft dodging and marital infidelity, Clinton responded by developing the persecuted victim dramatic narrative, which tied into his characterization of The New Covenant to become a part of his version of social reality.

The persecuted victim dramatic narrative is an old and familiar one in American rhetoric. Many individuals and groups have characterized their problems as the consequence of being unjustly victimized by the system or persecuted by villains out to destroy them. Clinton created a dramatic narrative in which he had followed the rules during the draft and now he was unjustly persecuted and victimized by villains like Bush's Republican operatives. He had also been unjustly persecuted by the tabloids, which had paid hundreds of thousands of dollars to unethical people for their stories.

These were villains who unjustly persecuted him for their own personal gain at his expense. However, in the Clinton version of the persecuted victim dramatic narrative, it was the American people who would ultimately suffer since he had to answer these accusations rather than addressing more important issues. Clinton characterized his accusers of being dishonest, pursuing their own agenda of distracting the people from the important issues facing the country, and derailing his candidacy. Clinton accused his opponents of trying to destroy his pledge to fight for the people. These villains could not win an honest debate, so they must resort to tactics abhorrent to the values he and the people shared.

This dramatic narrative was similar to the one Clinton used to control damage in the Flowers case. He reaffirmed past dramatic narratives of American values that he upheld and shared with the American people, but that were contrary to those of his persecutors. Whenever his version of social reality subsequently came under attack, Clinton used the persecuted victim dramatic narrative to support his version of social reality.

As the primaries continued, other issues surrounding Clinton's character arose. His Democratic opponent, Paul Tsongas characterized Clinton as dishonest and pandering to his audiences. Early in March, Clinton was questioned about his involvement in Whitewater Development, a real estate venture he had invested in with James McDougal his friend and aide. McDougal owned a failed Arkansas savings and loan that had subsidized their venture raising questions of conflict of interest, because it was a business regulated by Clinton. Later that month, Clinton admitted having tried marijuana a time or two, although he said that he did not inhale or like it. In a WCBS-TV interview, Clinton uttered the now infamous quote, "I didn't inhale." (The New York Times, March 30, 1992.)

In each case, Clinton characterized himself as an unjustly persecuted victim by using dramatic narratives, only changing the characters and plot lines to meet each situation. He characterized each dramatic narrative as a conflict between good and evil, and the unfair tactics of villains out for personal gain who victimized him. Meanwhile, he thought only of the greater good of the people. Attacks on Clinton were instigated by those who were trying to stop his program to help people, thus these attacks were victimizing the people themselves. These villains could not criticize what the people wanted nor could they stand up to the rigors of an honest debate, so they had to resort to dishonest means. Clinton was the hero in these dramatic narratives because he was the barrier between these villains and the people.

In a sense, by heroically fighting for the people, his own unjust persecution could represent the unjust persecution of the people by Bush and the Republicans, so he could fight the battle for them. This image served to reinforce his version of social reality and to galvanize support as people came to realize that this campaign must be defended. Not only was his version of social reality under attack, so were the basic values that it comprised, values that were the essence of the American people's legacy.

Because Clinton's dramatic narratives were primarily action based and not persona based, accusations surrounding his character were secondary to what he wanted to accomplish. This may account for why Clinton would continue to have persistent negative ratings and yet gain in public support against his opponents.

The Democratic Candidates' Debates.

The primary race found Clinton in a crowded field of Democratic contenders who participated in a number of debates broadcast on television and radio. The other Democratic candidates who participated in these debates included former California Governor Jerry Brown, Iowa Senator Tom Harkin, Nebraska Senator Bob Kerrey, and former Massachusetts Senator Paul Tsongas. The debates lend themselves to analysis as a group even though chronologically they overlap previously described events. When they do, instead of repeating them in detail they have been summarized.

In the primaries, the Clinton version of social reality had to face direct response and rebuttal by other candidates. During the debates, several of the dramatic narratives Clinton developed in his announcement and subsequent speeches were subjected to closer scrutiny. The Democratic debates represented one of the first tests of Clinton's campaign under fire from direct opposition. In these debates he utilized a different strategy than his response to scandal.

The Democratic candidates participated in a series of debates, beginning in New Hampshire and followed by other states, prior to their primary election. In these debates, Clinton's strategy first concentrated on criticizing Bush rather than his opponents in order to create his own identity and separate himself from the other Democrats. Clinton characterized several differences between himself and Bush. He said that he was tired of being on the receiving end of the Reagan Bush revolution, trying to help people in a poor state with no help from Washington.

Clinton used the debates as a forum to develop his version of economic change and demonstrate how his leadership had helped Arkansas. He reiterated his dramatic narrative of the nation's economy as distressed and the people as hurting by saying, "the middle class people worked harder, their incomes went down, their taxes went up, poverty exploded, and they were victimized by stupid policies." (Democratic Debate, January 31, 1992)

Clinton called for leadership and innovation as he put himself forward as an agent of change who had been proven, so he could lead the way. He explained, "I got into politics because I could not stand people's human potential going unfulfilled." (Democratic Debate, January 19, 1992)

When the other candidates questioned the credibility of his programs, he said all candidates should be required to say what they would do as president. He used the dramatic narrative of change to reorganize government. He said that he would pay for his new programs by controlling health care costs, cutting defense, and cutting administration costs. When his economic proposals came under fire, he defended them with his tax increase from 31% to 38% on incomes over $200,000 and his proposed reductions of administrative costs of government by 3% per year.

Characterizing his plan as restoring fairness by making the rich pay their fair share, Clinton would give tax relief to people whose incomes went down and taxes went up. All these people had told him to get tough, but Clinton said, "I don't see that there is any intrinsic merit in kicking the brains out of the middle class." He wanted to give "tax relief to people whose incomes went down and taxes went up." (Democratic Debate, January 31, 1992)

Other Democratic candidates criticized Clinton claiming that Arkansas ranked at the bottom of all the states. Clinton characterized his critics as "not doing such a hot job of running anything." (Democratic Debate, January 31, 1992) In defending Arkansas, he characterized his state as having accomplished amazing things without help from Washington to become fiscally sound improving economic and working conditions in one of the poorest environments in the country.

The New Hampshire Primary.

The New Hampshire primary turned out to be a major test for Clinton measuring his ability to control damage by characterizing events that could potentially end his campaign. Considering the eventual outcome, if he had planned the scandals himself and the timing of them being made public, the result could not have turned out better for him. The scandals may have cost him the New Hampshire primary, but they also registered low in importance to voters.

Tsongas won the New Hampshire primary with 33% of the vote and Clinton, who went in as the front runner, came in second at 25%. However, nationally among Democratic voters, Clinton led Tsongas 41% to 31%. On the positive side, the scandal did more for Clinton than he probably hoped for because it raised his name recognition from 50% in January to 86% by the end of the month. It also increased Clinton's support nationally 25 points from 17% to 42% in only a month. (Gallup Poll, February 23, 1992)

This bolstered Clinton's position as front runner with the strongest Democratic support of the candidates. After Clinton's response to his scandals, media narratives changed from whether Clinton was fit for office to the question of how the media was handling the story. They began to question if they should have ignored it altogether because now the handling of scandals relating to presidential candidates was coming under increased scrutiny.

Focusing on personal scandals was motivated by the media's own version of social reality that characterized reporters as duty bound to discover all possible evidence of wrong doing and report it to the public. While they still rushed to pursue such scandalous stories in regard to other candidates, the media pulled back from pushing stories about Clinton's womanizing. Perhaps the fact that the media stories failed to be widely shared after the Clintons' response had something to do with those decisions.

After the New Hampshire primary, the debates moved on to other states, however, the issues promulgated by Clinton changed little. In Denver, the exchanges between the candidates were much less congenial, even antagonistic as they focused their criticism on each other. The most dramatic exchange was between Clinton and Tsongas in response to a question about nuclear power. When Clinton referred to Tsongas as always being perfect, Tsongas replied, "I'm not perfect, but I'm honest." (Democratic Debate, February 29, 1992)

The debate aired by Maryland Public Television on March 1 focused on the economy and domestic issues. It was held at the University of Maryland and the candidates were asked questions by members of the audience. The candidates focused on the nation's problems and criticized Bush more than each other. Clinton again presented his dramatic narrative of change that went beyond the tired old ideologies and labels. Change was needed to compete and win in a global economy because the country was weak at home and abroad. To strengthen the country, the government had to put people first because Washington had abandoned them. Again the dramatic narrative of a troubled present was contrasted with a positive vision of the future obtainable only by Clinton being elected president.

In the Democratic debates, Clinton presented a dramatic narrative of America as the only industrialized nation with no long term economic strategy. He criticized Bush for having a tepid, stay the course attitude that had led the nation into trouble. It was these dramatic narratives of a weak Bush that provided part of Clinton's rationale for why the government needed to be changed. Clinton said that we had to go beyond the gridlock of the past to develop a new partnership between the public and private sectors. Much of our present economic trouble had resulted from the way people made money in the eighties, as well as the government's attitude toward the people.

In contrast, Clinton would reward people who wanted to make money the old fashioned way, by generating jobs. Clinton now began to focus on narratives concerning the issue of health care, which he characterized as overloaded and in need of reform. He had sought input from hundreds of people and developed a health care program to be responsive to the needs of the people. He would take on the insurance companies to save billions of dollars for them. The issue of health care came to be a centerpiece of his campaign and a part of his version of social reality.

Clinton would frequently characterize his own life as having to keep hope alive under difficult circumstances. He had said that, "Change is not easy, change is very hard." "It seems to me that life is a constant struggle to the end of our days." (Democratic Debate, January 31, 1992) He characterized the people of his state as wonderful and constantly working for change and put himself in the center of his social reality to show that the country needed a president like him who could get things done. He would be on the cutting edge of change by not defending the government, but rather by working to improve it.

Clinton reiterated his story of having the opportunity to realize the American Dream. He was running for president to give the American Dream back to the people. All people should have the chance that he and his family had been given to live up to their God given potential. Clinton felt his policy was a down payment on fairness. A president had to stand up and do what was right for the people who worked harder while their incomes went down and taxes went up.

Clinton said that he had run for president because he was fed up with being on the receiving end of the Reagan Bush revolution. He decided that he was the one to make the country great again. Clinton's role was to articulate a broad unifying version of social reality that would energize the voters by utilizing specific dramatic narratives to support his campaign.

During the debates, Clinton reiterated many of the same dramatic narratives that he had used earlier in the campaign. Although debates are commonly considered to be a forum for the exchange of ideas, the Democratic debates did not live up to that expectation. They were frequently punctuated by personal attacks, advertising pitches for 1-800 telephone numbers, and one-upmanship for the sound bite of the night. This was compounded by much repetition, rehearsed 'spontaneous' comments, jokes, and general piracy of the other candidates' ideas.

The purpose of single party debates is so that voters can see and compare the candidates to make an informed decision. However, they can more often serve to damage the party due to the tendency of candidates to resort to negative campaigning by criticizing their opponents. This can weaken a candidate in the general election because criticisms from a candidate's own party can be damaging to their legitimacy when used by an opposing party candidate. These debates seemed to have negligible impact on the eventual outcome, so another forum like a town hall or giving candidates free airtime would likely be more effective.

At the end of February, Clinton and Tsongas were in a dead heat with 35% to 34%. When asked what qualities people wanted in a president, more people saw Clinton as a leader than Tsongas 45% to 32%. However, a significant majority saw Tsongas as more honest than Clinton 56% to 39%. (Gallup Poll, March 1, 1992) Perhaps, people equated lack of honesty with leadership and presidential qualities.

As the campaign entered its next phase leading up to Super Tuesday, Clinton still suffered from character issues. This would not hold Clinton back because half of the people felt that he had good plans, 60% felt that he cared about people, and 44% felt that he was electable. He showed the highest rating of any Democratic candidate in terms of perceived ability to defeat Bush. (Gallup Poll, March 1, 1992)

This reaction in the electorate would support the notion that although people had concerns about Clinton as a person, they nevertheless felt better about his ability to get things done. This would mean that his dramatic narrative of change was being shared with the voters to an appreciable extent. A sign that Clinton's characterization of Bush was beginning to share meaning with the public was that approval of Bush's handling of foreign policy dropped from 65% in January to 55% in March. (Gallup Poll, March 10, 1992)

The previous year Bush had achieved an all time high of 84% approval of his foreign policy and his ratings of credibility, leadership, and caring about people remained strong at over 60% through January 1992. (Gallup Poll, March 10, 1992) The recent decline was most evident in marginal support groups including Democrats, independents, and moderates suggesting Clinton's dramatic narratives were breaking up Bush's version of social reality.

Following a clean sweep of the south on Super Tuesday, Clinton pulled ahead of his competition. In the media, he was generally considered the likely Democratic nominee despite concerns over the lasting affects of his scandals. (Washington Post, March 12, 1992) Democrats now supported Clinton by 54% to 23% over his closest rival Tsongas. A majority of voters felt that Clinton would be the nominee, yet 71% of those questioned thought that Bush would still win the election over the yet to be determined Democrat. (Gallup Poll, March 15, 1992)

The following week, after winning primaries in Michigan and Illinois, the media characterized Clinton as having gained enough momentum to clinch his party's nomination, but he had yet to convince the voters that he had what it took to lead the nation. (Washington Post, March 20, 1992) However, Clinton had not yet amassed the number of delegates needed to win at the convention, meanwhile Tsongas and Brown remained in the race.

By the end of March, the voters were sharing meaning with some of Clinton's economic plans. In tax policy, 75% favored increased taxes on high incomes and 80% wanted Congress to pass a middle class tax cut, with the tax cut ranked highest in importance by voters. (Gallup Poll, March 5, 1992)

Clinton, A Plan For America's Future.

Part of Clinton's version of social reality introduced during the primary characterized a grim vision of a troubled nation. He characterized the Republicans as the party of the rich who believed that if the rich prospered the money would 'trickle down' to the poor. For the traditional Democrats, this reference would convey the entire dramatic narrative to explain the current economic problems as being caused by Bush and the Republicans.

Clinton said that Congress should pass a 10% middle class tax cut to allow hardworking Americans to keep more of what they earn. Economic recovery would be accomplished through fast track spending on infrastructure to create jobs, help people buy homes, start small businesses, and lower interest rates.

Against his depiction of an economically troubled present, Clinton envisioned a better future with his plan to fix the troubled economy. As president, Clinton would take immediate steps to solve this problem. He would create an economic 'lifeline' to help those thrown out of work so they could make house payments and afford medical care. Within his first year in office, Clinton would help to improve the lives of all Americans by providing them with affordable health care, including preventative care and more choices.

In Clinton's version of social reality, education was equated with economic development that could empower every American. Everyone who wanted to could go to college and then serve their community. This would enable them to find good jobs with growing incomes. However, Clinton did not explain where these jobs would come from or how people would find them because, as he often asserted, good jobs were currently being lost.

In Clinton's plan for America's future, he developed a dramatic narrative of the current government that needed to be radically changed in order to become accountable to the people, to eliminate massive waste, and to balance the budget. This dramatic narrative of change was tied into a larger restoration of the best of America's past that would result in a better future. By presenting a dramatic narrative of a future that would be better than the present, Clinton provided motivation for the people to let go of their concerns about his character to vote for him.

Clinton Secures The Democratic Nomination.

In April, despite high unfavorable ratings, Clinton was closing in with 41% of the vote to Bush's 48%. (Gallup Poll, April 15, 1992) While still carrying negative baggage over his character issue, Clinton had been able to persist in steadily eroding Bush's lead suggesting that his message was sharing meaning with voters.

With the Los Angeles riots in late April and early May, the media spotlight was taken off Clinton and shifted to the nation's urban and economic problems. This was a situation from which he benefited, as during this time Clinton's unfavorability ratings fell from 49% to 36% and the public felt that he could do the best job to improve urban conditions. (Gallup Poll, May 3, 1992)

After victories in New Jersey, Ohio, and Alabama, Clinton had enough delegates to win the Democratic nomination making June 3 the starting point for his general election bid. Even though he had secured his party's nomination, Clinton continued to campaign. Now that the nomination was secure, Clinton would have to introduce himself to the nation as a presidential candidate representing his party in a wider contest. He would also have to do some image repair, so on June 3rd, he made a much publicized appearance on the Arsenio Hall show where he played his saxophone with the band. In the intervening month before the Democratic National Convention, Clinton continued to campaign on the dramatic narratives he had used in the primaries that shared meaning with the voters.

There was growing evidence that Clinton was touching on many of the issues that concerned the public as his dramatic narratives were being shared by a wider audience. Now, 72% of all voters supporting a candidate perceived their candidate as representing change, a clear sign this dramatic narrative was being widely shared, perhaps explaining why Bush would later pick it up. Followers of Clinton saw him as someone who cared about people with 81% sharing his putting people first dramatic narrative. As a result of his characterization of change, 77% felt he could bring about the change the nation needed. With his characterization of his record in Arkansas, 76% shared the dramatic narrative that he was best able to handle the economy. However, even among those who supported Clinton, only 51% saw him as honest indicating Bush's characterization of Clinton's character was having some effect, although 50% thought Clinton put the nation's interests above politics. (Gallup Poll, July 15, 1992)

A few days before the Democratic National Convention, Clinton chose Tennessee Senator Al Gore as his vice presidential running mate. The media speculated as to why Clinton chose Gore because it seemed to defy previous strategies of balancing a presidential ticket. They were both baby boomers, Southern Baptists, came from neighboring Southern states, and shared a similar political ideology. Gore seemed to bring nothing new to the ticket, except the only thing Clinton did not have and desperately needed at this time, credibility to give his candidacy legitimacy. Compared to Clinton, Bush, and Quayle, Gore had the highest favorability rating (64%) and the lowest negative rating (19%), which was better than the past Democratic vice presidential candidates Bentsen (48%) and Ferraro (52%). After the convention with Gore on the ticket, 73% said they would be more likely to consider voting for Clinton and his favorability increased to 63%, suggesting Gore had helped to bolster his legitimacy. (Gallup Poll, July 12, 22, 1992)

Through the sharing of several key dramatic narratives over the course of the primaries, Clinton changed the public's perception of himself on several key issues. The public's perception of him as honest and trustworthy improved from 25% to 56%. The perception of his ability to handle a crisis went from 36% to 52% and his ability to bring about the kind of change the country needed went from 35% to 44%. This would indicate that as the campaign progressed, the public was increasingly sharing meaning with Clinton's dramatic narratives. (Gallup Poll, March to July, 1992)

Bush's favorability rating dropped from 55% in April to 44% in July, and his unfavorability rating went from 41% to 50%. (Gallup Poll, July 2, 1992) Bush's high approval rating prior to election year had given way to a dramatic loss of support after the campaign began, which would suggest that Clinton's anti-Bush dramatic narratives were being widely shared by the public. Given the historical perspective of an incumbent never being reelected with an approval rating below an average of 50%, Clinton may have had a long way to go to victory, but he was closer than Bush seemed to realize.

The Republican Primary Campaign.

Early in the campaign, Bush faced a serious challenge from within his own party from conservative Republican television commentator Pat Buchanan. Buchanan characterized his candidacy as giving the country a vehicle of protest to bring Bush back to the party's conservative roots. As support for Buchanan grew, Bush was forced to begin campaigning in New Hampshire before he announced he was running as a candidate.

In the early primaries beginning with New Hampshire, Buchanan ran stronger than predicted against a popular incumbent of the same party. This encouraged the media to characterize Bush as being vulnerable. Early primary results gave Buchanan thirty to forty percent of the vote, compounded with his persistent attacks, contributed to making Bush appear weak.

Bush's legitimacy was damaged by a campaign in crisis that had been taken by surprise. Buchanan's message focused on the dramatic narrative of putting America first, so he criticized Bush's foreign policy initiatives by accusing him of abandoning the American people and losing the domestic agenda. These dramatic narratives were later picked up and effectively utilized by Clinton against Bush.

Buchanan Is Trouble For Bush.

Following the New Hampshire primary, Bush's approval rating dropped to 39%, the lowest rating of his presidency so far, and only 42% felt he deserved to be reelected. This drop was likely due to every other candidate in the race being critical of Bush. Winning 37% of the Republican vote in New Hampshire, Buchanan claimed victory and called for Bush to step aside. Buchanan did this despite the fact that only 35% of his voters strongly supported him and 75% voted for him simply to send Bush a message. Alternately Bush, who won 58% of the vote, was characterized as the loser, a candidate in serious trouble. (Gallup Poll, February 23, 1992)

The media characterized Buchanan as a serious threat and the upcoming primary battles could splinter the party. (Washington Post, February 19, 20, 1992) The media accused Bush of abandoning the conservative faction and the principles that had elected Reagan. (CNN, March 5, 1992) They characterized the Bush campaign as not going well, (ABC World News Tonight, March 6, 1992) that Bush was taking a beating, (Washington Week, March 6, 1992) and worried about Buchanan's support. (CBS Evening News, March 4, 1992) This media characterization followed Bush during the early primaries even though he led in all the polls at this time.

In the primaries, the contest between Bush and Buchanan had exposed the lack of any coherent Bush dramatic narratives. At first Bush tried to avoid attacking Buchanan, but as Buchanan's message began to catch on with voters, he found himself forced to get tough to eliminate Buchanan from the race. To bolster his candidacy, Bush ran television commercials that showed him in the oval office presenting his plan for economic growth to create new jobs. This dramatic narrative was designed to establish his credibility and answer his critics by demonstrating his concern for the issues, specifically the domestic agenda. To connect with the people, Bush asked them to help, not to win in November, but to gather public support in convincing Congress to pass his program.

In his television commercials, Buchanan raised the issue of the broken no new taxes pledge as a demonstration of the unfitness of Bush by attacking his credibility. During the 1988 campaign Bush had made his famous "read my lips, no new taxes" statement. (Bush Acceptance Speech, Republican National Convention, August 18, 1988) Bush was characterized as a president who made a promise and then broke it deceiving the American people. If he could not keep his tax pledge, then he could not be trusted on other issues. This dramatic narrative begun by Buchanan was later used effectively by Clinton and Perot against Bush to undermine his legitimacy. In attempting damage control, Bush said that his decision to go along with the tax increase was the biggest mistake of his presidency.

Bush characterized the tax increase as a compromise with Congress that was accompanied by much needed spending limits to reduce the deficit. He cast Congress as the villain who exhibited destructive behaviors and was unwilling to take responsibility. He had tried to compromise with Congress for the good of the nation and they had betrayed him by not staying within the spending limits that the compromise had set. He had hoped this compromise would guarantee no future need for tax increases. Admitting that he made a mistake, Bush vowed that he would no longer make compromises with Congress because they had not only deceived him, they had also deceived the American people.

Buchanan criticized Bush for his support of free trade at the expense of American workers who were losing their jobs to foreign countries. He criticized Bush for having foreign lobbyists as his top political advisors. Buchanan used the dramatic narrative of America First to illustrate his emphasis on the economy and domestic issues, while criticizing Bush for worrying about events around the world at American's expense. This was another issue raised by Buchanan that was later used effectively by Clinton and Perot to legitimize their right to govern. Buchanan also criticized Bush for abandoning the values of the Republican Party by presiding over a bloated government that created too much regulation and overspent while raising taxes. Buchanan's villains extended beyond the Democrats to include those in his own party, including moderates like Bush who wanted to help those abroad, while abandoning our own people here at home.

Aggravating increasing voter discontent and stimulating the desire for change, Buchanan focused his campaign on asking the people to send Bush the message that they were upset and wanted a change. Facing increased pressure in his own party, Bush ran television commercials to discredit Buchanan by questioning his patriotism in his opposition to Desert Storm. Buchanan's opposition was characterized as undermining basic American values and offending people who supported their country. As Buchanan hung on in the race, Bush used the issue of trust to directly attack Buchanan in the Michigan primary. In television commercials, Bush assailed Buchanan as deceptive and not truly concerned with autoworkers. While Buchanan called for America first in public, privately he did not mean it because he owned a foreign car that put Americans out of work, a message that hit home in Michigan.

As the primaries progressed, Buchanan continued to receive roughly one third of the Republican vote by exploiting Bush's vulnerability. Buchanan's attacks on Bush were contributing to Bush's rising unfavorability ratings. Buchanan's message was being shared with the voters as over half of his supporters were dissatisfied with Bush and agreed with Buchanan to send Bush a message. However, Buchanan's support would soon evaporate.

After a decisive Bush victory on Super Tuesday, 57% of Republican voters felt it was time for Buchanan to drop out of the race, a change from February when 62% thought he should stay in. After the Super Tuesday primaries Buchanan's support dropped to 11%, near his pre-New Hampshire levels. Republican voters seemed to agree with Bush that Buchanan was too extreme. Those voters who would not vote for Buchanan because his ideas were too extreme increased from 33% before Super Tuesday to 50% after. (Gallup Poll, March 15, 1992)

After Super Tuesday, Bush made a strong showing winning every primary and finally securing his party's nomination. Even with the media declaring that he had made a strong showing, they persisted to question his ability to convince voters that he could lead the nation. (Washington Post, March 20, 1992) In his dramatic narratives about Congress, Bush was not faring as well. Only 30% of the people agreed that their own representative should be removed. In the time since Bush began to campaign against Congress, the number of people who felt that members of Congress did not deserve to be reelected had only increased from 25% in January to 30% by the end of March. (Gallup Poll, March 25, 1992)

The Problems For Bush.

As the primary unfolded, Bush faced a new challenge quite different from the other candidates. He had come under assault from all the other candidates, even from his own party. In response, he was forced into a defensive position because he needed to reconstitute supporters through the process of shared meaning. His task was to maintain the support of voters who had shared his version of social reality, then to strengthen marginal supporters, and finally to bring back those who had gone to other candidates. It was not a good approach to criticize the present government or economy because Bush himself had participated in creating the present situation.

Because Bush could not utilize the same approaches as the other candidates and because he failed to develop his own, he appeared out of touch with the country. Should Bush acknowledge the validity of the problems that were being characterized by the other candidates, it would undermine his chances of being reelected. By making such a move Bush would seem to abandon his own past and confirm his opponents' criticism of it. So, he frequently reiterated that the country faced troubles, but was not falling apart as his opponents wanted people to believe.

In order to address their challenges, Bush stressed specific campaign issues characterizing past successes as evidence that he was the best candidate for president. Throughout the primaries, Bush's speeches tended to concentrate on issues and positions rather than developing a complete unified version of social reality comprised of various dramatic narratives that would share meaning with the public. Bush characterized peacetime prosperity aided by the defense cuts made possible by the end of the Cold War. America must remain strong and not ignore the lessons of history by proceeding recklessly with disarmament to create an ineffective army. He warned that there were still aggressors who needed to be contained by a strong deterrent. America needed to help other countries move toward democracy, so they could benefit from improved trade and economic relations. In a cautionary tone, Bush reminded Americans of the lessons of history that show the consequences of failing to support democracy abroad.

Bush characterized the changes that had taken place around the world to create a scene of a changing world where, "communism didn't just fall, it was pushed," and Iraq was kicked out of Kuwait. He characterized these as major successes, "and still some people say, hey what have you done for us lately?" (Bush, Small Business Legislative Council) This was a reference to the Democrats and Buchanan who criticized and recast foreign policy successes as failures. Bush used the dramatic narrative of change when he said, "If we can change the world, we can change America." (Bush, New Hampshire State Legislature) Bush tried to accentuate the positive aspects and alluded to successes in negotiations for change in China. An active, engaged interaction with China was the answer to this problem because such interaction would expose the Chinese leaders to western ways and values that would lead to a democratic market economy and expand personal freedoms.

Thus, Bush sought to build on his past popularity and successes in foreign policy to transpose the victories abroad to the domestic agenda. He had demonstrated an ability to solve difficult problems abroad and would now focus on difficult problems at home. His characterizations of foreign policy experience was a dramatic narrative he frequently utilized to present a vision of the future that concentrated on the domestic agenda. Bush said, "Now we can look past the burdens of the cold war, we can do what we do best." (Bush, Small Business Legislative Council) Bush wanted to reform government by eliminating regulation that slows down the economy and cost jobs. He characterized needless regulation as an evil that destroyed jobs and weighed down businesses.

Bush's speeches utilized dramatic narratives of the health care system to illustrate the differences between how he envisioned his own program and Clinton's plan. Health care was part of his plan for America because it was a problem for many people and it cost too much. Bush felt the present system provided the "highest quality health care on Earth." Even though it had its faults, it could be reformed, but he would not support a plan that did not allow for choice and put the government between the people and their doctors.

Bush characterized Clinton's plan as adopting a nationalized health care program that had been "proven a failure all over the world," other countries had been abandoning these kinds of socialist systems. (Bush, Small Business Legislative Council) Bush created a dramatic narrative of the struggle between building on success or adopting failure, and between individual choice or government imposition. Bush used this issue to demonstrate that it was necessary to reduce the power of government to restore individual freedom and choice.

Bush's opponents had characterized the economy as dismal and the country as in decline, so Bush responded, "The bottom line is we've got a lot of work to do." He said that those who wanted to believe that America's best days were past did not understand. Americans want to get things moving and "we can't let anyone stall us this time," including Congress. Bush called on Congress to pass his plan to get the economy going again. He said that there was an air of "cynicism and fear" in the country that must be dispelled. (Bush, Small Business Legislative Council)

Bush acknowledged the pervasive climate of "gloom and doubt" that surrounded the perception of the economy, however, he cautioned that this was not a reality, but was a perception that had been propagated by "professional pessimists." Bush characterized this group as detrimental to the country because they promoted bad feelings and "feast on bad times" at the expense of others. (Bush, Small Business Legislative Council) Bush's speeches characterized a more positive view of the present situation, although he was beginning to shift his position when he acknowledged that some things needed to be changed.

Bush and The Obstructionist Congress.

In several Bush dramatic narratives, Congress appeared as a villain who exhibited behaviors that were contrary to the nation's basic beliefs and values. Bush tended to personify Congress, but no specific members of Congress were singled out as villains. In a novel or film, a writer usually casts an individual as the hero who is pitted against another individual who is cast as the villain because it is easier for the audience to identify with an individual than a vague group. In his dramatic narratives, Bush did not cast a hero to stand against a specific villain. He was reluctant to put himself into his narratives, especially as the hero or central character. This made his dramatic narratives indistinct and lacking in any action or direction. They were mostly backward looking with little vision about the future.

Bush had entered the election without sharing any coherent version of social reality with the people. During the primary campaign, Bush did make an effort to create a patchwork of dramatic narratives with some coherence, but on balance he was never able to draw together a unified or intelligible version of social reality. Instead of developing his own version of social reality comprised of dramatic narratives, more often he presented issue positions, reiterated past accomplishments, and described programs that he had been trying to get through Congress. Bush's approach was to react to attacks and address specific issues as his opponents raised them, rather than setting his own agenda as did his opponents. The nature of these attacks and how he responded to them helped make him appear weak and under siege. This sense of incompleteness perhaps fueled speculation in the media that he had no plan for his campaign and did not know what he wanted to do if reelected. It also fueled speculation that Bush did not want to run for office or serve a second term.

As the primaries progressed, Bush did develop a limited version of social reality that gave a partial account of his foreign policy including the winning of the Cold War and foreign policy successes abroad. However, Bush himself did not appear in them and there was no real directive for action or a place for the people to participate to support him. Foreign policy was the most attractive and coherent of these dramatic narratives, but it tended to stress what had happened in the past. Although Bush mentioned the future, he did not seem to have a new policy to meet changing conditions and growing public dissent.

With unrelenting, and sometimes personal, attacks from a pack of Democratic contenders, and even an opponent from his own party, Bush was pressured from both sides of the political spectrum. On one side was a centrist moving, traditionally liberal Democratic Party and candidate. On the other side was a conservative Republican candidate whose stated objective was to bring a moderate president further to the right. As Bush was forced to move to the right in order to maintain his conservative following, Clinton was allowed to take the centrist ground in the campaign. While the primaries geared up, Bush attempted to stay out of the fray and maintain an appearance of being presidential. However, he was unable to maintain this posture and was pulled unwillingly into the campaign, as he later admitted.

Even after suffering a major attack from his own party and enduring constantly slipping ratings, Bush seemed to survive politically with the public and in the polls. After the threat from his own party was finally removed, on April 29th Bush claimed the number of delegates needed to win his party's nomination. In entering a new phase of the campaign, Bush continued to utilize many of the same dramatic narratives to finish out the remainder of the primary elections. After defeating Buchanan, Bush lost the only serious focus his campaign seemed to have. Instead of using this time to develop a clear version of social reality and shore up lagging support, the Bush campaign seemed to stall while waiting for the general election to begin.

During this time Bush was faced by several events that took his attention away from the campaign. Serious issues were raised by the Los Angeles riots and Hurricane Andrew that Bush as president had to address. Family values became an issue that would come to dominate the national convention after Vice President Quayle's speech about the media's depiction of single parents, exemplified in the television sitcom, Murphy Brown. (Quayle, The Commonwealth Club of California) The attacks from Clinton, and later from Perot, combined with lack of direction in the Bush campaign, registered with the voters as a majority felt that he was drifting without clear policies. (New York Times/CBS Poll, April 25, 30, 1992)

The media version of social reality continued to include the characterization of Bush as not running a strong campaign and lacking conviction on economic issues. They characterized uncertainty in the Bush campaign as stemming from confusion about the basic direction that his campaign should take. (New York Times, April 25, 30, 1992) Bush was characterized as realizing that he had not given America a good reason to reelect him, so he had instructed his staff to find one and define an agenda for the next five years. (New York Times, April 30, 1992)

Throughout this time, Clinton had steadily eroded Bush's lead with Clinton reaching 41% of the vote to Bush with 48%, suggesting Clinton's message was slowly taking hold with the voters. (Gallup Poll, April 15, 1992) The undeclared candidacy of Perot seemed to be taking a toll on Bush as well as Clinton because 43% of the voters did not think any of the candidates were a good choice and over half (60%) did not think they had any good ideas. (Gallup Poll, May 3, 1992)

Voters who continued to share meaning with the Bush version of social reality said that they supported him because they felt he had good judgment in a crisis and rated him high in honesty and trust. This would indicate that they shared his characterization of having the experience to be president. However, less than half of them thought he had a clear plan for the future of the country and the ability to solve its problems, which would eventually weaken his version of social reality motivating some supporters to switch to Clinton or Perot.

Perhaps a historical perspective helps to gain insight into why Bush seemed so unconcerned at this time. In March 1980, Carter led Reagan 50% to 42% in the polls and Reagan rebounded to win 50% to 41%. In 1988, in his first run for president, Bush's unfavorability rating climbed similarly during the primaries. After the Democratic Convention he trailed Dukakis by 17 points and still won 53% to 45%. Maybe, Bush anticipated an encore performance culminating in a second win. (Gallup Poll, March 22, April 12, July 22, 1992)

Perot's Unannounced Campaign.

During the primaries, Perot focused on forging his own mandate. As an independent candidate, he did not face the same problem of defending his candidacy against other candidates to win primary elections. Similarly, he did not have to worry about earning delegates to win a party's nomination at a summer convention. So, Perot was the only candidate in the race with the luxury of being able to define his campaign on his own terms. While the other candidates were fighting it out in primary contests being defined and damaged by their opponents, Perot was unopposed in creating his own popular mandate on his own terms.

However, Perot faced a task similar to Clinton in that he must create his own version of social reality to attract supporters in order to gain enough votes to win. Perot chose to meet this challenge in a much different way than did the other candidates. He did not traverse the country holding rallies and giving stump speeches, a traditional campaign mainstay. Instead, he used the media by appearing on television programs and organizing petition drives to get his name on the ballot. He did not seem to have clearly developed dramatic narratives at the outset of the campaign. Since Perot had little or no previous political experience, his version of social reality had yet to be developed.

The Perot version of social reality seemed to grow spontaneously creating dramatic narratives as it went along. As he was also a challenger like Clinton, Perot had to present his case for change by characterizing the present circumstances as unacceptable, while presenting himself as a better choice to motivate the voters to elect him. If the present situation is intolerable then change must be characterized as safe and attractive to reduce uncertainty in order to gain the voters' support. In order to do this, Perot utilized three basic dramatic narratives. The first centered on the mess in Washington that created a huge national debt and problems throughout the country. The second characterized him as a plain speaking candidate of the people. The third described his vision of the future as being better than today.

Perot entered the race later than the other candidates and did not campaign in the traditional manner. By not declaring his candidacy and characterizing his efforts as a petition drive, he escaped being subjected to the same media scrutiny as the other candidates. Perot enjoyed the luxury of not facing direct opposition from other candidates attacking him and he did not have to debate them. Unlike the other candidates, he did not have to run for months in numerous state primaries with the media deciding whether he was up or down, or when his candidacy was in the lead or finished.

Rather than crisscrossing the country making personal campaign appearances, Perot concentrated on exploiting free television appearances on news and talk shows to make his case to the voters. Thus, he was able to circumvent much of the early political process that was endured and in most cases not survived by other candidates. This approach enabled Perot to jump directly into the main election and run against the incumbent president without any opposition or the burden of having to follow the rules. This may be why Perot was able to criticize Bush and gain high ratings without accruing the negative baggage of high unfavorable ratings that the other candidates amassed.

The focus of Perot's campaign was to describe what he thought was wrong with Bush and the government. Perot was prolific in his criticism of the current government in Washington, but provided few specifics for change. He was often criticized in the media for not being forthcoming with his own proposals for change and only being critical of others. In many instances, he claimed that he was studying the problem and would get back later with what he would do about it. When Perot entered the race, Bush's approval ratings as president were below 50% and both Bush and Clinton shared high negative ratings.

The media characterized the candidates as being so bad that another unnamed candidate would be better. So, it was not surprising that an independent candidate would eventually share the media's dramatic narratives and enter the race. The situation looked bad for Bush and Clinton, but more optimistic for an independent candidate like Perot. History would suggest that third party candidates tend to do well initially and then their support tapers off. In the 1980 presidential race, John Anderson initially drew 20% support in April, peaking at 24% in June, and then dropped to 14% after the summer conventions, to win only 7% of the vote in the fall election. (Gallup Poll, April 5, 1992)

On March 24, Jerry Brown solidly won the Connecticut primary and Clinton's support decreased suggesting that he would not be able to profit from Bush's increased vulnerability. Between March 22 and April 1, Clinton's support dropped from 43% to 34% and Bush gained from 52% to 54%, reversing past trends. In a three way race, early polls indicated that Perot would tie Clinton with 24% to 25% of voters with Bush leading at 44%. (Gallup Poll, April 5, 1992)

Not being a politician initially helped Perot as 32% of the people found him favorable, while only 10% did not. This was the first election since 1956 where both the incumbent and the major party challenger had negative ratings above 30%, with Clinton at 33% and 35% for Bush. These negative ratings later climbed to 34% for Clinton and 47% for Bush, which suggested large numbers of those polled were sharing Perot's dramatic narratives regarding Bush, Clinton, and the government in Washington. By mid-April over half the voters were dissatisfied with the political process and the current candidates, so much so that 61% felt the Democratic convention should consider new candidates. (Gallup Poll, April 5, 12, 15, 1992)

By the end of April, Bush had 50% of the vote with a 42% approval rating, while Clinton was at 34%, which may indicate that dramatic narratives against Bush were working. However, the people may not have been willing to change and for the time being they continued to support Bush despite their dissatisfaction with him. This would keep Bush's support higher than his opposition, even though he had a higher negativity rating. Clinton was also losing ground as now half (49%) of the people had a negative impression of him. Perot's name recognition nearly doubled in a month and he had the lowest negative rating of all candidates at 23%, with 41% favorable. (Gallup Poll, April 26, 1992)

Perot and The American Dream.

As the campaign progressed, Perot began to add more specific dramatic narratives until a clear and coherent version of social reality had emerged. Perot employed this version of social reality throughout the campaign. He often utilized the familiar dramatic narrative of restoration. Perot said he would be the voice of the people and would restore the government to the people to whom it rightfully belonged. This dramatic narrative was reminiscent of one in Ronald Reagan's version of social reality, restoring the American way by getting the government off the backs of people.

Perot utilized a dramatic narrative characterizing the people in Washington who had created the mess in which the country now found itself immersed. The government could no longer be tolerated by the people and must be changed in order for the country to solve the problems it faced. This dramatic narrative of Washington in disarray was similar to a mainstay of Clinton's campaign. Even though he claimed his candidacy was only a petition drive to get his name placed on the ballot in all fifty states, Perot was in essence running primarily against Bush rather than Clinton or any other candidate. Characterizing his candidacy as a petition drive also served to insulate him to some extent from the scrutiny directed at other candidates.

Perot described the lives of ordinary people who lived in fear of crime with bars on their doors and windows, a court system that most people could not afford, and a health care system that was not available to all people. With these dramatic narratives he characterized America as the most violent, crime ridden nation, with the highest number of functional illiterates, ranking at the bottom of the industrialized world in academic achievement. He said that the government had let the job base deteriorate, creating tax users when we needed to foster business growth to create taxpayers. It was fiscally irresponsible for the government to finance long term projects with short term debt held by foreign interests. Employing interpretations of breaking news to characterize a present that was unacceptable, Perot tried to discredit the current positive characterizations of America, like Reagan's famous "Morning in America." (Reagan Television Ad, 1984)

Against a negative scene of the present, Perot presented a positive depiction of a future achieved through change. In presenting a vision of a better future, he felt that American jobs must be protected and businesses kept strong in order to provide jobs to keep people off government rolls. He felt that industries of the future should be targeted with investment strategies to make the words 'made in the USA' mean something as a standard of excellence in the world. Education was another investment that we had failed to make, it was a national failure so it must be remedied in the future. The government must stop its adversarial relationship with business and form partnerships to compete in a global economy, as had been done in Germany and Japan.

According to Perot, it should be illegal for former public officials to serve as lobbyists for companies or foreign interests to influence our laws for five to ten years after leaving government because, "you don't come to Washington to cash in, you come to serve the people," and now they are on both campaign staffs. We own this country, so the government should come from us, instead it comes at us. The country has to be put back under the control of the people who are the owners. Perot added, "In plain Texas talk, it's time to take out the trash... or it will be too late." The people have to be "fully informed" and "stay in the ring," not just elect someone and then go home. Important decisions including pay raises should be put on the ballot for the owners to decide. Perot got involved because he loved this country, the people, and the principles it was founded on, and because he was "sick and tired of seeing these principles violated." (Perot, National Press Club)

In creating his version of social reality, Perot used a dramatic narrative of himself as a plain speaking, straight talking, get the job done alternative to the deception and inaction in Washington. He had the business experience to solve the country's problems by getting people to work together through consensus, which he characterized as linking arms together. Perot was the quintessential reluctant leader, he would not seek office, but if drafted would work for the people as their servant. Perot would get rid of special interests and foreign lobbyists. He would demand integrity and experience from those in government.

Perot developed his own version of the American Dream dramatic narrative. He said that he wanted to give future generations the American Dream that he had been fortunate enough to live. In this way, he connected his populist candidacy to his characterization of the American Dream. Coming from humble beginnings, Perot had been blessed with prosperity through hard work and helping others because America was the land of opportunity unlike any other nation on earth.

Perot's speaking style added to his public persona of an ordinary guy who had done well. He described himself as not a polished orator, but spoke truth from the heart. His populist, euphemistic, plain style of speaking, and ready wit was reminiscent of early rhetorical styles deeply rooted in the American political tradition. To show that his dramatic narrative of being a plain speaking candidate of the people shared meaning with the people and the media, as he was often compared to Harry Truman who had many of the same qualities.

In order to gain support during this phase of the campaign, Perot needed to shake people loose from their old version of social reality by characterizing the current administration as repugnant in the worst possible terms, just as Clinton had done. There must be a compelling reason for change and for persuading the voters to switch to a new and unfamiliar version of social reality. So, the new one must be made to be more appealing than the old social reality to reduce uncertainty about him. For Perot, the people in Washington did not understand how to solve the people's problems because they did not know how things worked. If they did, they still could not do anything about them because they had no idea what the problems even were. What they did know how to do was to take money from foreign lobbyists and profit for themselves.

The president and Congress blamed each other when they should have been working together to solve the country's problems. Instead, they bickered, fought, and pointed fingers to avoid responsibility. Yet, they spent money at an amazing rate, creating the largest national debt in history. He equated the government's approach to that of a financial officer in a corporation who, if they did the same things would go to prison.

Characterizing the tax code as unfair, Perot said it was "a tire with a thousand patches," with each patch added by a special interest. It should be thrown out and the government should start over with a blank sheet of paper. The people must demand long term solutions because the country could no longer afford to let the economy deteriorate. Because the other candidates had ignored the national debt, Perot made it the focus of his attention by characterizing the present government's economic policies as spending our children's money to mortgage their future, so it was irresponsible for the government to put this burden on them.

The Perot Conundrum.

When Perot entered the campaign, Bush's lead in the polls eroded from 50% (in a two-way race) on April 22 to 35% (in a three-way race) by May 10. Despite this drop of fifteen points, he remained in first place. Perot followed in second place with 30% of the voters supporting him. Coming in third, Clinton had dropped 5 points during the same period from 34% to 29%, but with a much smaller loss in support than Bush had suffered. (Gallup Poll, June 10, 1992)

Perot's unannounced candidacy was hurting Bush the most. Bush's dramatic narratives were not gaining many new supporters and their ability to hold current supporters was slipping. Neither Bush nor Clinton were attacking Perot clearing the way for him to gain support. Perot's attacks on Washington had drawn voters away from Bush, increasing Bush's unfavorability rating. Even though Bush was still leading in the polls, it began to look like he was in serious trouble. While 35% of the people shared Bush's dramatic narratives, 58%, well over half of the people now shared anti-Bush dramatic narratives. This change represented a significant shift in the electorate.

By the end of May, Perot had tied with Bush in the polls and by June Perot surpassed him, leaving Clinton a distant third. By June, Bush's favorability rating was 44%, with 48% for Perot and 45% for Clinton. On the eve of the Democratic convention, Bush had 35% of the vote with Perot at 30% and Clinton trailed them both with 28%. However, with Perot in the race, for the first time in the campaign, Bush had lost the support of the majority of the people. (Gallup Poll, July 2, 15, 1992)

The most significant obstacle for Bush was the change in how people perceived he was performing his job as president. From the first of the year to the Democratic Convention, Bush went from an approval rating of 46% to 38% and his disapproval rating went from 47% to 55%. (Gallup Poll, January 19, June 26, 1992)

This trend would suggest that Bush's characterization of his past experience was not gaining support, while negative characterizations about him by his opponents were sharing meaning with the voters. Despite these low ratings, Bush continued to lead in electability suggesting that some of his dramatic narratives were still holding, but they were under tremendous pressure and in serious danger of collapsing.

Even as Clinton's ratings improved, Perot still continued to keep Clinton in third place. It looked like Clinton had slowed down in his ability to attract more supporters. It also appeared that Perot had drawn voters away from Bush further increasing Bush's unfavorability rating, which was considered a determinant of Bush being reelected. Because Perot was relatively unknown, he generated a low negative response. However, this was expected to change as Perot became better known to the public.

Even though Clinton had lost ground, this shift in the electorate would ultimately benefit him the most. Although Clinton was in third place at 28%, what was significant was that with Perot in the race, only 35%, less than half the people, now shared the Bush version of social reality, but 58%, well over half of the people, now shared the anti-Bush dramatic narratives of Clinton and Perot, which were similar in many important respects. This gave Clinton the potential to attract many of Perot's supporters.

Perot had succeeded in converting a large block of Bush supporters to Perot's version of social reality. This conversion was observed in the polls with the increase in angry voters. This change represented a major shift in the electorate because now Bush had lost the support of the majority of the voters. Perot had been able to accomplish in a comparatively short time what Clinton could not, to lure a majority of the American people away from Bush.

The Year Of The Angry Voter.

Beginning in April, the Gallup Poll observed a growing public discontent with the candidates, which they called "the angry voter." The media shared this dramatic narrative of the angry voter and it became a dramatic narrative in media interpretations of the campaign. Comprising 39% of the electorate, the angry voter was characterized in the media as being dissatisfied with both Bush and Clinton. Their anger was evidenced by Bush and Clinton's unfavorability ratings reaching a record 49% and 62% respectively. (Gallup Poll, April 12, May 3, 1992)

From January to April, the number of people who felt proud of the election process dropped to 39%. Almost half, 43%, felt that none of the candidates would make a good president and 60% thought that none of the candidates had any good ideas to solve the nation's problems. Those who felt that the candidates did not address important issues increased from 28% in January to 44% in May. Despite their anger with the candidates, more voters indicated that they would vote for Bush at 43% over Clinton at 29% or Perot at 21%. Even among angry voters Bush led with 38% to Clinton with 22% and 30% for Perot.

This voter anger had not transferred to members of Congress despite Bush's negative characterizations of them. When asked if their congressional representative should be reelected, voters said yes versus no 54% to 26%. The subgroup of voters labeled angry indicated that they would vote to reelect their congressional representative by a 45% to 40% margin. In spite of a widely reported dissatisfaction with Congress, a majority of voters and even angry voters thought their representative should be returned to office. (Gallup Poll, May 3, 1992)

With a strong Perot showing, the media began to share meaning about a dramatic narrative involving an electoral crisis in which none of the candidates would have the number of electoral votes needed to win. This would mean that the House of Representatives would decide the election. Perot's ratings had improved since April, moving from 23% to 16% unfavorable and from 41% to 48% favorable. Late in May, Perot tied with Bush for the lead in the polls at 35%, with Clinton trailing at 25%. As Bush and Clinton's favorability ratings declined, Perot's rating increased to a 50% favorability rating. (Gallup Poll, May 24, 1992)

Even though Perot was vague on the issues, his dramatic narratives about Washington and the state of the nation were catching on with the voters. Perot's dramatic narratives enticed those with feelings of uncertainty about the present candidates as he presented an alternative to politics as usual. Public response to Perot would support the notion that skill in sharing meaning with the voters utilizing dramatic narratives can be more significant to gaining voter support than having actual positions on the issues.

The attraction of his dramatic narratives was in their explanatory nature and Perot seemed to be able to provide an appreciable faction of the electorate with a believable explanation of events, at least in the present. This notion would seem to be evidenced by the polls as 56%, over half of the electorate and 33%, a third of those who supported Perot felt that they knew little or nothing about him. While only 11% claimed to know a lot about him. (Gallup Poll, May 24, 1992)

Among those who supported Perot, 77% felt that he had strong leadership abilities, 73% felt that he could get things done, 62% felt that he would have good judgment in a crisis, 53% felt that he cared about people, and 51% felt that he could enact change. These numbers would suggest that the electorate was sharing meaning with several Perot dramatic narratives. (Gallup Poll, May 24, 1992)

By June, for the first time in history, an independent candidate led in the national polls. With 39% of the voters supporting him, Perot led Bush with 31% and Clinton with 25%. In a two way contest Clinton still trailed Bush 40% to 46%, even though Bush's approval rating had fallen to 37%, indicating that Clinton had yet to capitalize on Bush's approval rating dropping from 46% in January to 37% in June, its lowest level of the year.

The economy was the issue voters said they were most concerned about and 39% felt Perot was best able to handle it. Bush followed with 23% and Clinton was perceived as the least able to handle the economy with 22%. Perot was perceived as best able to facilitate change with 38%, Bush had 20%, with 24% for Clinton. At this time 72% of all voters supporting a candidate perceived their candidate as representing change, a clear sign that this dramatic narrative was being widely shared, perhaps explaining why Bush later shifted his campaign to promote the need for change. (Gallup Poll, June 8, 10, 14, 1992)

It seemed that Perot's dramatic narrative of the Washington mess had the ability to capture the public's dissatisfaction with government. A historic high of 75%, felt that Washington did the right thing only some of the time or not at all. Only once since 1958 had trust in government fallen so low. In 1980, after an economic downturn and the Iran Hostage crisis, only 25% rated the government as positive. (Gallup Poll, June 14, 1992, University of Michigan, American National Election Study)

Historical precedent would suggest that the groundswell of support Perot received would not last and in July this prediction began to be realized. Perot fell from a high of 39% to 32%, behind Bush at 33% and ahead of Clinton at 27%. The media explained this drop largely on Perot's rising unfavorability ratings stemming from voters finally getting to know him. Since May, Perot's unfavorability had gone from 25% to 34%, moving more closely to the ratings of his opponents. (Gallup Poll, July 2, 1992) The longer he was in the race, the more his unfavorability rating increased suggesting that voters' dissatisfaction may be more the result of the electoral process than their perception of a candidate's qualities.

The media explained the public's favorability of Perot as being due to his personality and individual style. About a third (31%) of the people shared the dramatic narrative of Perot running the country like a business and 33% that he was a man of action, while 23% thought he could bring the kind of change the country needed.

What was hurting Perot was his lack of specific ideas on the issues as 38% felt his not taking positions on some issues troublesome because they did not know what he would do if elected. About 40% worried that he would assume too much power and not respect limits on presidential powers. Lack of political experience ranked low with only 18% concerned that he had no training to be president. (Gallup Poll, July 2, 1992)

Perot Withdraws From The Race.

The events in this section overlap in time with the next chapter, but are included in both places because of their significance to the outcome of the election. As an independent candidate, Perot had a unique problem that neither of the other two candidates shared. He did not have the public forum of state primaries or a national party convention to use as a platform to get his message out to the voting public. Even though he did not have primaries, a convention, or a political party to support him, he was still able to capture the nation's attention.

Since Perot was an unconventional candidate, the events that transpired should not have carried the surprise they did. In the midst of the television coverage of the Democratic National Convention, Perot dropped a bombshell that upstaged them and brought him national television coverage when he announced his withdrawal from the race. In doing this, he cited his reason for withdrawing was that the Democratic Party was now revitalized and had the ability to bring the party together to address important issues facing the nation.

Perot said that the motivation for his withdrawal was that he was thinking of what was in the best interest of the nation and the people. He characterized the Democratic Party as now being much stronger and revitalized. It had pulled itself together in order to address important issues. So, he no longer thought that he had a chance to win. He expressed concern that his candidacy might needlessly divide the nation in a three way fight. Perot had invited speculation that he might win enough electoral votes, so that no candidate would have enough to claim victory throwing the election into the House of Representatives assuring a Democratic victory, which might not be the people's choice. Here, he played the hero falling on his sword doing what was right and noble by sacrificing his own ambitions for the greater good of the country. This action would later have the reverse effect by damaging his own legitimacy eliminating any chance of electoral success.

Despite his strong showing in the polls, on July 16 Perot unexpectedly withdrew from the race. Recent polls placed Perot with 28% of the vote, down from a high of 39% compared to Clinton's 31% and Bush's 32%, making the race a statistical dead heat. (Gallup Poll, July 15, 1992) Much to the surprise and anger of his supporters, Perot took this dramatic action despite unprecedented support for a third party candidate. Even though he withdrew as a candidate, he continued his petition drive to be placed on the ballot in all fifty states.

In June, Perot was considered the candidate most likely to effect change by 38%, followed by 24% for Clinton and 20% for Bush. Perot was considered best to handle the economy by 39%, followed by 22% for Clinton and 23% for Bush. Perot rated highest in putting the country's interests above politics 41%, in getting things done 36%, and caring about people 31%. Perot had a slight edge in having a clear plan to fix the nations problems 25% to 21% for Clinton and 19% for Bush, even though he had few issue positions. (Gallup Poll, June 21, 1992)

Many voters expressed concern over his lack of developed positions on the issues because Perot had avoided them in his campaign. However, his support remained high suggesting that it was not issue positions that motivated voters to share meaning with candidates, but rather how they characterize events. During the primaries, Perot had essentially campaigned for Clinton because Perot's version of social reality was so similar to Clinton's it would be relatively easy for voters who shared the Perot version to switch to Clinton rather than to Bush. It was to Bush's credit that he received as many converts as he did from the Perot camp in spite of their fundamental differences.

In the days leading up to his withdrawal, Perot had slipped slightly in the polls, but he still maintained a historically unprecedented showing for a third party candidate. His campaign had lost several well known political consultants including former Reagan consultant Ed Rollins and former Jimmy Carter Chief of Staff Hamilton Jordan over rumored personal disputes. These events alone do not seem to provide sufficient reasons to support such drastic action. This action suggests that now that there was a real possibility of being elected, he really didn't want it.

Perot dropping out of the race during the Democratic National Convention, on the day of Clinton's most important speech, gave Clinton the best chance of gaining the most benefit from Perot's action. People who shared the Perot version of social reality had their candidate suddenly taken away, so they would be searching for a new one at a time when the Democrat's were presenting their plan for America. Clinton had created a version of social reality that would be more attractive to Perot supporters than Bush's loosely connected visionless dramatic narratives. Now, it would be up to Clinton to maintain that support. If he could do that, he would be assured to win.

Given this dramatic turn of events at this particular time, the question of motivation naturally arises. What would prompt one of the most successful independent candidates in history to abruptly drop out of the campaign? Considering how long he had been in the race, why was such drastic action taken at this particular moment? Why not wait until after the convention or at least a few more hours until after hearing Clinton's speech? This raises the question, why did Perot really get into the race in the first place? Perot's lack of criticism of Clinton and the timing of his withdrawal suggested that part of his motivation might have been to give Clinton maximum support or to inflict maximum damage to Bush, or both.

If that was not the intent, it was the result.

Chapter 5
The Conventions

National political party conventions at one time chose presidential candidates, wrangled over political policies, and hammered out party platforms. Decisions and deals were made in smoke filled back rooms by political bosses.

Today, the primary system selects the party's nominee through a series of state primary elections before any candidate ever gets to the convention. Conventions now function more as a choreographed media event extolling the virtues of the presidential candidate and the party. Everything is planned in advance of the convention to avoid any conflicts that might be played out on live television before the entire nation.

Conventions of the past have been more uncertain being marred by conflict, controversy, and even violence. Perhaps, the most infamous being the 1968 Democratic Convention in Chicago. Since then, very little is left to chance because the public airing of conflict at a convention would reduce the chances of electoral success in November.

In the 1992 presidential election campaign, the two major party conventions marked a definite turning point that would ultimately determine the political fortunes of the candidates. Going into the Democratic National Convention, Clinton was gaining momentum with 28% of the voters supporting him, nearly tied with Perot at 30%, but still trailing Bush who led them both with 35% of the voters. (Gallup Poll, July 12, 1992)

Problems with Clinton's character stemming from his infidelity and draft dodging still contributed to his negative image. The negatives had risen from 40% in March to 49% in July. His favorability rating, however, had also improved from 37% to 41% during the same period. (Gallup Poll, March 26-29, July 6-8, 1992) Those who disapproved of Clinton most often cited character (39%). Character issues of this sort seemed to have had less importance overall as 56% felt that Clinton had the honesty and integrity to be president, up from 47% in April.

These improvements in public perception indicate that Clinton's own characterizations of himself may have had a positive effect. Clinton came across as thoughtful, with 71% feeling that he had a good understanding of the issues, but 53% did not think that he had a good plan for solving the nation's problems. In countering foreign policy attacks, 62% felt he would defend our national interests abroad and 52% felt that he would show good judgment in a crisis. His dramatic narrative of restoration had less effect because 48% of voters felt that he could not bring about needed change. (Gallup Poll, July 15, 1992)

The Democratic National Convention.

From July 13th to the 16th in New York City, the Democratic Party came together to anoint Bill Clinton and Al Gore as its candidates for president and vice president of the United States. In a striking coincidence there was a sense of déjà vu mentioned by several speakers. Sixteen years before, in this same place at Madison Square Garden, the Democratic Party met to nominate an unknown governor from another southern state in hopes that he would unseat an incumbent president. It was that nominee, Jimmy Carter who went on to defeat incumbent President Gerald Ford. The convention emphasized The New Covenant dramatic narrative as the core of the social reality that Clinton had carried through the primaries.

The following are some of the featured convention speakers.

Bill Bradley, A Vision Of Teamwork.

New Jersey Senator Bill Bradley developed the part of the Clinton version of social reality that characterized the need for change by comparing the differences between Bush and Clinton. In characterizing the Bush years, Bradley went through a litany of examples of Bush not showing decisive leadership. He said that Bush had "waffled and wiggled and wavered." Bradley spoke of his playing basketball for the New York Nicks, where players worked together for the good of the team. The American people should develop a similar kind of teamwork to have a better future. Now the country faced a crisis of no hope, so he called for a return to those things that made America great. Personal achievement and mutual cooperation would create a better America and a better world for the future that could be realized by following Clinton.

Zell Miller, A Plain Speaker From Appalachia.

Georgia Governor Zell Miller used a dramatic narrative characterizing the Republicans as villains, a party of divisiveness and diversion, robbing people of hope as "the voices of anger rise up, rise up from working Americans..." Bush was a "timid man who only hears the voices of caution and the status quo." Miller characterized Bush as a man who just did not get it, did not see it, did not feel it, and did nothing about it. He characterized Perot as someone who gave us salesmanship rather than leadership. Miller compared all three candidates, summing them up as an "aristocrat, an autocrat, and a Democrat." (Miller, Convention Address)

In contrast, Miller called Clinton a hero who might not be book smart, but need not be because he had experienced the struggle with poverty and came from a single parent family. Clinton never had a free ride, he had achieved everything through hard work. Miller called Clinton a man of courage who would stand up to both liberals and conservatives for reform. Miller characterized himself as an unpolished, plain speaking person from a corner of Appalachia in a remote valley hidden among the peaks and hollows.

Nominating a man for president from a remote part of Arkansas was testimony to the American Dream that lived on in the Democratic Party. Miller was an ordinary man who may not speak eloquently, but spoke from the heart. Coming from a poor family, Miller's father died soon after he was born, a circumstance he shared with Clinton.

His mother worked hard, clearing the land and building a house from stones collected in a mountain creek. She had mixed the cement in a wheelbarrow, cement that today still bears her handprints and those of her small sons. Miller added that, not everyone could be born with everything, so that was why there was a Democratic party with heroes like Roosevelt, Truman, Kennedy, Johnson, and Carter. These were men of decency, honesty, and integrity.

This dramatic narrative illustrated the Democrats as a party of hope, not just for his mother in the past, but for all people in the future. Miller compared his background to Clinton's background. Each came from humble beginnings to become governors of their states, which was a tribute to the American Dream. Even with success, Miller never forgot his roots because that very night his children and their children who lived in the same mountain valley were watching him on television right now in the very stone house built by his mother.

In this dramatic narrative, he compared his house to every house to let the people know that they would fight for working people to "ease your burden," "carry your cause," and "hear all the voices of America." The Democrats would "answer their call," "keep the faith," and "restore hope." (Miller, Convention Address)

This dramatic narrative played on the double meaning of Hope, Arkansas and human hope. It was one that would be employed often throughout the convention. Reiteration of similar stories and the play on words regarding hope by different speakers shows that these dramatic narratives were widely shared. (In 2004, Miller would give a keynote speech at the Republican National Convention criticizing Democrats and supporting the reelection of George W. Bush.)

Paul Tsongas, Heals Political Divisions.

Former Massachusetts Senator Paul Tsongas ran for the Democratic presidential nomination in the primary elections against Clinton. His presence at the convention as an opponent who was now a supporter symbolized that the divisions in the party were now healed. In speaking to the convention, Tsongas began by retelling the Clinton version of the American Dream dramatic narrative. He characterized immigrants coming to America in search of freedom, of men and women laboring and dying to build and defend it.

Utilizing the dramatic narrative of restoration, he said that we must restore the past principles of our forebears and abandon present day indulgences. Clinton would restore economic security, which was the foundation of everything we hope to do. He said that Americans knew we were in trouble. They knew we must invigorate the economy, create jobs, cut taxes, reduce deficits, and make things fair. The country was ready for sacrifice because what was done must be paid for, not borrowed from our children, so fiscal discipline must prevail.

Tsongas characterized Bush as the villain who had shamefully created a legacy of the greatest debtor nation on earth, unable to compete in the world. He said Bush's "record is generationally immoral. It violates the legacy of our ancestors. It violates the promise to our children. It is spiritually bankrupt." It is our responsibility to restore the country, economic growth, and fiscal responsibility. In order to do this, he concluded, the people must unite and choose a path of responsibility by electing Clinton. (Tsongas, Convention Address)

Ronald Brown, Unites The Party.

Democratic National Party Chair Ronald Brown, recalled sixteen years ago when the Democratic Party met in the same place to nominate the last Democrat elected president. His dramatic narrative was of a party celebrating their unity, strength, and leadership to shed the shackles of a failed presidency. Brown repeated the dramatic narrative of the American Dream. Having been entrusted with leading and rebuilding, the Democratic Party was an example of the American Dream. Brown painted a picture of a united Democratic Party that had put aside internal fights and avoided primary battles to target Bush for defeat.

In contrast to this upbeat characterization of a new Democratic Party, he created another dramatic narrative of the upcoming Republican Convention. He sketched a hellish scene in which the Republican Party would be divided and dispirited by problems with the economy. He envisioned a convention full of "supply siders," "race baiters," and " S & L looters," telling lies and breaking promises. (Brown, Convention Address) Bush would ask for a second term based on his record of tax breaks for the rich and no tax cuts for the poor, on broken promises on the environment and jobs, on racing speedboats and golfing, and on blaming the recession on the media. Bush was characterized as a president of privilege who knew nothing of the plight of ordinary people and blamed his problems on anything he could find.

These dramatic narratives formed the basis of his restaging of the Clinton characterization of the need for change by saying that the American people would not be fooled again. They were a party that brought all people together to fight for the country's potential, justice, and equality. He described the party as standing with a litany of heroic persona including Roosevelt, Truman, Kennedy, Johnson, and Carter. It would be Clinton who would restore the country's principles and values to which our lives, our fortunes, and our sacred honor were pledged.

Barbara Jordan, Agent Of Change.

Former Texas Representative, Barbara Jordan reiterated the dramatic narrative of change to reinforce Clinton's version of social reality. First, she characterized the other candidates, who argued about which one was the agent of change as not comprehending the public's apprehension about the future. She saw the Democratic Party as the catalyst of change, a party that knew what needed to be done and could do it as they had done in the past. The party had to change its reputation from one of tax and spend to investment and growth.

As her justification for change, Jordan reiterated the Clinton dramatic narrative of economic crisis. She said that America was a place where people feared losing their jobs and were trying to survive, so economic growth and environmental protection must become compatible. She then tied the dramatic narrative of change to the American Dream because, "the American Dream is slipping away from too many people." In order to change we must move away from the "greed and hatred and selfishness" of the eighties when executives prospered, while people lived without sanitation and working people lived in decaying inner cities. (Jordan, Convention Address)

Trust and character were other elements in her dramatic narrative of change. In order to change, the party had to convince the people to trust them to govern. Public apprehension and fear created cynicism, so reason must prevail for the country to win. She cast her party as the purveyor of reason and as the provider of solutions, who could best lead the country at this time in our history. The assumption was that the nation was in disarray and that the unmentioned villains were the Republicans. So, if change was to be achieved, the best alternative was to choose the Democrats to lead the nation.

Al Gore, The Accidental Candidate.

"Pledging to pour my heart and soul into this crusade," Tennessee Senator Albert Gore accepted his party's nomination to run for the Vice Presidency. He began by characterizing himself as the unlikely candidate who did not seek nor expect this honor, but would uphold the office. For the love of his country, Gore had worked for the forgotten majority that the government was failing. Hearkening to the restoration dramatic narrative, he would renew the journey begun by our country's forefathers because, "We were not put here on earth to look out for our needs alone." (Gore, Convention Address)

Evoking the American Dream dramatic narrative, Gore told of his father who was a teacher in a one room schoolhouse and went on to represent Tennessee in the House and Senate. Gore had experienced adversity, including what it was like to lose a father and a sister. He had experienced what it was like to have his son struck by a car and fight for his life while he stayed at his bedside. His family was healed by the love, prayers, and kindness of people he did not know.

In comparing his personal experiences to that of the nation, he said that we were all a part of something larger, you hear it in quiet voices crying, see it reflected in weary eyes. "You will see that our democracy is lying there in the gutter waiting for us to give it a second breath of life." In this direct reference to his son's crisis, he equated this family experience with the crisis of the nation. He rallied his audience in a call for the renewal of the country and of ourselves, admonishing people not to lose heart for together, "We will rekindle the American spirit and renew this nation for generations to come." (Gore, Convention Address)

Gore reiterated the dramatic narrative of a troubled country that had been utilized by previous speakers. He amplified the charges against the Republicans and characterized them as villains who had failed. They lacked moral courage, had given the people false choices, ignored suffering, endangered America's interests, betrayed cherished ideals, and embarrassed the country in the eyes of the whole world. Like other speakers, Gore repeated the dramatic narrative of restoration by depicting an America in despair. He characterized an alternative scene of his party to bolster its own legitimacy by connecting his values with the values of the people. Gore characterized a scene of a better future that had become a hallmark of the Democratic platform as presented at the convention. In closing, Gore admonished the people not to lose heart for together they would rekindle the American spirit to renew the nation for generations to come.

Mario Cuomo, People Want Change.

The speech to nominate Bill Clinton as the Democratic candidate for president was delivered by New York Governor Mario Cuomo. His appearance was important to the Democrats because early in the campaign Cuomo had been a media favorite to run for president and the media had speculated about his potential success, even though he had never chosen to run. When the Gennifer Flowers scandal surfaced, Clinton was reported to have made disparaging remarks about Cuomo and Italians that was released to the media. Clinton was forced to publicly apologize to Cuomo. The presence of Cuomo was key to repairing the rift between him and Clinton as well as signaling to the public the unity of the party.

In his address, Cuomo developed the dramatic narrative of change by using a comparison between the disastrous course led by the Republican administration and another choice where Clinton was the nation's only hope. He contrasted the Republican's "shining city on the hill" with the reality of a real city where "people were struggling, many of them living in pain." (Cuomo, Convention Address) Cuomo described the state of the country as being intolerable for the people and then offering a better alternative with Clinton in order to convince voters that there was a need for change.

Cuomo used Perot's popularity as proof of how desperate people were for change. He warned the party to not fail to bring their message to the people as they had in the past because they wanted something better than Bush, something that only Clinton could provide. In order to make his case, he employed the analogy of the ship of state as being about to sink. He said that the crew knows it, the passengers know it, but only the captain of the ship, President Bush, did not know it. This was the president who said there was no money to do what needed to be done for children or for jobs, yet had billions to bail out crooked bankers and for war.

Cuomo characterized Clinton as a born leader who was the solution to the nation's problems because he had the ability to get the country back on course to advert disaster. In his dramatic narrative of change and prosperity, Clinton was the hero as the agent of change. Cuomo also employed Clinton's dramatic narrative of hope in the future as a means of justifying his call for change. He concluded that Clinton would lead a "victory parade" through the streets where there is opportunity and jobs making "America surer, stronger, and sweeter," Clinton was "the comeback kid, a new voice for America." (Cuomo, Convention Address)

Bill Clinton, The New Covenant.

In accepting his party's nomination as their candidate for the office of the president of the United States, Clinton took the major features of his original version of social reality and developed several of his dramatic narratives to exemplify them. He focused on the core narrative of The New Covenant, but also included the dramatic narratives of hope, restoration, and family values, as well as the American Dream.

In his acceptance speech, Clinton expanded on his frequently utilized version of The New Covenant dramatic narrative. According to Clinton, The New Covenant was about benefits the government would bestow on the people like creating jobs, promoting investment, improving the economy, giving people opportunity, providing health care, helping to raise middle class incomes, lowering taxes, reforming welfare, protecting global interests, promoting the cause of freedom abroad, and reducing spending to remain strong. The New Covenant was also about responsibility, which according to Clinton starts at the top with our leaders. It was also about opportunity for everyone, like in Arkansas where a lot of great people, working together made amazing progress.

Clinton characterized this dramatic narrative as opportunity, responsibility, and community with everyone pulling together to seize the moment to "renew our faith" and "restore our sense of unity and community." Clinton called on the people to join in his campaign, acknowledging that he could not do this alone. Only through combined mutual effort, commitment, and creativity could we "chart a bold new future." Now was the time that the nation must again renew their commitment to the future and to future generations in an effort to give something to our children, community, and country. We must lift our spirits and inspire the world in a New Covenant because Clinton still believed "in a place called Hope." (Clinton, Convention Address)

In his speech, Clinton repeated his dramatic narrative of hope by telling the story of his growing up in Hope, Arkansas as illustrating the ideal America he sought to restore. Then Clinton moved to include the dramatic narrative of the American Dream that he had used extensively throughout the campaign. The American Dream had been destroyed by the people in Washington through "brain dead" politics and a president "caught in the grip of a failed economic theory." (Clinton, Convention Address)

In concluding his speech, Clinton repeated his dramatic narrative of restoration that began with the need for change. It was the Democrats who were the agents of change to make government work and even Perot believed that they were a revitalized party that would change America. Clinton said a new approach of empowerment, not entitlement was needed giving people more choices, expanding opportunity based on old values, and demanding responsibility. Clinton recognized that there was change occurring around the globe and appreciated that now there needed to be change at home. He would defend hard working people who raise children, pay taxes, and "play by the rules." He would defend the "forgotten middle class," against the "forces of greed and the defenders of the status quo." (Clinton, Convention Address)

Democratic Convention Themes.

During the Democratic National Convention, the speakers presented to the American people a unified version of their party's social reality. In various ways, they characterized the dramatic narrative of The New Covenant. Repetition of the same dramatic narratives during a convention can be used to provide evidence that they had shared meaning with the public as speakers tend to repeat ideas that share meaning with their audience. During the convention, the speakers presented a choice to the voters, to continue the past twelve years of waste and greed that hurt the middle class and working people while the rich and crooks benefited or to support Clinton and the Democratic Party as an agent of change to provide a better future for all Americans. Clinton and the other Democrats presented dramatic narratives representing their personal experiences illustrating how they had benefitted from the American Dream. They recalled their past of hardship and struggles that made them feel the pain of average working people who struggled daily. These were people they would not forget and for whom they were dedicated to making a better tomorrow.

Post Convention Response Unprecedented.

The dramatic narratives presented by the convention speakers were widely shared by the media. The Democrats were characterized in the media as a new party, different from the Democrats and Republicans of the past. They were a party with a plan for a smarter government. (CNN, July 14, 1992) Clinton was characterized as a moderate and an instrument of change. (NBC Nightly News, July 14, 1992, New York Times, July 17, 1992)

The dramatic narratives utilized during the convention were not only shared with the public, but by the media as well. After the convention 61% of the people believed that the Democratic Party had changed for the better, including 42% of Republicans. Clinton's favorability rating increased from 41% to 63%, while his unfavorable rating dropped from 49% to 25%. Bush's favorable rating further eroded from 49% to 40%, while his unfavorable rating increased from 45% to 53% during this time. (Gallup Poll, July 22, 1992)

Historically, this mark is significant for Bush because an incumbent president running for a second term would not likely be reelected with an average approval rating of less than 50% for the year. Clinton gained in several key areas that he had characterized frequently during the convention. This indicated that the dramatic narratives of the convention were working and that his version of social reality was being more widely shared with the public. With the convention delivering an estimated audience of 95% of the electorate, it provided a great potential for gaining support.

The effectiveness of the convention's dramatic narratives is supported by poll data that indicated Americans who believed Clinton had the honesty and integrity to be president increased from 56% to 69%. The dramatic narrative of restoration also seemed to be more widely shared as 64% of the voters now believed that Clinton had the ability to bring about the change the country needed, up from 44%. When asked if Clinton had a clear plan to solve the nation's problems, 53% felt that he had a plan, up from 38%. (Gallup Poll, July 15, 26, 1992) These changes would indicate that several of Clinton's dramatic narratives, including his New Covenant, had been widely shared by the public and the media.

The most dramatic outcome of the Democratic National Convention was Clinton's record 16 point post convention bounce. This was the largest post convention increase recorded in the 32 year history of Gallup polling. In comparison, a 6 point increase is considered normal after a convention. This change may have resulted from the convention speakers or Clinton's dramatic narratives connecting with the audience. Or, it may have been because he was the beneficiary of what was perhaps the most bizarre move in political history.

On the final day of the convention, before Clinton gave his acceptance speech, Perot unexpectedly announced that he was withdrawing as a candidate. After Perot's withdrawal, Clinton's political fortunes changed dramatically. Clinton went from trailing Bush 40% to 48% the week before to leading Bush 56% to 34%. (Gallup Poll, July 22, 1992) Bush would never be able to overcome this change in public opinion for the rest of the campaign. This would demonstrate Perot's influence in assuring Clinton's victory, as it was the first time in the campaign Clinton had a decisive lead over Bush.

Clinton was clearly the beneficiary of Perot's withdrawal, as this was the best time for those who shared the Perot version of social reality to move to a new version. Perot supporters flocked to Clinton two to one over Bush, 62% to 26%. This shift demonstrates just how similar the Clinton and Perot versions of social reality really were. Both were critical of the state of the nation and both stressed the need for change in Washington. Voters who shared these dramatic narratives would not as readily identify with those of Bush.

Those who shared the Perot version of social reality could easily move to Clinton by rearranging only a few details of their views. In order for Perot supporters to shift to Bush, they would have to reject the Clinton dramatic narrative of restoration that emphasized change. Perot supporters would have to modify their perception of the villainous persona of Bush to a more positive one. More importantly, returning to Bush would require a major shift from the negative Clinton and Perot characterization of the present conditions in the country to the mildly optimistic dramatic narratives of Bush.

Poll results also indicate the degree to which the people shared meaning with Clinton's version of social reality. Among those supporting the two candidates, Clinton now held a higher percentage of core supporters than Bush. Prior to the convention, Clinton had 13% core supporters and 46% of the voters said there was no chance that they would vote for Clinton. After the convention, Clinton's core support increased to 44% and those who would not consider him dropped to 24%. During the same time Bush's core support increased from 17% to 22% and those who said there was no chance they would vote for him increased from 40% to 46%.

This would indicate that those voters with a preference of supporting Clinton shared his version of social reality more strongly than those supporting Bush, and consequently would be less likely to defect to another candidate. Compared to other conventions more people were likely to vote for Clinton (60%) than for Dukakis in 1988 (56%) or for Mondale in 1984 (45%), indicating that some of the success lay in the ability of the convention speakers to share meaning with the public. (Gallup Poll, July 6-8, 17-18, 1992)

In the month between the conventions, the campaign messages of both candidates changed little. Clinton held on to his lead while Bush continued to lose ground. By August 4th, Clinton's bounce was still evident as he held a 25 point lead over Bush with 57% to 32%. This was one of the largest leads on record, only Johnson's lead over Goldwater by 36 points in 1964 was larger. Bush continued to drop in approval ratings to 29%, which compared to Carter's rating of 29% in July 1979 when he gave his famous Malaise speech.

Nixon's approval went below 30% following Watergate and Truman's fell similarly during the Korean War. In comparison, Bush's approval rating did not slip below 50% during his first three years in office and only fell after the campaign began. This would suggest that Clinton's and Perot's negative dramatic narratives about Bush and the state of the nation were sharing meaning with the public.

Since 1950, no president had been reelected with approval ratings below 50%. By the Republican Convention, Bush was at 29% averaging 40% for the year. In comparison, since large scale polling began no president had fallen so far so fast as Bush with a loss of 60 points (89 to 29) in a year and five months. Only Truman fell further, losing 64 points (87 to 23), but over a period of six years and five months. Going into the Republican National Convention, Clinton led in the polls on many of Bush's core issues. Clinton was seen as best able to handle the economy (60% to 30%), best able to deal with crime and drugs (51% to 35%), and with family values (48% to 41%). Bush continued to lead Clinton in foreign affairs (62% to 30%) and in having made the nation more secure (57% to 36%). The race had tightened as fewer voters (43%) viewed Bush favorably and 47% would not vote for Bush. (Gallup Poll, August 4, 9, 1992)

It is interesting to note that voters now saw Reagan less favorably than Carter, 48% to 50%. Reagan's unfavorability rating was also higher than Carter, 49% to 43%. This suggests a recent shift in public perceptions of them. In 1990, Carter had a 45% approval rating and Reagan had 54%. In comparison, Reagan's approval rating was 56% in 1984 and Carter's was 39% in 1980, the respective last years of their first term in office. This trend suggested that Clinton's dramatic narratives about the eighties had some effect on voters' perception of how Reagan had handled his job as president. (Gallup Poll, August 16, 1992)

The Republican National Convention.

The Republican National Convention was held from August 17th to 20th, at the Astrodome in Houston, Texas. As announced by Republican National Committee Chair Richard Bond, the convention was centered around the theme of The American Spirit, which focused on issues affecting the world, the nation, and the family. The focus was on how Republican ideas of freedom and democracy had changed the world, making it a better place. The Republican Party would rise to the challenge of the future by concentrating on family and traditional values, a central theme that would be employed throughout the convention. President Bush would be put forth in the convention as the embodiment of those values and principles, leading the drive to recapture the American spirit.

Each day of the convention was organized to focus on a specific theme that would illustrate how Bush and the Republican Party had made the country better for everyone and each speaker would follow that theme. The first day focused on worldwide change and how they had made America prosper including the loss of the Soviet threat and increased trade. The second day focused on domestic issues and policies to promote reform and economic development. The third day focused on family values, volunteerism, school prayer, welfare reform, and education by promoting the idea that strong families and communities were an essential part of the American Spirit. The fourth and final night was dedicated to the presidency and its powers and responsibilities, featuring the accomplishments of Bush and how he was the embodiment of American values and the American Spirit.

The following are some of the featured convention speakers.

Richard Bond, Sets The Convention Tone.

On the first day of the convention, one of the featured speakers was Republican National Committee Chair Richard Bond. His task was to set out the theme of the convention by reminding America what George Bush was all about and what he had done for them. Bush had ended the cold war, brought freedom to Eastern Europe and the Baltic, and had stood up against Middle East dictators. Bond characterized the Bush family as role models who believed in family, community, enterprise, and individual dignity, so they deserved the people's support. Bush was cast as the hero in Bond's dramatic narrative as the defender of American values and freedom throughout the world.

Bond characterized Clinton as the failed governor of a small state who was taking the country for a ride. Clinton had to change his public image for the country because of his poor record in Arkansas. In contrast to Clinton, Bond cited several issues illustrating how Bush had tried to solve the country's problems. In balancing the budget, reforming education and health care, and in cleaning up crime, drugs, and violence, Bush had been blocked by Democrats in Congress who opposed him and did nothing.

Bond hearkened back to the last Democratic Congress and president, which was a time of high inflation when America was a laughing stock around the world. He sought to connect Clinton to the Carter Presidency by characterizing a Clinton Presidency as being similar to Carter, so it would be unacceptable to the American people. Bond characterized Congress and Clinton as the villains in his dramatic narrative, with Congress on the "road straight to failure" and Clinton on "a journey to disaster." (Bond, Convention Address)

Pat Buchanan, Polarizes the Audience.

Bush's rival in the primaries, Pat Buchanan, developed another dramatic narrative to undermine the Democrat's legitimacy. Buchanan spoke on the first night of the convention after Bond and before Reagan. In a highly dramatic speech, largely consisting of extreme characterizations he equated the Democrat's national convention with a masquerade ball to which "radicals and liberals came dressed up as moderates and centrists," calling it the "greatest single exhibition of cross dressing in American political history." (Buchanan, Convention Address)

This created a dramatic narrative of a party hiding from its true identity, a party that was trying to defraud the public. Buchanan associated the policies of Clinton and the Democrats with the extreme elements of society promoting values that were, in his opinion, not desirable for the country. He recalled how Hillary equated marriage to slavery, her radical feminism, and environmental extremism as examples of their true ideology that hurt the economy and cost jobs.

Buchanan's speech was significant because he had posed the strongest op-position to Bush from a member of his own party. He exploited a strong conserva-tive faction that supported Reagan and whose support Bush would need to win in November. Buchanan's speech at the convention served two basic purposes. First, the speech tried to mend the rift created during the primary campaign when he opposed the president. This was now remedied by Buchanan supporting him and demonstrating how Bush's accomplishments had helped the American people. The second purpose was to undermine the legitimacy of the Democrats by expos-ing their false image and demonstrating how their actions had hurt the American people. The effect of his speech may not have created an image of unity, but rather to characterize divisiveness and extremism that served to polarize the electorate.

Ronald Reagan, Restoring the Past.

Certainly the most celebrated speaker of the Republican Convention was former President Ronald Reagan. Reagan was the final speaker on the first night of the convention following Bond and Buchanan. He began by recounting a now familiar dramatic narrative of sweeping changes taking place around the world. He had personally witnessed many pivotal events in history like the development of television and the birth and death of communism. As Reagan told the story, the Democrats were the major cause of the country's past troubles, such as double digit inflation, the threat of nuclear annihilation, gas lines, shrinking incomes, and a much more dangerous world.

Reagan next depicted a better future based on twelve years of Reagan Bush leadership. Reagan developed a dramatic narrative of Bush as the average, or-dinary guy who was quiet, trustworthy, level headed, and respected around the world. Reagan tried to defuse the dramatic narratives of the need for change, say-ing that this is not a time for change. If there was to be a change it should come at the other end of Pennsylvania Avenue with Congress.

Reagan then invoked his own dramatic narrative of change, forecasting a new beginning for those bereft of hope. He noted that the country was at a cross-roads asking for change and reform. He extolled the Republicans as being ready to be the party of change. With a new Congress, they could enact the kinds of pro-grams and changes the people wanted. It was the Democratic Congress that was the villain who stood in their way.

In evoking the restoration dramatic narrative he characterized the election as a crusade, a journey of renewal that had begun twelve years ago, so now our commitment must be renewed. Reagan sought to reconstitute his audience by re-calling past shared meanings to remind them of his version of social reality. He concluded with a familiar dramatic narrative when he said, "May every dawn be a great new beginning for America and every evening bring us closer to that shining city upon the hill." (Reagan, Convention Address)

Newt Gingrich, Calls Democrats Obstructionist.

The keynote speaker on the second night of the convention was Georgia Representative and Minority Whip Newt Gingrich. His convention speech characterized the Democrats in Congress as obstructionist. They were villains who posed a threat to individual freedom. To illustrate this point, he used a dramatic narrative of a housewife from Georgia who with ten dollars started a business that now employed over 500 people in 28 states, Gingrich praised free enterprise and castigated the Democrats who extolled taxation, legislation, and regulation because they encouraged waste, arrogance, and inefficiency.

In another dramatic narrative, Gingrich characterized Congress as being obstructionist to progress. He illustrated this by speculating that if electricity was invented today, it would be taxed and declared a health hazard. Then, Congress would pass legislation to protect candle making. Republicans want to make government more like business, Democrats want to make business more like government. Republicans would replace welfare with work, cut taxes, and encourage families. He summarized his speech by saying that change was a given, but asked, at which end of Pennsylvania Avenue would it take place? If the people wanted change, they should elect a Republican president and Congress because this fight was not just Bush's, it was everyone's. Concluding, "Your country needs you, your children need you, your president needs you." (Gingrich, Convention Address)

Marilyn Quayle, and The Family.

On the third day of the convention the wives of the President and Vice President spoke about the issue of family values. Marilyn Quayle, wife of Vice President Dan Quayle, took a decidedly different approach than the previous speakers. In her address, she touched on several major points including the baby boom generation, the woman's movement, her experiences, and the qualities of the Bushes and of her husband. In doing so, she sought to bolster her husband's and Bush's legitimacy, but did not seek to attack the opposition as previous speakers had done.

Instead, she presented the distinct differences between the views of the Democrats and the views of herself and her husband regarding family, society, and the changing roles of men and women in their families and careers. She and her husband were a part of the much touted baby boom generation, for which Clinton and Gore received much publicity. However, she and her husband were examples that not everyone protested, dropped out, or did drugs during the sixties.

Mrs. Quayle utilized the dramatic narrative of family values to promote the Republicans as the party of the people in touch with what they value. This view of a strong family and community was enmeshed in the fabric of the nation because as she said, leadership had everything to do with character and principle. Her husband and George Bush were leaders of principle, integrity, and wisdom. She explained how these qualities made a good president who was ideal for America. Barbara Bush was also included in this dramatic narrative as an example of a dedicated, strong, and generous woman.

In her speech she characterized Bush, Mrs. Bush, and her husband as heroes by virtue of the qualities they possessed making them ideally suited to lead the nation. In this way she took on the issue of trust and character combining it with the dramatic narrative of family values that was used by other speakers. President Bush had provided the linkage between these different perspectives by exhibiting the outward signs of family values as evidence of the inner qualities of trust and character.

Barbara Bush, A Conversation With America.

In her speech to the convention, First Lady Barbara Bush took what she said was a different approach than the other convention speakers. She too promoted the dramatic narrative of family values, characterizing an administration in touch with mainstream American values. However, she began by stating that she did not come to the convention to give a speech, but rather to "have a conversation."

She spoke about families including her and her husband's experiences meeting many families around the country and learning from them. These families included many kinds of families, including single parent families. These families, like her own, were not so different. They teach their children the values of, "integrity, strength, responsibility, courage, sharing, love of God, and pride in being an American." She explained, "However you define family that's what we mean by family values." (Barbara Bush, Convention Address)

Mrs. Bush told about her personal experience when, after the war she and her husband headed west and settled in Midland, Texas, a wonderful place to start a family. She characterized this as the best years of her life. She told stories of her children growing up and described her husband as a quiet, kind, and wise father. When her husband was asked what accomplishment he was most proud of she said he would always answer, "that his children still come home." The dramatic narrative presented here was not of an idyllic family, but rather one that was caring and compassionate, with Bush as the central figure. These qualities of integrity, love for family, and America were ones that a president should possess.

This speech was directed to support Bush's legitimacy and did not seek to undermine Clinton's. There were several indirect references to Clinton, but they arose out of extolling Bush's qualities. She characterized a side of Bush that the Republicans felt was an important issue for the election. Since Clinton had run into scandal over his personal life, the Republican's tried to heighten and elaborate the differences between Clinton and Bush by calling on an expert on the subject, his wife, to present a dramatic narrative of Bush as a dedicated family man.

Dan Quayle, The Cultural Divide.

On the fourth and final night of the convention Vice President Dan Quayle began his acceptance address by evoking a dramatic narrative of his personal experiences. Confronting his critics who didn't like his values, looked down on his beliefs, and were afraid of his ideas, Quayle referred to the two parties' differences as a cultural divide "between fighting for what is right and refusing to see what is wrong." (Quayle, Acceptance Address)

The family values dramatic narrative was an underlying component of the larger American Dream dramatic narrative, in that these values were essential to fulfilling the promise of the American Dream. In making this connection, Quayle tied into the dramatic narrative of the American Dream when he characterized his own life in a small town in Indiana that exemplified the traditional values he had tried to teach his children.

For Quayle, family came first and when it was undermined and belittled it was the country that suffered. Family values could be strengthened to empower people by lowering taxes, by providing choice in affordable health care, by ensuring safe streets, and having a clean environment. Although these were elements of the Republican plan of reform that would strengthen families and the nation, Congress had stood in the way.

In his speech, Quayle turned to the typical Bush castigation of Congress while also casting lawyers as villains who abused, "the finest law system in the world," a legal system in which both he and his wife participated. He admonished Congress for their failure to properly run the house bank, post office, and restaurant, asking how they thought they could run the country. The leaders of Congress were so corrupt that they had to be kept hidden during the Democratic National Convention.

Quayle characterized Bush as the hero who made the country strong and the world safer in contrast to Clinton who saw America as, "the mockery of the world." Bush represented what was good about America. He was the "embodiment of character." Every day Quayle saw, "The dedication of a husband, father, and grandfather, the self-reliance of an entrepreneur, the courage of a Navy pilot, the dependability of a loyal friend, and the compassion of a man of faith." It was these values, beliefs, and the hope of "faith, family, and freedom" that Quayle, Bush, and the Republicans were fighting for in this election. (Quayle, Acceptance Address)

George Bush, Change To Renew America.

In his convention address to accept the nomination of his party for the office of president of the United States, George Bush replayed several dramatic narratives developed throughout the convention. He reiterated the foreign policy accomplishments of the past. He discredited the opposition's revisionist accounts that criticized his emphasis on foreign policy. These outcomes were not inevitable or mistakes as some had claimed. They took strong leadership, vision, and the support of the American people. Now the nuclear threat was gone and, "more people have breathed the fresh air of freedom than in all of human history." (Bush, Acceptance Address)

Bush contrasted his decisive leadership with Clinton's wavering on issues. He recalled the problems of the last Democratic president, Jimmy Carter, reminding the audience of hostages, gas lines, and inflation. Projecting this dramatic narrative into the future, he said that there would be more tough decisions because the world was still dangerous. Bush asked if the nation should be led by someone who claimed that America was ridiculed abroad or by someone who was respected by world leaders. Relating his foreign policy experience to his personal experience, Bush again recounted the history of his war service.

Bush then turned to the dramatic narrative of change, which he stated was what the election was all about. He countered Clinton's claim that America was in decline, citing positive attributes of America including strong exports, high worker productivity, low interest rates, and no inflation. All this good news had not been covered by the media that only concentrated on what was bad. Then Bush described legislative changes that he had accomplished including the disabilities act, clean air act, rebuilding roads, and civil rights.

Bush told of two different characterizations of America today. One was of a strong America that had faith in the individual. The other was one that looked inward, was self protecting, and put faith in bureaucracy. After employing his familiar depiction of an obstructionist Congress, Bush then focused on Clinton who was a man who believed in big government and would enact new payroll taxes as well as the biggest tax increase in history. He would do this Bush said, because "his passion to expand government knows no bounds."

A dramatic narrative of conspiracy was alluded to when Bush inferred that Clinton and Congress were in 'cahoots,' a reference to the tax deal that the Democrats pushed him into signing so that they could later use it against him in the campaign. Bush had extended his hand to Congress and "they bit it." He said that the programs he had proposed, "Have not failed. They haven't even been tried." (Bush, Acceptance Address)

Bush put the American people at the center of his dramatic narrative of change by giving them the choice of, "the tattered blanket of bureaucracy that other nations are tossing away? Or do we give our people the freedom and incentives to build security for themselves?" (Bush, Acceptance Address) This compared Clinton with failed Communism as the enemy of freedom. He recalled the malaise of the Carter Presidency by dubbing a first Clinton administration as Carter II.

Bush then connected his dramatic narrative of change to restoration. He hearkened back to the war when he kept watch on the bridge of a submarine watching the sunrise. Today he could see a sunrise for America. He appealed to the "American Spirit," and to a "commitment to renew and rebuild our nation" by shaking up a Congressional leadership entrenched for thirty eight years and entangled in, "PACs, perks, privileges... and paralysis." Bush quoted Truman's nomination speech, in which the people were asked to, "Give me your help, not to win votes alone, but to win this new crusade to keep America safe and secure for its own people." (Bush, Acceptance Address)

Republican Convention Themes.

The theme of the Republican National Convention as stated by party Chair Richard Bond was The American Spirit. However, in the speeches at the convention this slogan seemed to have been forgotten. The American spirit was mentioned from time to time, but the greatest amount of time was devoted to restatement of dramatic narratives previously developed in the campaign. During the convention, the Republican version of social reality was more fully developed than in the primary and several new dramatic narratives did surface throughout many of the convention speeches including change and family values.

The notion of change was a particularly difficult problem for the Republicans to overcome. The convention speakers reiterated the dramatic narrative of America at a crossroads with a time of change abroad and problems at home. This served to transform the earlier Bush approach to simply recognize that the people wanted change. The dramatic narrative of change was perhaps borrowed from the Democrats or based on public sentiment. So, the Republicans tried to cast themselves as the party of true change. The question then became, not whether there should be change, but what change was best and who was best to carry it out.

The Republican convention presented two contrasting views of the nation and the audience was asked to choose between them. The people could take the road back to the failed policies of the past characterized by the similarities between Clinton and Carter or they could embark on a new journey. That journey represented a continuation of the last twelve years that had brought change based on the restoration of basic American values and opportunities. The issue of trust and each candidate's record in office was used to illustrate the differences between Bush and Clinton.

Bush was standing up for what was right and good, for family, community, and defense of freedoms at home and abroad. He was cast as an ordinary guy and family man who was qualified to lead the country through what was characterized as a dangerous time abroad and a difficult time at home. The question became, which candidate had experience and commanded the respect of the world to be an effective president?

The dramatic narratives of change and family values formed the core of the American Dream, which both parties sought to preserve and restore. Here evolved a social reality shared by the two parties. Both Clinton and Bush used the American Dream dramatic narrative to connect their values to those of the people to gain voter support. Both parties characterized the need for change in order to restore the American traditions of the past. It was the details of how that restoration was to be realized that formed the basis of the differences between them.

Post Convention Response Below Expectations.

The Republican Convention appeared to have presented many dramatic narratives that were shared by the voters, but not as widely as the Democrats had done the month before. Bush gained a respectable 5 point post convention bounce and cut his gap with Clinton to 10 points, but Clinton still led Bush 52% to 42%. Bush improved his favorability rating from 43% to 50% and cut his unfavorability rating from 51% to 47%. (Gallup Poll, August 25, 1992)

Similarly, Quayle improved his standing with voters from 32% to 40%, suggesting that positive dramatic narratives about him had helped to sway public opinion. Bush's approval rating as president went up to 40% with a 54% disapproval rating. However, negative dramatic narratives about the Democrats failed to make the public perceive Clinton less favorably, as Clinton had done so successfully to Bush in July. Clinton was perceived as 57% favorable and 37% unfavorable, the same as his preconvention ratings. (Gallup Poll, August 25, 1992)

Several Bush dramatic narratives seemed to have been shared in the electorate as demonstrated by the number of voters who felt that Bush handled several issues better than Clinton. Bush now led Clinton in family values 51% to 33%, a marked change from when Clinton led Bush before the convention with 48% to 41%. In foreign affairs, the public's perception of Bush improved with his rating increasing from 62% to 73% and Clinton's rating dropped from 30% to 19%. In handling the economy, Bush went from 30% to 37%, but still trailed Clinton who went from 60% to 52%. In health care, Bush increased his approval rating from 20% to 33% compared to Clinton's loss of 62% to 54%. And Clinton was now perceived as the candidate most likely to raise taxes. (Gallup Poll, August 25, 1992)

Negative dramatic narratives of Congress convinced 39% of the people that a Republican Congress would bring better change, compared to 41% who thought a Democratic president would bring better change. The 20 point Democratic lead over Republicans in the voter's preference for Congressional candidates was cut to 5 points. This decline for the Democratic Congressional majority suggested that Bush's anti-Congress message was working, but was not strong enough to convert the number of voters he needed to win. However, more people came away with a lowered image of the Republicans than an improved image by a margin of 41% to 35%. While, 39% saw Bush more favorably, an almost equal 35% saw him less favorably. (Gallup Poll, August 25, 1992)

The Republicans were able to share meaning in areas in which they were traditionally strong, but made little headway in areas where Clinton had gained support. In essence, Bush seemed to have been preaching to the already converted without gaining many new converts. Perhaps this was due to the Republican's tendency to concentrate on areas that were already their strengths, like foreign affairs and family values.

In contrast, Clinton focused on areas of weakness in order to strengthen them. He had spent months hitting areas where he had low ratings, like character and the economy, until he gained ground with the voters. This was exemplified by how public perception had changed regarding character issues and his ability to effect change. These were issues where Clinton was weak at the beginning of the campaign, but he gained ground and now led Bush. This also may confirm the notion that the process of rejecting the old shared meanings of Bush to sharing new meanings about Clinton, began in the primaries and consummated during the Democratic convention, had now taken hold with the electorate.

Media Demonstrates Liberal Bias.

During the two national conventions, many similar issues were reported, however, it is insightful to consider differences in how the media reported them and shared the candidates' version of social reality. The media shared dramatic narratives about the Republican and Democratic National Conventions very differently. Some of the narratives presented were shared by the media while others were not, which may have affected the wider acceptance by the electorate. Several of them bear examining as to their impact on the election's outcome.

One example of these differing characterizations of the conventions was illustrated by how the CBS Evening News employed different dramatic narratives in covering the opening day of each of the two conventions. On the first day of the Democratic Convention, CBS reported that the delegates were upbeat and in a spirited mood as they expected that this year the party would effect real change. CBS reported that it had uncovered a dirty tricks campaign against Clinton. (CBS Evening News, July 13, 1992) The Republican Convention opened with CBS reporting that Bush denied any allegations of sleaze in his campaign, claiming that the real issue was leadership. While Clinton stressed the importance of national security on domestic issues of concern. (CBS Evening News, August 17, 1992)

The media characterized the Democratic Convention as a success in bringing the party together, while the Republican Convention was leaving a legacy of desperation politics by resorting to dirty tricks because they were weak on the issues. (CNN, August 23, 1992) The media's dramatic narratives involved asking if the slash and burn tactics the Republicans used to attack the Democrats in 1988 would work or if the public would tire of dirty politics. (This Week ABC, August 23, 1992)

During the conventions, the media shared a dramatic narrative that characterized New York City as tinged with optimism as it opened its doors to convention delegates. The media characterized the Democratic Convention as the least contentious and most confident in years, with traditional brass bands, balloons, and hoopla. Party leaders sought to assure the television audience that the Democratic Party had moderated its policies and could be trusted to govern again. They denounced Bush as a failed leader who broke his promises and allowed the country to sink into recession and division. (New York Times, July 12 to 16, 1992)

Media reports reflected their characterization of Clinton as believing in people while having the strategic vision to realize his goal of leading his party to an inevitable victory. (New York Times, July 12, 1992) The media characterized Al Gore as playing a strong role in taking the lead with Congress, breaking the log jam and not just sitting back waiting to break ties, so we can have a government that works for the people again. The media saw Gore's experience in foreign policy and the environment as making him an attractive running mate for Clinton. The convention was characterized as presenting a new moderate party and candidate that had won wide support with the electorate. (New York Times, July 10, 11, 17, 1992) The Democrats smelled victory ending the convention on a high note full of hope that they could win. (CNN, July 16, 1992)

In contrast, the media shared dramatic narratives that characterized Houston as suffering through hard times and in no mood to be host to the Republican Convention. As the convention was set to begin, the media reported that the Republicans were mindful that they were behind in the polls and hoped to prevent the convention from becoming a nationally televised airing of Bush's problems. The media characterized traditional Republican delegates to the convention as bitterly disappointed with President Bush. They were a party deeply divided against itself so partisans may be reluctantly voting for Clinton.

The media interpreted Bush's speech as containing vague promises, noting that family values references were perceived by half the people as cynical or irrelevant. (New York Times, July 23, August 10, 12, 16, 17, 18, 1992) The media did not share many of Bush's dramatic narratives. They characterized Bush as searching for a message that would help him connect with the voters. This was difficult for Bush to sell since his message kept changing and the Democrat bashing by convention speakers was disliked by most viewers. Any help Bush might receive from the convention would be too little too late. (CNN, August 17, 1992)

Not only did the media not share the Republican dramatic narrative of family values, they actively rejected it. It was criticized in the media, which featured Republican delegates who expressed views critical of the issue and asking if the government should even be involved in these matters. (CNN, August 18, 1992) (However, at the next Democratic convention in 1996, Hillary would speak to the delegates on the subject of family values. August 27, 1996)

Shortly after the Democratic Convention, rumors circulated in the media about Bush and Quayle, including their health and futures. Days before the Republican Convention, it was speculated that Quayle would be dropped and another candidate for vice president would replace him on the ticket. In this media dramatic narrative, Republican leaders felt such a move might have been in Bush's best interest for reelection because of the success of the Democratic Convention.

When Bush and Quayle denied reports of Quayle being dropped, the media made the denial a lead story. (CNN August 22-27, 1992, NBC Nightly News August 22, 1992, ABC World News, August 26, 1992, CBS This Morning, August 4, 1992) Overall, the media shared the dramatic narrative that the Republican convention was unorganized, creating dissension while doing little to dispel voter uncertainty. (New York Times, August 21, 22, 1992)

During the Democratic Convention, Bush maintained a long standing tradition of keeping out of sight and out of the media by going on a fishing vacation in Wyoming. (Washington Post, July 12, 1992) On the first day of the Republican Convention, Ross Perot who was officially out of the race, publically attacked the convention for failing to address the country's economic problems. This was significant because his supporters would be the swing vote in determining the outcome of the election.

Clinton, however, did not take the Republican criticism during the convention silently. (National Public Radio, August 18, 1992) During the convention he broke with the tradition of keeping out of the public eye to barnstorm in Michigan.

By the end of the summer the Republicans were still looking for a way to connect with the voters, while Clinton's general election campaign was well underway.

Chapter 6
The General Election

Once the candidates had accepted their respective political party's endorsement at their convention, the campaign enters a new phase. In recent times this rite of passage has become largely symbolic. With the rise of the primary system, the party conventions have little real significance. They mostly serve as free advertising for candidates to promote themselves and bash the opposition.

From the conventions to Election Day, the candidates focus on one another in their quest for office. During this time, candidates will employ dramatic narratives to establish themselves as having the legitimate right to govern, while also trying to undermine their opponent's legitimacy. Ideally, the result of this process is the establishment of each candidate's right to govern by providing voters the information necessary to cast an informed and thoughtful vote based on the issues. However, it is more likely that the candidate who can scare the most people into fearing their opponent, will motivate enough people to vote for them to win.

Due to the adversarial nature of the American political system, the general election is often a time of accusation and refutation. There is a tendency for a candidate to grow more strident and negative to galvanize their supporters and shake loose those who share their opponent's version of social reality. Negative campaigning, dirty politics, and mudslinging with candidates exchanging charges and counter charges are encouraged by the media who often share these dramatic narratives because they have a tendency to view them as 'newsworthy.'

The proportion of logic and evidence diminishes during the general election as more emotional dramatic appeals, usually in the form of television commercials increases. This tendency towards television ads enhances the potential attractiveness of the use of dramatic narratives. The political television commercial is often a short dramatic narrative filled with actors in a melodramatic format that casts a heroic persona who represents good that is pitted against the villainous persona of the opposition candidate.

It is these shared dramatic narratives that become the major battle ground in the approaching final days of the campaign. It seems that a rational argument is relatively ineffective when used against previously shared dramatic narratives. A dramatic narrative that is widely shared by the public is unlikely to be stopped with reason or explanations. In order to attack a shared dramatic narrative, a candidate might use the same facts or events, but interpret them in a new or different way. They may turn the dramatic narrative against their opponent with a turn of phrase or reinterpretation of the same events. Or they may create a new dramatic narrative to divert public attention in a different direction.

This chapter examines the exchanges between the candidates in their speeches, use of television commercials, and the way the media shared or rejected their dramatic narratives in the general election campaign between the conventions and Election Day. It analyzes how the candidates selected and adapted their version of social reality to undermine their opponent's legitimacy and bolster their own. Because the conventions were a month apart, there is some overlap in the time frame and material covered in this chapter and other chapters.

Clinton Makes The First Move.

After winning his party's nomination, Clinton wasted little time in beginning his general election campaign. It would be yet another month before the Republican National Convention when Bush would introduce his campaign to the public giving Clinton the advantage of time to establish his legitimacy. At the onset of the general election campaign, Clinton had the advantage of a large post convention bounce to lead Bush in the polls for the first time. History would suggest that this lead would dissipate over time, so Clinton's challenge would be to galvanize the support that he had gained as quickly as possible.

During this phase of the campaign, the dramatic narratives of hope and change were utilized as exemplified by his speech to the Los Angeles World Affairs Council on August 13th. Clinton characterized a world of hope and opportunity as demonstrated by the people of Europe and Russia who overthrew oppression and tyranny. Clinton argued that even though Bush claimed credit for the victory of the Cold War and promised to bring that success home in a second term, such claims ignored the facts of history. In Clinton's view, the test of leadership included understanding how the world has changed "to assert a new vision of our role in the world," and to summon our values, economic and military strengths to support the new vision. Bush had failed to meet these new challenges because he held on to old assumptions and policies that maintained the status quo.

Bush's foreign policy plan was designed for Cold War ways of thinking and did not fit the new challenges of a changing world. Characterizing a specific instance, Clinton said Bush had failed to aid the new Soviet Republics even referring to Ukraine's independence as "suicidal nationalism." In sending secret emissaries to China after Tiananmen Square, Bush undermined freedom by "failing to stand up for our values." (Clinton, Los Angeles World Affairs Council) Clinton stressed that Bush had ignored human rights atrocities in China and Haiti and was hesitant to support the new democracies of the Soviet Union and Eastern Europe. Bush had even stood by as Yugoslavia slipped into chaos.

In a reinterpretation of a Republican dramatic narrative, Clinton claimed that the fall of Communism was a result of the work of many presidents and Congressional leaders, past and present, Democrat and Republican. It was the people of the former communist countries who were the heroes, not Bush. Clinton described the Republican view as akin to, "the rooster who took credit for the dawn."

(Clinton, Los Angeles World Affairs Council) The Republican's claim of changing the world was just as flawed as their contention of changing things at home. This turned the Bush dramatic narrative of success abroad around and characterized the Republicans as false and ineffective, content to let opportunity slip by instead of reaching out to embrace it.

Clinton even attacked Bush's biggest foreign policy success, the Gulf War. Clinton recast the history of the Gulf War by saying that it was Bush who had created the conflict in the first place by supporting Iraq and not supporting government opposition before the war. Furthermore, Bush had missed the chance to create a democracy in Kuwait. The burden of the Gulf War had been born by America, so any future involvement abroad must be shared with our allies.

Clinton warned that Bush would refer to his past accomplishments in foreign policy as the basis of his claim to office. These issues should not be the measure of leadership, according to Clinton, who preferred to define leadership as opportunities seized and crises adverted. Clinton characterized his leadership as "strategic, vigorous, and grounded in America's values" compared to Bush who was "reactive and tied to a status quo that cannot prevail." The Gulf War victory was a foreign policy defeat for Bush because it was a war that, in Clinton's judgment, should have been avoided. Bush had supported "familiar tyrants" and "the old geography of repression rather than a new map of freedom." (Clinton, Los Angeles World Affairs Council)

In another Clinton characterization of Bush foreign policy, he called Bush's trade mission to Japan a failure and an embarrassment. This was demonstrated by the Japanese Prime Minister who told Bush that he felt sympathy for the United States. For Clinton, this was further indication that we had a second rate economy in decline, so there was a need for new economic leadership to inspire respect abroad. In this manner, Clinton took the dramatic narratives of Bush and attached new characterizations to them in order to support his candidacy. Bush was cast as being anti-freedom and opposing traditional American values. Unlike Bush, Clinton would stand up for the American values of democracy and freedom by working for human rights and standing against aggression.

In order to promote our national interests, Clinton asserted that we must promote the growth of democracies because they provide the most stable trading partners and rarely create military threats. Clinton would be concerned with how others govern their people, so he would 'put people first' in other countries by making human rights a primary consideration in foreign policy decisions because foreign policy could not be divorced from our moral principles. Clinton characterized a new world, "tolerant of diversity and respectful of human rights," and "united against the common enemies of mankind," so we can pass on to our children and their children, "the knowledge that we rose to new responsibilities in our world and in our age," and we can turn "vision into reality." (Clinton, Los Angeles World Affairs Council)

In creating a dramatic narrative linking foreign policy to domestic policy, Clinton sought two objectives. First, he sought to blunt growing criticism of his lack of foreign policy experience by characterizing such experience as not of primary importance. Second, he sought to make success in foreign policy contingent on success at home. This approach was in opposition to Bush who was using characterizations about foreign policy success to enable change at home. Clinton also tried to change the public's perception of Bush's foreign policy successes by presenting a different dramatic narrative surrounding world events. So, Clinton's first priority as president would be the domestic agenda because it was important to revive the economy first. America needed to be strong at home in order to be strong abroad because foreign policy and domestic policy were, "two sides of the same coin." (Clinton, Los Angeles World Affairs Council)

Clinton asserted that the lack of a national strategy had hurt the people and had not allowed us to reap the benefits of recent changes around the world. Change was inexorable, so our actions would determine whether it would be to our advantage or disadvantage to reestablish America's military and economic leadership in the world. The nation needed an Economic Security Council of equal importance to the National Security Council. Clinton defined himself as a leader who would mobilize the public and private sectors in the country to champion world trade to benefit American workers. Leadership demanded an intelligent assessment of future dangers and establishing new modes of cooperation to maintain a force that was ready to meet future challenges. Even though the mission of the military had changed, our interests must be maintained. Some saw defense cuts as a piggy bank for other programs, but this was a mistaken notion. Remaining a world power was essential to successful diplomacy and international relationships.

The Clinton Economic Plan.

In speaking to the Economic Club of Detroit on August 22, the day after Bush's convention acceptance speech, Clinton characterized his view of the nation's current domestic and economic problems, their cause, and his solutions. Clinton reiterated his version of social reality about the economy by utilizing the dramatic narratives that had been a mainstay of his campaign from the beginning. He spent much of his speech refuting what the Republicans had said the night before at their convention and attacking Bush for what he had done as president. Bush was avoiding responsibility for the country's economic problems and had resorted to lies and distortion about Clinton and his record. Clinton characterized Bush as personally untrustworthy, "desperate for reelection," and someone who "would say anything to get reelected." (Clinton, Economic Club of Detroit)

Utilizing the dramatic narrative of change, Clinton reaffirmed his belief that tomorrow could be better than today. There was an immediate need for change to create an "Economic Security Council" and to expand trade to create a level playing field. Clinton was "offering a vision" of "millions of new jobs in thousands of new companies, in dozens of new industries." He characterized his program called Putting People First as new and different, neither Republican nor Democrat, neither liberal nor conservative. Rather, it was the charting of a new course for the nation, in a radically new direction. He said that he would, "Not embrace the old Democratic theory of tax and spend and regulate." He rejected the "brain dead politics in both parties in Washington." (Clinton, Economic Club of Detroit)

Not only did the dramatic narrative of change apply to Clinton's plan to change Washington and the nation, it also applied to the Democratic Party and even to Clinton himself. For months, he had made the case that the Democratic Party had changed and he rejected the failed economic theories of trickle down and tax and spend with big government offering a program for every problem. Instead, he cast himself as an independent interested in change.

In this approach, Clinton characterized the old dramatic narratives of the past administration as the source of the nation's problems, demonstrating the need for change. Clinton had to connect Bush to Reagan because of their similar programs, so he could not criticize one without the other. One of them could not be characterized as a hero and the other cast as a villain because this would create a contradictory narrative. As a part of his rationale for change, Clinton responded to several Bush dramatic narratives by repeating his reinterpretation of past events. The past decade of the eighties was evil, the cause of the problems with which Clinton now contended. Twelve years ago, Reagan promised growth, tax cuts, and debt reduction, but instead he left inequality, economic decline, and the nation in debt. Four years ago Bush promised jobs, a balanced budget, no new taxes, and an environmental and educational presidency. Instead, he brought deficits, slow growth, tax burdens, and a decline in productivity. These promises were characterized as hollow because they betrayed the people's trust.

Using a quote from Bush's 1988 presidential campaign, Clinton redefined the famous 'read my lips' quote by reinterpreting the phrase from its original meaning as a promise not to raise taxes as proof that Bush was dishonest. In this dramatic narrative, Bush was characterized as offering the people the "cynical read my lips, promises," while millions of jobs were lost, wages fell, and there were record bankruptcies. Bush deplores bureaucrats, but he also ignores workers because "now more people were working for the government than for the private sector." Bush told the people that the election was about trust, yet he lied to them when he said, read my lips, "No wonder Americans hate politics." (Clinton, Economic Club of Detroit)

In his campaign speeches during the general election, Clinton frequently returned to the same dramatic narratives about Bush. He attacked Bush as being self centered, caring only about winning the election rather than serving the people. Bush did not have a record to legitimize his being reelected and he lied about the significance of his accomplishments. He had not helped average working people who made less and paid more, instead he had made things worse for them and he had no serious programs to help the people or the nation's problems.

To counter several Bush attacks and to provide evidence for his credibility, Clinton accused Bush of continuing to lie about Clinton's record of raising taxes in Arkansas. Bush also lied when he said that Clinton would raise taxes if elected. Despite Bush's claim that Clinton was bad for Arkansas, Clinton had created jobs at ten times the national rate and increased income at twice that rate. Bush talked about cutting taxes and helping education, yet Clinton characterized himself as actually doing something about these issues. Bush took credit for everything that had happened around the world, but accepted responsibility for nothing at home.

In response to what the Republicans had said the night before, Clinton said that family values were not about whether "Al Gore and I love our wives and our children as much as George Bush and Dan Quayle," but whether we are concerned about "your children and your future." The Republicans lectured the nation about family values, but they had abandoned families who, because of their policies, had to work harder while falling behind. (Clinton, Economic Club of Detroit)

(Years after making this statement, Clinton would be accused of marital infidelity leading to his impeachment. After 40 years of marriage, Gore and his wife would separate, but not divorce and he would live with his girlfriend. (New York Daily News, April 25, 2014) Both Bush and Quayle remain married and the Bushes are the longest married presidential couple.)

The Clinton Television Campaign.

Following the Republican National Convention, Clinton launched a series of national television commercials. In these commercials, he characterized the core dramatic narrative of The New Covenant by pledging to repair the bond between the government and the people, changing the nature of government by putting people first. These ads were designed to share meaning with the voters to bolster Clinton's legitimacy by demonstrating that his version of change was safe and secure.

In order to counter the Bush dramatic narrative of experience, Clinton's commercials praised his record as governor and helping the people of Arkansas. Service to others and changing people's lives was his life's work. These accomplishments were not easy because Clinton had to fight for change and battling the odds in one of the nation's poorest states. As a result of his work, Arkansas led the nation in job growth with incomes rising at twice the national rate with seventeen thousand people moved off welfare to work.

Several Clinton commercials utilized his dramatic narrative of doing for the nation what he had done for Arkansas by stating, "Bill Clinton has an economic plan to rebuild America, invest in our own people. Education, training, eight million new jobs in the next four years, a new direction. Those making over $200,000 have to pay more, the rest of us get a break. It's a plan to put people first again, and six Nobel Prize winning economists say it will work." (Clinton,

Television Commercial) For those who shared this dramatic narrative, it provided evidence of what Clinton could do for the country. It persuaded the public that since Clinton could make economic conditions better, change was nothing to fear.

As evidence that his plan for change would work, Clinton presented another commercial about a specific part of his plan that would get people off welfare and into productive work. This dramatic narrative characterized Clinton as having the answer to a major problem facing America to, "end welfare as we know it, to break the cycle of welfare dependency. We'll provide education, training and child care." (Clinton, Television Commercial)

This was a typical example of how he used The New Covenant dramatic narrative to share meaning with the public. This was used to define Clinton's view of the relationship between a leader and the people in which benefits were given freely to the people. It was the government's responsibility to care for its people, with the understanding that the people would have to take responsibility in order to receive this assistance.

The Great Conversion, By September It's All Over.

By September Bush trailed Clinton 39% to 54% in the polls. This was a significant point in the campaign because no candidate this far behind, at this stage of the campaign, without gaining momentum, had ever made a comeback to win. A major problem for Bush was his approval rating as president, which was now at 39% and had averaged below 50% all year. Only one president, Harry Truman, had an approval rating below 50% in an election year and had come back to win. Perhaps, this was the impetus for Bush making comparisons between himself and Truman. (Gallup Poll, September 5, 1992) However, Bush encountered criticism from Truman's daughter for comparing his campaign to Truman's campaign. (Los Angeles Times, August 28, 1992)

With only 15% of the voters now uncommitted, 46% of them said that they would not vote for Bush under any circumstances. Bush had a 45% favorable to a 49% unfavorable rating. In comparison, the public's perception of Clinton had improved dramatically because 57% now viewed him as favorable to 37% unfavorable. This turnaround for Clinton would suggest that his dramatic narratives about himself were creating shared meaning by reducing uncertainty about him with the public more than those of Bush. (Gallup Poll, September 5, 1992)

The primary campaign seemed to have reduced uncertainty about Clinton, while it increased uncertainty about Bush. This was likely due to Clinton attacking the old Bush dramatic narratives that had previously shared meaning with the electorate. At first, Bush maintained a strong lead and his opponents had little effect in eroding his support. However, as the primary races geared up, the Bush version of social reality had come under attack from Clinton and Republican candidate Pat Buchanan.

As the Clinton and Buchanan dramatic narratives became more widely shared in the electorate, more people began to express their discontent with Bush as demonstrated by the number of people who voted for Buchanan to send a message of their dissatisfaction with Bush. When Bush came under attack, he did not adequately defend himself while his opponents relentlessly hammered away at him. By May, all of these factors had steadily eroded Bush's lead, with Clinton reaching 41% of the vote with Bush at 48% (Gallup Poll, April 15, 1992) suggesting that Clinton's message was slowly taking hold with the voters.

The undeclared candidacy of Perot also seemed to be taking a toll on Bush because 43% of the voters did not think that any of the candidates were good ones and 60% did not think the candidates had any good ideas. (Gallup Poll, May 3, 1992) Public perception of Bush was becoming more like Perot's characterization of the corruptness of government and the influence of special interests on party candidates. This perception was also similar to Clinton's characterization of Washington and the bankrupt nature of politicians. During the primaries it seemed that Clinton had been successful in recasting Republican dramatic narratives, causing a major block of the electorate to be separated from their old version of social reality. One indication of this was the emergence of a high percentage of angry voters, which can be a typical reaction to the process of changing social reality.

While shifting from a previously held social reality to a new one, people may feel angry or confused. Beginning in April, the Gallup Poll observed the rise of the angry voter with a significant portion of the people expressing anger with the system and dissatisfaction with the candidates. This anger reached its peak in June when a record 84% felt dissatisfied with the state of the country, with only 14% feeling satisfied. (Gallup Poll, June 21, 1992) If the voters were unhappy with Bush, it would seem that they would simply change allegiances and support another candidate. However, over half the people wanted another unnamed candidate to enter the race and half of the current candidates' support was considered soft. This supports the perception that a majority of the people were searching for another version of social reality at this time.

The people were increasingly dissatisfied with the old version of social reality as evidenced in Bush's rising disapproval ratings. Even so, during the primaries Bush remained in the lead. Although these views of Bush would seem to conflict, the people who were dissatisfied with Bush continued to share dramatic narratives that characterized him as the best candidate. With half the voters considered angry, it would seem that the focus of their anger would be directed at the incumbent, however, the polls indicated that a majority of the voters still supported Bush and less than half wanted to change their congressional representative. Even among angry voters, the majority still supported Bush.

The ongoing attacks from Clinton and later from Perot, combined with the lack of Bush dramatic narratives, registered with the voters as 58% felt that Bush was drifting without clear policies. (New York Times/CBS Poll, April 25, 30,

1992) The media reflected this characterization of Bush as not running a strong campaign and lacking conviction on economic issues. They characterized a confused Bush campaign as stemming from uncertainty within the campaign itself about the direction it should take. (New York Times, April 25, 30, 1992)

When Perot dropped out of the race during the Democratic Convention, voters who shared Perot's dramatic narratives would be looking for another version of social reality. They would likely find the Clinton version attractive to them, which would explain why Clinton received a historically high post convention bounce. With the Bush campaign in disarray and Bush on vacation, there would be no one to defend his version of social reality making it unlikely for voters to return to the Bush or the Republican version of social reality in any significant numbers.

This shift in public opinion during the convention left a majority of people separated from their old version of social reality and searching for a new one. Although a few returned to their previously shared version of social reality, an overwhelming number shared a new one. It was here that the core support for Clinton rose above that of Bush. Even though public opinion suggested that Clinton's issues existed before the campaign began, he was able to exploit them by panicking people into believing that the state of the country was so bad something drastic had to be done to avert a total crisis.

The inability of Bush to recapture voters during the Republican Convention would seem to demonstrate the significance of the great conversion to the new Clinton version of social reality. If Bush was unable to regain those who had lost his version of social reality in significant numbers, he would not be reelected president. So, even before Bush had announced his main campaign initiative or had even begun to campaign, it looked like the election was all over.

A Change In The Bush Campaign.

Not until after the conventions did Bush finally begin to set out a version of social reality that would form the basis for his reelection campaign. The lack of his ability to share meaning with past Reagan Bush supporters likely cost him vital support. During the time before Bush created his version of social reality, both Clinton and Perot had time to create and share their versions and to gain converts to their candidacy by separating people from previously shared meanings like the weak Bush version of social reality.

At the beginning of the general election, Bush was faced with a challenge different from that of his rival. Bush had to keep the support of people who had voted for him in the past. This could be accomplished through the skillful process of sharing meaning with them. However, Bush emerged from the convention and moved into the general election with the dramatic narrative of family values as the core of a loosely cobbled together version of social reality. This contributed to the perception that his campaign was adrift with no discernable direction.

Problems developed when the Bush campaign came under intense criticism in the media. The campaign's use of family values was characterized as an intrusion into personal morality (Washington Post, September 8, 1992) that seemed to repel voters. (New York Times, August 30, 1992) Bush's view of family values was considered to be unclear for two reasons, the campaign did not tell people specifically what those values meant and different groups viewed family values in very different ways. (Chicago Tribune, August 6, September 6, 1992) While 47% of the voters felt that Bush handled the issue of family values best, compared to 38% for Clinton, only 52% felt this issue was important. In comparison, 89% felt the economy was important and Clinton led Bush 55% to 34% as the candidate best able to handle it. (Gallup Poll, September 13, 1992)

At this point, the media characterized Bush's attempt to attract voters as ineffective because public opinion on these values was divided. (Los Angeles Times, September 8, 1992) Because the dramatic narrative of family values was not shared by the general population or with the media, Bush seemed to back away from it. The media then shared a dramatic narrative that characterized this change in direction as evidence that Bush was struggling to find a clear message and consistent campaign strategy. The Bush campaign was adrift and left with only one consistent issue, criticizing Clinton. (National Public Radio, Morning Edition, September 7, 1992)

This failing may have contributed to the media perception of Bush's lack of direction. During the primaries he had been criticized for not campaigning or having a plan. After the convention, the media began to share dramatic narratives that characterized the Bush campaign as having become a real campaign, a reawakening after months of presidential apathy and self imposed exile that allowed Clinton to take the lead. (Washington Post, August 23, 1992)

However, the reorganized campaign ran into difficulties. Bush was further distracted by the demands of conducting the nation's business and dealing with the effects of Hurricane Andrew. The slow relief effort contributed to the erosion of Bush's recent gains. (Chicago Tribune, September 1, 1992, New York Times, August 29, 1992) In late August, Bush cancelled campaign appearances to survey the relief effort. Clinton followed with a visit to the disaster area the next week and criticized Bush's slow response and having cut social programs. (In a twist of irony, the slow response to another hurricane, Katrina, would later come to plague another President Bush.)

In response to criticism of his lack of campaigning, Bush developed a damage control strategy. Bush characterized himself as facing a situation for which he was criticized from all sides, sustaining one assault after another while he had tried to run the country and do what was best for the people. Bush was unfairly attacked by an opponent who had not done in his own state what he criticized Bush for not doing. Clinton had attacked Bush for months while he had, "sat back trying to get things done for this country." (Bush, Tulsa, OK)

In order to counter the public perception of weakness, Bush explained that he had chosen not to fight back until now because he believed Americans wanted action, positive ideas, and real solutions to challenges. This approach amounted to utilizing a strategy of running for president by being president, in essence using governing as a form of campaigning. In the media, Bush was characterized as emerging from his self imposed exile after months of apathy. (Washington Post, August 23, 24, 1992)

Bush, An Agenda For American Renewal.

In September, Bush unveiled an economic plan for the nation's future entitled An Agenda for American Renewal. In a speech to the Detroit Economic Club on September 10 and appearing in a five minute network television address on September 12, Bush introduced his plan to the public. In his campaign book, *Agenda for American Renewal and Accomplishments Through Leadership*, Bush presented a dramatic narrative of renewal as the primary initiative for his campaign and to legitimize his candidacy. Immediately after Bush's speech was aired on C-SPAN, a Clinton rebuttal of Bush's program was aired raising the question of how Clinton obtained this information in order to have time to produce his response.

An Agenda for American Renewal began by citing the challenges that faced the nation while at the same time it recalled Bush's accomplishments as president. It utilized the dramatic narrative of restoration to legitimize his campaign. Bush had proven his ability in the past and that experience could provide a better future under his leadership. Bush used An Agenda for American Renewal to build his version of restoration based on basic American principles. It was characterized as being comprehensive by restoring power to people, not to government. In his plan, initiatives and successes gained in past foreign policy would be applied to the future domestic agenda. The dramatic narrative of renewal characterized this transference from the past to the future, identifying the economic problems and setting out Bush's approach and guiding principles. As there was no single cause for our problems, there could be no one cure. This program was his vision of a better America and his plan for getting there.

Bush's plan began with the dramatic narrative of a golden age around the world with the first peace in five decades. Bush characterized this as a historical watershed having, "completed the greatest mission in the lifetime of our country, the triumph of democratic capitalism over imperial communism." Meeting the challenges facing the nation required sound policies by recognizing the unfinished work and unsolved problems at home. Because, "While we face an era of great opportunity, we face great risks." So, we need to be engaged in the world to "transform uncertainty into opportunity." (Bush, Economic Club of Detroit)

Bush's dramatic narrative was forward looking, promoting capitalism with free international markets that fostered growth at home "that begins on Main Street and extends to Wall Street." Having won the Cold War was not good enough, now we must win the peace. The dramatic narrative of foreign policy as domestic policy was created when Bush characterized advances in either realm as essentially bound together. Bush spoke of turning "our strength as a world power to our advantage as an economic power." (Bush, Detroit Economic Club) For Bush there was an inseparable link between foreign and domestic policy because engagement abroad created growth and stability at home.

Bush characterized America as being well positioned to achieve this goal with the passage of NAFTA and GATT to open free markets and create high wage American jobs. Just as during the cold war military alliances were forged, now a strategic global economic and trade policy must be forged to shift from a military superpower to an economic superpower. Global military alliances must be turned into a strategy for global economic trade policy. The weight of the largest export market could be used as leverage to create reciprocity with other countries. By staying strong abroad, opportunity would be created at home to increase our competitive edge. Thus, Bush envisioned a future with an America restored through "her most cherished principles" to empower economic growth.

Bush repeated his charge that Clinton was exploiting the economy's weaknesses for political gain by creating a false perception of America in decline. In responding to his critics' criticism of the economy, he said that the economy was one of the best in the world. Bush did not mean to say that all was well, but that the economy was better than his opponent wanted the nation to believe. The opposition looked only at America's problems by telling the people that its best days were past. Bush's approach was one of opportunity for all Americans through a reduction in the intrusion of government to provide incentives for growth. The past decade had witnessed unprecedented growth and we could do this again.

In this dramatic narrative, the villains were government bureaucrats who would impose unfair restrictions to hurt the economic growth of the nation. Bush characterized Congress as 'apple polishers' for the special interests who resisted this revolution. They were the villains who obstructed Bush's plan for the future. Trial lawyers were characterized as large financial contributors who were a powerful special interest well represented in Congress. Lawyers had created a state of crisis, so to solve our problems we must, "sue each other less and care for each other more." (Bush, Agenda for American Renewal)

Just as businesses downsize to stay competitive, government needed to become more streamlined to be productive. Bush proposed cutting federal staff and salaries, capping growth, freezing spending, passing the line item veto, and allowing people to apply tax payments directly to reducing the deficit. Congress spent money because it brought individual members more power. They would spend "every last dime they can squeeze from the working men and women of America." So, our interests will lose out to the business as usual tradeoffs with Congress. (Bush, Agenda for American Renewal)

Bush characterized this time in history as a turning point for the nation to be a better America through change and renewal. In Bush's plan, economic growth came from businesses that took risks. The government should keep taxes, interest, and regulations as low as possible to encourage growth. If capital was taxed heavily, it would be available only to the wealthy. In his program for renewal, Bush defined a view of the world and created a dramatic narrative of the future. He looked forward to working with a new Congress to meet new challenges. He put the public in the dramatic narrative because it was their choice to decide which plan fit their principles, values, and hopes for the future. These principles of freedom that had made the United States the most dynamic society in the world were fundamental to defending the personal freedom of all Americans.

Clinton, The Rebirth and Restoration Dramatic Narratives.

Between the conventions and Election Day, Clinton frequently utilized a number of dramatic narratives to legitimize his right to govern. In his speech at Notre Dame on September 11th, Clinton utilized the rebirth dramatic narrative by characterizing the events that brought him into public service to explain why he was running for office. This served as a sanctifying agent to legitimize him seeking the presidency. It also helped provide the basis of a populist mandate by presenting him as a candidate that understood the problems of ordinary people because he was one of them who had suffered similar problems.

The rebirth dramatic narrative has a long history in secular and religious rhetoric. It focuses on a person who experiences a defining moment in his or her life that changes or shapes it in a new direction. For the person who uses the rebirth dramatic narrative, it often begins with them living an aimless life. Then comes a dramatic experience that is characterized as a defining moment, which changes the course of their life. The circumstances of the moment of their rebirth are often recounted in detail and are characterized in a dramatic narrative style. Evangelical ministers would recount their personal conversion experience of being born again or receiving the call to the ministry as an example of their faith to congregants and potential converts. This dramatic narrative is important to a candidate because if it is shared with the public, it can help to legitimize their right to govern.

The Clinton rebirth dramatic narrative began when he recounted the hot summer afternoon when, as a sixteen year old delegate to the American Legion Boy's Nation, he met then President John F. Kennedy in the Rose Garden at the White House. That meeting was repeatedly characterized during the campaign as a defining moment in his life that motivated Clinton to begin a purposeful life of public service. A photo of a young Clinton meeting Kennedy was frequently used as a symbolic passing of the torch between generations. It served as a powerful image to help legitimize Clinton's claim to office. When Clinton shook hands with President Kennedy, he assumed some of the Kennedy mystique. Years after this meeting, Clinton decided that he wanted a life of public service in the spirit of Johnson's Great Society.

In his speech at Notre Dame, Clinton spoke about the history of the University, about religion and religious freedom, about his own experience attending Catholic schools, and about what his faith meant to him. However, breaking from his normal remarks, he did not mention by name or refer to his campaign mainstay, the dramatic narrative of The New Covenant. Instead, he developed several other dramatic narratives that he had used previously in his campaign. He characterized his campaign as one to restore hope and the forgotten middle class by putting people first. His campaign was about bringing people together because, "We are all in this together and we will rise and fall together." (Clinton, Notre Dame)

Clinton reiterated his version of the restoration dramatic narrative when he urged the country to embrace a renewal in the American spirit to bring it together with a greater sense of community. He was grateful for being born in a country where more people put religion in their lives than any other in the world, a country made great by religious freedom, an "offering of a free and joyous spirit." This freedom was a "tribute to the genius and the courage of the American experiment. That the government can be the protector of the freedom of every faith because it is the exclusive property of none." For Clinton, faith was a source of strength, hope, and challenge because, as he put it, "None of us is a stranger to sin and weakness." (Clinton, Notre Dame)

The restoration dramatic narrative begins with a depiction of a time of troubles. So, in order to demonstrate a sense of purpose for his candidacy, Clinton characterized the present as a time of troubles caused by twelve years of neglect that created the need for restoration. Setting his dramatic narrative of America within a larger context Clinton said, "We must know we are in a quieter crisis of a fraying society and a declining economy, of an educational system unequal to the task of global competition, of an environment slowly coming apart." (Clinton, Notre Dame) This troubled time provides the motive for change and the restoration dramatic narrative allows for a reform movement to develop that would correct the evils of society and reaffirm people's faith in the institutions of society without destroying them.

Whenever Bush or the Republicans attacked him, he was quick to answer them, often by trying to recast their dramatic narratives to bolster his legitimacy and undermine theirs. For instance, he answered the familiar Bush dramatic narrative of family values when he said, "I want an America that does more than talk about family values, I want an America that values families." He went even further to attack the legitimacy of Bush, with a direct reference to the Republican convention when he said, "I have been appalled to hear the voices of intolerance raised in recent weeks." Yet, he extolled the virtues of having free speech and debate as illustrated when Clinton quoted Mario Cuomo when Cuomo had spoke at Notre Dame in 1984, "The price of seeking to force our ideas on others is that someday they might force theirs on us." (Mario Cuomo, Notre Dame)

At this point in the campaign Clinton utilized the dramatic narrative of putting people first. His campaign commercials and literature utilized this narrative, including a book titled *Putting People First, How We Can All Change America.* This book was characterized as having been developed by Clinton from having a "continuing conversation with the American people." This helped him to claim a popular mandate for change as the representative of the people. Clinton would institute a new approach to reinvent government that was "neither liberal or conservative, neither Democratic nor Republican." This helped him to escape past negative connotations that could hurt his campaign. (Clinton, Putting People First)

Putting People First was presented as Clinton's plan for what he would do as president. It was characterized as, "a revolution in government." However, rather than simply outlining his policies and programs, it consisted of a series of dramatic narratives casting the past twelve years of Reagan Bush as villainous in the harshest terms. They had damaged the country by violating the people's and the nation's values. First, it sought to recast people's perceptions of the last decade, "During the 1980s, our government betrayed the values that made America great." These statements were not a part of Clinton's program, but rather a series of dramatic narratives designed to separate people from their current version of social reality by characterizing it as repugnant, so they must change. (Clinton, Putting People First)

People who shared meaning with the Bush version of social reality were now being told that their beliefs were wrong, because Bush had betrayed the people, "This betrayal of democracy must stop." For each point of his plan, he began by demonizing Bush and the Republicans as villains, "For 12 years the Republicans in Washington have praised the virtue of hard work, but they have hurt hard-working Americans." Clinton would help them to fix their problems, "We can provide opportunity, demand responsibility... We can give every American hope for the future." Clinton then made his version of social reality as appealing as possible by casting it in the best possible terms, " It's time to honor and reward people who work hard and play by the rules." (Clinton, Putting People First)

This approach to changing public perception was used to characterize every problem facing the nation as being caused by Bush and the Republicans, "The Republicans in Washington have compiled the worst economic record in 50 years." Clinton would then cast them as the villains, "For twelve years Republicans have divided us against each other pitting rich against poor, black against white, woman against man." He characterized their actions as destructive, "the Bush administration has been an environmental disaster." Clinton then presented himself as the hero who would save the people, "Putting people first demands, above all, that we put America back to work." He would help them prosper, "America needs a new approach to economics that will give new hope to our people and breathe new life into the American dream." And he had the solutions people wanted, "Our plan will cut the deficit in half within four years and assure that it continues to fall each year after that." (Clinton, Putting People First)

Clinton added several other dramatic narratives. He attacked the nature of government itself, "Our political system isn't working either. Washington is dominated by powerful interests and an entrenched bureaucracy." He attacked their perception of the American Dream, "Home ownership and decent housing are essential parts of the American dream. But for too many Americans, that dream is unattainable." He even attacked people who worked for Bush, "During the 1980s the White House staff routinely took taxpayers for a ride to play golf." For each problem, he had the solution, "Putting our people first means honoring and rewarding those who work hard and play by the rules." (Clinton, Putting People First)

Bush, Conservation Dramatic Narrative.

In a speech at the Burrill Lumber Company in Medford, Oregon on September 14th, Bush spoke about his agenda for American renewal. Although renewal suggested restoration, as it unfolded it became clear that Bush was using a conservation dramatic narrative. Conservation is about keeping those things that are good or valued, but not necessarily lost, as with restoration. It is often used when referring to the prevention of wastefulness or the protection and preservation of a valued resource, like the environment. Bush's speech noted that America faced, "foreign, domestic, economic, and environmental challenges" that called for an integrated approach to solving these problems, because "the balance has been lost." (Bush, Burrill Lumber) Bush characterized himself as a person who through a lifetime of experience appreciated, revered, and respected the wilderness because it deserved sound management.

Bush cited his accomplishments in environmental protection by establishing the Clean Air Act, instituting offshore drilling restrictions, and expanding the national parks and services. However, there had to be a balance between protecting lands by conserving the best, but also helping the people. To illustrate his point, Bush told the story of a paper mill that closed because of legislation to protect owls, which resulted in the failure of other local businesses and an increase in violence. Where local mills had been closed, workers had lost their jobs, schools were closed, and local services were cut. Even the original author of the bill to protect the owls characterized it as having gone too far. Environmental regulations were meant to protect endangered species, but were not meant to hurt jobs, families, and communities.

Using the dramatic narrative of conservation, Bush was the candidate who would restore the balance between the economy and the environment, conserve the best, and change the rest for the betterment of the people. Legislation protecting the owls was a noble concept, but it was being used by extremists who worked through the courts to wipe out jobs, families, and even entire communities. Bush characterized the laws as broken and in need of fixing. He had asked Congress for a more reasonable plan and they had refused.

In addition to environmental extremists and Congress, Bush added Clinton to the group of villains who hurt people when he said, "My opponent talks about putting people first. Well, we can start right here in the Pacific Northwest." (Bush, Burrill Lumber) Even worse than Clinton was Gore who Bush characterized as a preservationist in league with environmental extremists who were out to protect owls regardless of the costs to people and families. The restoration of the balance between the environment and the economy would protect "endangered species" and "endangered jobs" in future legislation by considering the interests of people as well as owls. In an unusual melding of restoration and conservation, Bush sought to claim the middle ground between the two.

This dramatic narrative exemplified larger issues in which, for Bush, the balance between important interests had been lost. Bush possessed the character to be balanced and presidential in his decisions to work out a fair resolution of important issues. Bush put himself in his own dramatic narrative as the candidate who would restore the balance to solve the problems facing the country. In contrast, he said that Clinton did not possess the character to balance differing sides of critical issues to work out equitable solutions.

Bush, Military Service Dramatic Narrative.

Expanding on his agenda for American renewal, Bush addressed the issue of national defense in a speech to the 114th General Conference of the National Guard Association on September 15th. Bush began with the familiar scene depicting past events, including the end of communism and the fall of the Berlin Wall to characterize his view of the world and America's role in it. These events represented a victory for the ideals of men and women who fought for freedom, because "communism didn't just fall. It was pushed."

To establish his credibility and undermine his opponents' legitimacy, Bush compared his military service with Clinton's, because whoever was the president would be the commander in chief of the military. He spoke about the recent controversy over Clinton's military service, but Bush said that he had not come to attack Clinton. Instead, he defended Dan Quayle, who served in the National Guard and was exposed to the brunt of savage and unmerciful attacks by villains who called the Guard a "haven for draft dodgers." (Bush, National Guard Association)

Quayle had "stood his ground" with calm and candor, so Bush was very proud to have served with him. The issue for Bush was that the president led the military and had the authority to send "sons and daughters in harm's way." (Bush, National Guard Association) To illustrate this point, Bush told of events on the night Desert Storm began. After having dinner with Billy Graham, his thoughts were thousands of miles away. He walked down to the Oval Office to await the results of the initial strike and wondered if our forces would be as effective as he had hoped. He thought about the men and women who had been sent there as well as their parents back home.

Characterizing Clinton as irresponsible, Bush described Clinton's proposed defense cutbacks as going beyond what all experts said was advisable. Bush had protected the country from inadvisable defense cutbacks. This was a pattern that history had demonstrated would result in Americans paying a big price. The Congress would waste any defense savings in a rush to "get busy beating the swords into pork barrels." (Bush, National Guard Association) In an era of downsizing, Bush felt that the nation must remain committed to maintaining a strong, capable force in order to avoid straining people and families who serve in the Guard.

We now inhabited a world where the single threat of the Soviets had been replaced with many smaller threats. The end of the Cold War did not mean that the work in defense was finished. Recognizing that a conflict could arise with little or no warning, Bush was resolved to maintain the military to ensure that we had the best trained and equipped forces to guarantee the peace. He was proud to be the first president in five decades not to preside over any war, hot or cold, and to have given the order to reduce the nuclear alert. For all these successes Bush cautioned, "the world remains a dangerous place" with many potential threats to peace, so we must remain strong. (Bush, National Guard Association)

Bush, American Renewal Dramatic Narrative.

On September 18th, Bush spoke to the employees of AT&T at their corporate headquarters in Basking Ridge, New Jersey. Tying into his dramatic narrative of an agenda for American renewal, Bush presented his plan for economic security. He wanted to provide economic security for all Americans to preserve the American Dream for them and future generations. Bush was offering an alternative to Clinton who put his faith in government by giving government increasing power. Instead, Bush wanted to give people the power to help themselves.

To illustrate this dramatic narrative, Bush told the story of the German Kaiser, William II, who drew up plans for a new battleship that would be the best ever built except that if it were ever put in the water it would sink. He compared this ship to the proposals that came out of Congress that sounded good, but would not work. One example was the Family Leave bill, which sounded noble, but had the effect of discriminating against women who might leave to have children or take care of their families. Instead of overloading businesses with federal mandates, Bush wanted to provide incentives for growth since the economy was sluggish and businesses were laying off people.

In his dramatic narrative about the economy, Bush again characterized an obstructionist Congress as the villain who would hold up legislation all year, pass it two weeks before adjourning, and then dare him to veto it. Responding to accusations that he promoted the rich, Bush said that helping businesses was not protecting the rich as all business owners were not rich and many were owned by women.

Bush characterized his opponent, whom he did not mention directly, as promoting big government and restricting personal freedom by taking an approach that was counter to his and the people's shared values. The finest health care system in the world, a system that attracted people from all over the world would be threatened if taken over by government. Bush would provide incentives and use competition to keep costs down.

The importance of this election was characterized by Bush as not having to do with individual policies or programs, but rather with the philosophy behind them. Bush advocated a philosophy of personal empowerment, so that the people would retain control over their own lives to make their own decisions. The power of government must be used to help us move forward to create opportunity. These opportunities were contingent on less government and less regulation for families and individuals. Economic security could be created on the basis of traditional values that would guide us to build a safe and more secure America. Thus, Bush claimed a mandate based upon the communal values he shared with his audience.

Bush Makes Some Gains.

By mid-September, Bush was making some headway in regaining the status he once enjoyed in the polls. Bush had increased his standing from 37% in August to 40% in September. The public was sharing his dramatic narrative of Clinton's dishonesty as those who saw Clinton as honest dropped from 70% in August to 62% by September 19th. And Clinton fell from 56% to 50% as Bush began to close the gap. (Gallup Poll, August 16, September 23, 1992)

This change in public opinion would suggest Bush was having some success in promoting his program of renewal. By basing his latest speeches on a plan of restoration and adding a philosophy of leadership, he was finally sharing meaning with the voters to develop his version of social reality. However, the Bush dramatic narratives about Clinton were having less success in sharing meaning with the voters. Raising the issue of Clinton's character was having little effect as 60% of the voters were satisfied with Clinton's explanation of his draft status, 72% no longer doubted Clinton's ability to be Commander in Chief, and 62% thought that he had the honesty and integrity to be president.

Many of Clinton's dramatic narratives remained shared by a majority of the people on issues that people felt were important. On the handling of the economy, Clinton led Bush 52% to 36%, a slight gain for Clinton since March when he led Bush 49% to 37%. Clinton was preferred 51% to 31% as the candidate best able to bring about change. This would suggest that Clinton's dramatic narrative of change, with himself as a competent leader who would fix the economy was still being shared by the majority of the people. In foreign affairs Bush led Clinton 73% to 20%, up from August when he led Clinton 62% to 30%. (Gallup Poll, September 19, 1992)

Clinton Runs The First Negative Ads.

In every election there inevitably arises accusations of negative campaigning and charges stemming over who started it first. In the general election, the Clinton campaign ran the first negative television commercials in which he criticized the Bush economic record. (New York Times, September 21, 1992, Washington Post, September 23, 1992, The World Today CNN, September 20, 1992, Chicago Tribune, September 22, 1992)

Clinton's first attack commercial characterized the Bush record on jobs and unemployment as evidence that he was out of touch with the people. This commercial sought to discredit Bush to change people's perception of actual events, so that Clinton's plan would appear better. Video of the 1988 election depicted Bush saying that thirty million jobs would be created in the next eight years and that we were not in a recession. These quotes were contrasted with news reports that the jobless rates had hit new highs. This characterized Bush as not only out of touch with what was happening in the country, he did not even understand the problem, so it did not matter what kind of program he might have. This commercial promoted the need for change because we could not afford four more years of an administration that could not even help its own people.

Several television commercials developed Clinton's dramatic narrative of Bush lying to the people, which were very similar to those used effectively by Buchanan to undermine Bush in the primaries. The commercials showed Bush saying "read my lips," which the Clinton campaign repeated so often it lost its original meaning and became a new dramatic narrative for Bush's broken promises. This commercial asked the audience to remember when Bush had said that they would be better off in four years and asked viewers how they were doing now to remind them that Bush had made things worse for them. These quotes were contrasted with headlines reporting that health care costs went up $1,800 in four years and that Bush had passed the second biggest tax increase in history. In comparing Bush's remarks against recent events, the commercials characterized differences between the past and present, a dramatic narrative Clinton employed often in his version of social reality.

Clinton frequently used the bad economy and the loss of jobs to discredit Bush as ineffectual and not deserving of a second term. Clinton appealed to the voter's self interest and desire to be better off in the future, implying that any change would be better than the present to reduce uncertainty about a Clinton presidency. To counter Bush's dramatic narratives, Clinton's commercials characterized a deceptive, misleading Bush whose ideas were scary. Clinton's commercial quoted the Washington Post when it characterized the Bush commercials as misleading, observing that his 'read my lips no new taxes' pledge was broken when, "George Bush signed the second biggest tax increase in American history," increased middle class taxes, and "now George Bush wants to give a $108,000 tax break to millionaires." (Clinton, Television Commercial)

The source of this information was identified as the Congressional Budget Office, which was presented as credible and impartial. In these attack commercials Clinton was not directly mentioned, a tactic that was intended to keep him above the perception of being negative. These commercials promoted change that was justified by the lack of trust in the current government. They did not seek to directly help Clinton bolster his own legitimacy, but rather to lower the public's perception of Bush to make Clinton look better in comparison.

Clinton's characterization of the ailing economy continued to be shared by the media, which began to report that the voters also believed the economy was bad and blamed the Republicans. (Chicago Tribune, August 30, 1992) The media's dramatic narratives characterized the condition of the economy as the fault of the Republicans who had the worst economic record in fifty years. (Houston Post, August 28, 1992) Bush aided in the sharing of the Clinton dramatic narrative when Bush characterized the economy as 'lousy,' promising never again to agree to a Democratic tax increase. (Los Angeles Times, New York Times, September 10, 1992)

The media shared Clinton's dramatic narrative of Bush breaking his no taxes pledge, which was even shared by Bush as he had spent much of the campaign apologizing for raising taxes explaining that he had found out the hard way that it was a mistake. The media also characterized Bush as taking credit for what went right and blaming Congress for everything that went wrong during his administration. (Washington Post, September 10, 1992)

A New Characterization Of Clinton.

In a change of strategy, Bush adopted a different characterization of the election and specifically of his opponent. In the next series of speeches, Bush set out the differences between himself and Clinton. Bush characterized how Clinton had, in effect debated himself by changing his mind on every issue. Although he did not want to be critical of the people of Arkansas, Bush remarked that they were good and decent people, but were deserving of better treatment than they had received from their governor. Bush said that he would tell the people what Clinton had actually done in Arkansas or as Bush turned the phrase, what he had done to the people of Arkansas.

In his speech in Tulsa, Oklahoma on September 22nd, Bush began by affirming the dramatic narrative developed in previous speeches of his agenda of American renewal that would stimulate markets in order to create new jobs. In a change of tactic, he characterized the country as coming out of tough times, warning his audience not to believe the pessimists who tear the country down. Pessimists, like Clinton took unfair advantage of the economy and had attacked Bush for months while he "sat back trying to get things done for this country." He characterized many of Clinton's attacks as personal, unrelenting, and distorting his record. (Bush, Tulsa, OK)

Clinton was the first candidate to use negative campaigning in the general election campaign by airing the first negative television commercials. Bush called this act firing the first shot in a negative campaign, giving notice that he was not going to take it anymore. He would now present Clinton's record to the American people to compare with his own. Bush characterized Clinton as bringing the campaign into its first negative debate when the country wanted a positive addressing of the issues. Doing so separated Clinton from the values of the people whom he sought to serve.

Bush reiterated that many of Clinton's attacks had grown increasingly personal in nature. In contrast, Bush chose to focus on Clinton's record recognizing that Americans wanted a positive debate of the issues. The stakes were too high to be drawn into the negative debate that Clinton had begun. Bush would concentrate on the facts about Clinton, which he characterized as a Grand Canyon that separated Clinton's rhetoric from the reality of his actions.

Using the debates as an example, Bush characterized a debate between the two Clintons. Candidate Clinton was "a promising young man who seems to be willing to promise anything to get elected," and Governor Clinton, "whose record in Arkansas is a series of broken promises." (Bush, Tulsa, OK) To illustrate this difference, Bush repeated the story of a debate between the two Clintons emphasizing how his record differed from both. Civil rights, education, and equal opportunity were issues candidate Clinton used to criticize Bush, yet Governor Clinton had done nothing about them.

Bush accused Clinton of playing the old game liberals use to divide the rich from the poor by using divisiveness to further his campaign through class warfare. Candidate Clinton criticized Bush's civil rights record, yet Governor Clinton led one of only two states that did not have a civil rights law guaranteeing equal opportunity. Bush had voted for the Fair Housing Act in Congress in 1968, yet Arkansas had no law banning such discrimination.

Bush cautioned his audience that as governor, Clinton had talked a lot and done nothing. When they hear candidate Clinton, remember Governor Clinton's record because "his actions betray his words." While continuing to contrast the differences between the two Clintons in his dramatic narrative, Bush concluded that it did not matter which one you heard, the result was the same because Clinton was the "wrong man to accept your trust to be president." America deserved better and could do better to confront the challenges it faced. In this regard, Bush reiterated his approach to resolving important issues such as improving schools, improving health care, and getting on "with the business of governing this nation and solving our problems." (Bush, Tulsa, OK)

Bush asked for the audience's support and expressed the hope that his character would "pass muster" with the American people. As part of his emerging version of social reality, Bush developed a dramatic narrative of trust and experience in order to contrast himself with Clinton and Congress who had faith in government instead of faith in people.

Bush likened the election to interviewing for a job noting that the people knew him, his record, his strengths, and his mistakes. He spoke about the opportunities and challenges that he would confront as he built on his record. He felt a great optimism for the country, which would rise above today's conditions to achieve a better tomorrow. Bush characterized himself as differing sharply from his opponent who sought to tear down the last ten years by focusing only on what was wrong with America.

Clinton Solidifies His Lead.

As the campaign moved into the final month, a larger number of Clinton supporters shared their candidate's version of social reality than did Bush supporters. Recent polls gave Bush 38% of the vote with 54% for Clinton. Since August, those who strongly supported Clinton had grown from 44% to 46%, while strong support for Bush dropped from 57% to 37%. In September, Bush's approval rating had declined to 36%, which was lower than Carter's (39%) in September 1980. In October, the number of angry voters had declined from 38% in April to 23%. These changes in the electorate suggest that people were converting to a new version of social reality. (Gallup Poll, September 23, October 3, 1992)

To help bolster his legitimacy, Clinton had succeeded in enticing most of the people into sharing the dramatic narrative that his draft record did not matter as 70% said that it was not important and only 26% felt that he was not telling the truth. (Gallup Poll, September 23, 1992) Bush's criticisms of Clinton's honesty and character had been shared little among the public and in the media as Clinton's image had actually improved. (Los Angeles Times, September 17, 1992) The middle class was anxious about what the future held for them and their children, and they were concerned about their ability to achieve the American Dream. (Chicago Tribune, September 13, 1992)

Bush was seen as trying to change the negative image of family values from the convention, an image that was characterized in the media as being hostile to gays, feminists, and welfare recipients. (New York Times, September 21, 1992) However, according to the media, Republican plans to redefine family values may have come too late, as the polls showed that it had already alienated many voters. (CBS Evening News, September 21, 1992)

In mid-September, when people were asked what was the most important problem facing the country, 66% indicated economic issues and 37% specifically indicated the economy. However, when it came to naming specific economic issues they ranked much lower, 27% said unemployment, 9% said cost of living or inflation, 2% said the trade deficit, and 1% said recession or depression.

The majority of the people who indicated concern for the economy gave few details, suggesting that the Clinton and Perot dramatic narratives were being shared, since they both criticized the economy with few specifics. The Gallup Poll noted that most people were focusing only on the economy in general, not on any specific problem. (Gallup Poll, September 17, 1992)

In past polls, when people had expressed a concern over the economy they usually cited a specific issue such as unemployment, the deficit, or inflation. This perception would again tend to support the public sharing meaning with the Clinton and Perot dramatic narratives about the economy. Bush administration officials even conceded to Clinton's characterization of the economy as most economic indicators confirmed that the economy had slowed under Bush. (Los Angeles Times, September 25, 1992)

In an incursion into traditionally Republican areas, Clinton announced that he had been endorsed by one hundred business executives, including the support of the CEO of Apple Computer. (New York Times, September 17, 1992) The dramatic narrative of Clinton having been endorsed by many business leaders soon became a shared dramatic narrative in the media. (All Things Considered, National Public Radio, September 23, 1992)

Meanwhile, the media continued to depict the Bush campaign as showing weakness and uncertainty. Media stories reported that the Bush campaign welcomed a Perot bid due to frustration with their inability to close Clinton's lead. (Los Angeles Times, September 28, 1992) They had hoped to benefit from the uncertainty that a change in the campaign would create.

They couldn't have been more wrong.

Chapter 7
The Race Widens

In mid-September, Ross Perot's name was placed on the ballot in Arizona, the last of all fifty states. Still Perot did not reenter the race, even though he had spent $7 million to sustain volunteer activity since leaving the campaign in July. Despite Perot's denials, he would eventually reenter the race as his supporters were continuing their campaign efforts. (Houston Post, September 12, 1992, CNN, September 18, 1992, Washington Post, September 30, 1992)

A few days before announcing, Perot met with Democrat and Republican leaders to discuss the type of debates that would be held indicating his interest to run. (CNN, September 28, 1992) The media reported that Perot wanted to begin a television campaign as soon as possible and that he might reenter the race in order to make it easier to buy television time. (New York Times, September 19, 1992)

Perot's withdrawal and loss of visibility in the intervening months had alienated him with the voters. Only 20% now viewed him as favorable, with Clinton rating the highest at 54% and 40% for Bush. Prior to announcing his reentry, Perot received only 7% support in the polls falling from a high of 39% before he dropped out. Now a majority of voters, 60%, opposed his return to the campaign regardless of whom they supported. The media was sharing a dramatic narrative that Perot was trying to gain attention and wanting to save face from increasing embarrassment. His public image had now turned negative as 66% viewed him unfavorably compared to 56% for Bush and 38% for Clinton. (Gallup Poll, October 3, 1992, CNN, September 28, 1992, New York Times, October 1, 1992)

By the end of September the phenomenon of the angry voter that arose during the spring primaries had subsided suggesting that public conversion to Clinton's version of social reality had stabilized. The number of voters considered angry had dropped from 38% in April to 23% in October. Voter opinion of the candidates had changed as well. From January to October those who thought that the candidates had good ideas increased from 29% to 50%. Those who thought at least one candidate was a good candidate increased from 40% to 61%. (Gallup Poll, October 3, 1992) Perot said that he had reentered the race because the candidates were not addressing the issues the people wanted, yet recent public opinion seemed to indicate they were being addressed more than when he dropped out.

Since Perot's first run, voter anger had dropped and support for Clinton had solidified essentially closing the window of opportunity for a third party candidate. Given these feelings and change of climate within the electorate, one might well ask why Perot would subject himself to the tough scrutiny that reentry into the campaign would surely bring.

The Perot Announcement.

On October 1, Ross Perot ended weeks of speculation in the national media, which was partially fueled by statements from Perot himself. In a news conference in Dallas, he announced his reentry into the election. Perot began by evoking a grassroots dramatic narrative to support his popular mandate when he said, "The volunteers in all fifty states have asked me to run as a candidate for president of the United States." (Perot, Dallas Announcement) After taking time off to evaluate his candidacy, Perot had returned to the campaign not as a presidential hopeful, but as the sanctified choice of the people who had spoken.

In his announcement, Perot acknowledged the commitment of all the volunteers who had carried on to put him on the ballot in all the remaining states after he had dropped out. Apologizing to the volunteers, he expressed his concern that they were hurt by his actions when he stepped aside in July. Back when he dropped out of the race, he had characterized his actions as the right thing to do, which he now called a mistake.

Since dropping out of the race, he said that he had given the other candidates a chance to address the problems facing the country and they did not do it, so he was forced to take on these issues himself. The two parties were not providing solutions for the problems the people wanted resolved, so the people had asked him to get back in the race. Perot was in the race because the national debt was threatening the American Dream for future generations. Looking to the future while diminishing his past actions, Perot said it did no good to look back as there were problems that must be solved and that he would not spend a minute talking about anything other than the problems the country faced.

Perot Dramatic Narratives.

In his announcement speech to reenter the race, Perot utilized the following dramatic narratives. He had used many of them in the primary and continued to use them for the rest of the campaign.

1. The American Dream. Perot characterized himself as an example of the American Dream, as he had done earlier in the campaign. He had benefited from the American Dream with a wonderful family and successful business, which gave him an obligation to serve his country and the people by dedicating himself to passing on the American Dream to the next generation. To illustrate his point, Perot told the story of a little girl who wrote to tell him that she felt everyone should have a say in how things were done, not just a small group of people.

Perot recalled retired people who went through the depression, then fought and won the Second World War. Back then everyone participated and now we needed "fair, shared sacrifice" from everyone to solve our problems. Many veterans had asked him to run on their behalf, veterans who had served their country with no thanks. It was these people who deserved a country that fulfilled the ideals they had fought for on the battlefield.

A soldier who was ambushed in the Vietnam War and received the Purple Heart had sent his medal to Perot on loan, to carry with him through the campaign as a reminder that he was running for ordinary people. By evoking the American Dream, Perot shared common traditions and values to establish a common bond with the voters. Perot had connected his vision of the future and the American Dream with his audience's values and beliefs to motivate them to support him.

2. The Washington Mess. In developing his version of social reality, Perot returned to two previous dramatic narratives, one of the American people and the other of the American government. As he had done in the past, Perot characterized the American people as heroes, good people who had figured out that there was something wrong with the government, so it needed to be changed. Perot characterized the government in Washington as mired in gridlock and in a mess. People who came to serve rejected taking responsibility, made excuses, and cashed in for themselves. They answered to special interests and foreign lobbyists instead of the American people. Washington had attracted ego driven, power mad people when it should attract the best qualified to serve.

After setting up the characteristics of these two groups, Perot compared them on specific issues. He said, "The people know that it is wrong to spend our children's money," yet the government would "pass on a four trillion dollar debt." The people wanted the government to rebuild and reorganize the job and industrial base, keep industry from going abroad, put people back to work, and make "the words made in the USA once again the world's standard for excellence." (Perot, Dallas Announcement)

3. A Man of the People. Ordinary people had asked him to run, many had written him, and some had even traveled at their own expense just to see him. Perot repeatedly characterized himself as a candidate of the people who owed nothing to anyone but them. He called for their help because, as he told the audience, one person could do nothing, but millions could do anything. Characterizing himself as their servant, Perot would give it everything he had. He was indistinct on what he would do, but this approach placed the people at the center of this dramatic narrative as the sanctifying agent.

Finally, Perot called for the people's support, as he could only do this work if they were with him. He loved his country, the American people, and the principles on which it was founded, and he didn't like to see those principles violated. Perot was the central character in this action that could only be completed with the support of the people, as he told them, "it is up to you, it's up to all of us." The final result was up to the people, so Perot gave them a choice by telling them, "The final result is in your hands because you own this country and you're the voters." (Perot, Dallas Announcement)

Bush Television Commercials Stress Trust And Experience.

After Perot's reentry into the race, the Bush dramatic narrative of American renewal seemed to erode as another one became more dominant. In television commercials and during the debates, Bush focused on dramatic narratives that characterized himself as having demonstrated his ability to govern. In order to legitimize his candidacy, Bush stressed that he was the only candidate who could be trusted and who had the experience to govern. Bush concentrated on the difference between himself and Clinton, their records in office, and their plans for the nation.

In an effort to characterize Clinton as a traditional liberal, Bush revived the dramatic narrative of tax and spend to cast him as a villain who supported high taxes and government programs that wasted the people's money. To pay for his increased spending in Arkansas, Clinton had raised taxes not just on the rich, but also on the middle class. If elected president, Clinton had promised to increase spending by $220 billion. The people were drawn into this dramatic narrative to confront Clinton who had a record of being a tax and spend liberal because he had frequently tried to deny that he was one.

The Bush commercials characterized Clinton as having been dishonest in the past, so the country could not trust him in the future. One ad featured Time Magazine with a picture of Clinton on the cover and the headline, "Why voters don't trust Clinton." This ad said, "he was never drafted, then he admitted he was drafted. Then he forgot he was drafted. He said he was never deferred from the draft. Then he said he was. He said he never received special treatment, but he did receive special treatment. The question then was avoiding the draft. Now for Bill Clinton, it's a question of avoiding the truth." (Bush, Television Commercial) This ad characterized Clinton as frequently taking both sides of issues, never making his position clear. It asked people to consider the question, what did Clinton have to hide because he was avoiding the truth? This commercial included the commonly used dramatic narratives of trust, credibility, and honesty, which Bush often used to demonstrate that Clinton was unfit for office to undermine his legitimacy.

Another Bush commercial employed a similar argument as proof of Clinton's unfitness for office. In this instance, specific examples of tax raises under Clinton's economic plan were shown. Using Clinton's own words, the commercial said that he would only tax the rich to pay for his campaign promises, however, "100 Economists say his plan means higher taxes and bigger deficits." (Bush, Television Commercial) These issues were made more personal by showing various people and estimating how much their taxes would increase under the Clinton plan. This was done to discredit Clinton's plan and cast him as deceptive, as well as a liberal tax and spend Democrat. The people could not trust Clinton economics because it was wrong for them and wrong for America. Thus, a dramatic narrative was created of a dishonest Clinton whose programs would make things worse for ordinary people.

After the Bush commercial was released, Clinton was reported in the media to be steamed. (CNN, October 2, 1992) Clinton responded by airing a commercial of his own the next day. (New York Times, Washington Post, October 3, 1992) Clinton's commercial showed the actual Bush commercial and pointed out which of its assertions were false. A similar incident had occurred on September 10th when Bush released his campaign agenda for a second term to the Detroit Economic Club. When Bush's speech aired on C-SPAN, a pre-taped video with Clinton's response was aired immediately afterwards.

It is helpful for a candidate to have a rapid response team to reply to their opponent's charges, and this type of response was typical of the Clinton campaign. However, considering the time needed to produce and air such a response, it seems reasonable to question how the material was obtained and produced. Bush charges against Clinton were often covered in a news report followed by coverage of Clinton's response. However, the reverse rarely happened. Slow responses to Clinton attacks by Bush gave the appearance of weakness and an admission of guilt. By responding to Bush's charges so quickly, Clinton created an impression of being unfairly attacked and competent enough to deal with these situations. Not only was this an attack on Clinton, it was also an attack on the American people, considering that Clinton only sought to help the people. Any distraction or attack on Clinton prevented the people's problems from being solved.

Clinton, A New Kind Of Democrat.

In Clinton's television commercials, he was characterized as a new type of politician, "a new generation of Democrat, Bill Clinton and Al Gore, and they don't think the way the old Democratic Party did." The commercial separated Clinton from the old dramatic narrative of liberal Democrats by saying that he had "rejected the old tax and spend politics." This commercial gave examples, without being too specific, of how they differed from Democrats in the past such as calling for an end to welfare as a way of life. This dramatic narrative sought to characterize a departure from what was typically perceived as old Democratic programs. (Clinton, Television Commercial)

This approach was designed to neutralize Bush's accusation that characterized Clinton as a tax and spend liberal. Clinton demonstrated his credibility in solving problems by having "balanced twelve budgets and they've proposed a new plan investing in people, detailing 140 billion dollars in spending cuts they'd make right now." (Clinton, Television Commercial) This commercial reaffirmed two familiar Clinton dramatic narratives, putting people first and change. Another Clinton commercial designed to characterize himself as an experienced head of state showed him sitting behind a desk in the governor's office with the American and state flags behind him. The time of the scene appeared to be late at night, as the lights were on and he had his jacket off and sleeves rolled up to show him being thoughtfully engaged in the people's business.

This commercial sought to establish the credibility of his program by marshaling an array of endorsements including six Nobel Prize winners, more than four hundred of America's most respected business leaders, a panel of independent experts gathered by Time Magazine, and even the author of Ross Perot's plan joined Clinton in pronouncing his program as the nation's best hope for reviving the economy to get the country moving again. The purpose of this commercial was to counter Bush's criticisms of Clinton's program as being detrimental for the people and the nation. Since so many successful business people and experts backed Clinton, their credibility should transfer to him legitimizing his candidacy.

Another commercial showed Clinton campaigning combined with images of people along the bus tour route cheering and waving flags. This scene depicted a candidate of the people who was in touch with the average person and who understood their needs and problems. Clinton offered, "no easy or simple solutions, but a real plan to jump start our economy, to put people first with education, job training, health care we can afford. Together we can get this country moving again. It won't be easy, but let's get to work." "That's what it's all about. It's time to unite this country for a change." Clinton's campaign slogan was not only an allusion to two familiar dramatic narratives, but it was also an artistic play on words, "Clinton Gore, for people, for a change." (Clinton, Television Commercial)

These scenes of Clinton and Gore mingling with the people during their bus tour served to characterize them as one of the people. The candidates were shown with their sleeves rolled up, ready to go to work. Clinton was shown speaking to a crowd at an outdoor rally, then talking to individual people, holding a young girl, and being surrounded by a crowd of exuberant people waving flags and Clinton signs. These scenes visually reinforced the dramatic narrative of putting people first. These familiar narratives of change and putting people first were supported with visual images that captured their spirit. These commercials put Clinton in the center of his dramatic narratives as a catalyst for change. The kind of change that would improve the lives of people who were currently forgotten by their government and who would come first in a Clinton administration. These were people with whom Clinton had personal contact and that he understood.

Response To Perot Returning To The Race

Following his reentry to the campaign, Perot was not initially very successful in obtaining widespread sharing of his version of social reality. After Perot announced that he would again be a candidate for president, 80% of the electorate did not trust him and 72% said that he should not reenter. His favorability rating was only 20% with an all time high unfavorability rating of 66%. In voter preference, Clinton led with 52%, followed by Bush at 35%, and with 7% Perot found himself now in third place. (Gallup Poll, October 3, 1992)

Bush was also having a problem getting the public to share his dramatic narratives. Bush's commercials were believed by only 38% of the people compared to 51% who believed Clinton. (Los Angeles Times, October 9, 1992) These trends may have led the media to begin sharing the dramatic narrative that the Bush ads were backfiring. (Washington Post, October 10, 1992) Around the same time, a story surfaced in the media that a hundred banks were facing impending failure and that this crisis was being covered up by Bush and Clinton until after the election. (Los Angeles Times, October 11, 1992) This story is significant in that Perot would characterize this as a defining issue during the debates.

Perot's Television Campaign.

If ever a presidential candidate's public image could be said to be a creature of the media it was that of Ross Perot. He entered the presidential race as an independent candidate on a national cable talk show having had no history of holding political office. In the primary, he rose to the top of the polls before dropping out. His challenge would be to gain back the lost support for his candidacy. After returning to the race, Perot ran the bulk of his campaign on television, not opting for the more traditional political rally and stump speech circuit. He was innovative and unique in how he used television by running several thirty minute programs he financed himself. In these programs he talked to the American people about issues that he felt were important to the country.

In order to establish his legitimacy as a serious candidate, Perot had to present his view of the problems facing the country and his plan to fix those problems. He had to demonstrate the ability to accomplish the task and that he still had a mandate of popular support for himself and his plan. Now that he had been placed on the ballot in all fifty states, he would claim that he was chosen as a candidate of the people.

Perot's first television program aired shortly after his reentry in October and drew an audience of 20 million viewers. He characterized his program as the first town hall to keep the "American people informed so that they can make intelligent decisions as owners of this country." The program presented Perot's solution to the economic problems the country faced. Using the Washington mess dramatic narrative, he characterized those in power in Washington as villains who had perpetrated troubles upon the people. Perot said the American people are good, yet "we have a situation where the president blames the Congress, Congress blames the president, Democrats and Republicans blame one another, nobody steps up to the plate and accepts responsibility for anything." (Perot, Washington Mess)

As the basis of his call for change, Perot returned to his earlier characterization of the dismal scene of the present state of the country. America had become "the most violent, crime ridden society," with the "least effective school system in the industrialized world." (Perot, Washington Mess) No longer able to stand idly by, Perot offered to examine what had happened. In order to illustrate his point, He said that we needed to raise the hood to diagnose the problem and having found that a tune up would not work, we would have to do a major overhaul.

Stressing the dangers of a large national debt, Perot used a play on words to recall a previously shared dramatic narrative from the 1980 primary campaign when Bush called Reagan's economic program 'voodoo economics.' Perot used a play on words to describe how we had gotten ourselves in 'deep voodoo' through reckless spending. Perot compared the folks in Washington to Willie Sutton the famous bank robber who robbed banks because 'that's were the money was.' To illustrate how they had become out of touch with the people, he compared them to Marie Antoinette who was also out of touch and unsympathetic with her subjects. Campaign aides to the other candidates had been lobbyists for foreign countries, who sold out the American people by sending jobs overseas. Instead of coming to serve they cashed in, which Perot characterized as akin to economic treason.

For Perot, America was not a shining beacon to the world. We needed to leave the American Dream of a better life to future generations. Perot felt that we were losing our standard of living, because more children now lived in poverty. To solve the challenges we were facing, we had to just go and do it. Every day was important and we had to start now to get the job done. Perot asked the people to think of their children, who were their hopes and dreams because they needed to do it for them and for the future.

In another television program, Perot focused on his plan to solve the nation's problems by presenting his ideas in a business presentation format, complete with charts and graphs. Once again he reminded the audience of voodoo economics by using his 'voodoo stick' to point to his charts. Past economic programs had not worked because trickle down economics had not trickled. The nation had to learn to balance its budget like ordinary people had to balance theirs. Perot would increase taxes, like taxes on gas and on the wealthy in order to be more in line with other industrialized countries. In presenting his view of the tax system, Perot used a metaphor about an old inner tube with a thousand patches that should be discarded, so that we could start over with a new and fair system. Acknowledging that this proposal would be painful, he said if others could come up with something better then he would drop his plan and go with that. Some had criticized his plan claiming that it would cause a recession, but once his plan was in operation if things did not seem to go well, he would slow the plan down.

Perot characterized these issues as a part of his plan for a new America as a country restored. It could be purposeful and thriving, a place where people work hard, not look for work. Where people save, not spend what they earn. Where the country leads, instead of falling behind. He envisioned a nation strengthened by diversity, focused on solutions, and not quitting until the job was done, so we could pass on the American Dream to future generations.

In order to share meaning with the people, Perot used the dramatic narrative of restoration to characterize his plan as the solution to the nation's problems. He identified traditional values as part of what made our nation great and our falling away from them was the source of our recent problems. We needed a candidate who could "restore the meaning of made in the USA." (Perot, Red Flag) Another ad featured a letter he received from a veteran who was awarded the Purple Heart he lent to Perot for the campaign, so he would remember ordinary people. The letter comprised the text of the ad. It encouraged him to "restore honesty, integrity, and responsibility to our government." (Perot, Purple Heart)

Perot frequently used the dramatic narrative of restoration by emphasizing the values he sought to preserve. He concentrated on his past business success and recognition by presenting a dramatic narrative of an ailing nation returning to prosperity under his leadership. One of his television ads told the viewers, "In this election, we have the opportunity to choose a candidate who is not a career politician, but a proven business leader with the ability to take on the tasks at hand, to balance the budget, to expand the tax base, to give our children back their American dream." (Perot, Our Children) Another television ad characterized his campaign as a new war. With the Cold War over, we no longer had to fight the "red flag of communism, but the red ink of our national debt, the red tape of our government bureaucracy" as our enemy. (Perot, Red Flag)

In his television program, Perot characterized a crisis that demanded immediate solutions to save the nation and its people. We were engaged in an economic war in which "the threat of unemployment is greater than the threat of war" and "the national debt demands as much attention as the national security." (Perot, Time) The solution was Perot, who had proven business experience. He was not a 'business as usual' politician, but someone who could get the job done.

As a late arrival to the general election campaign, Perot was able to be selective about his campaign strategy. He had the advantage of seeing what had worked for the other candidates, so he could carefully assimilate the positive elements of other campaigns while avoiding the negative ones. He utilized dramatic narratives that had rated high with voters like the economy, job creation, education, and the mess in Washington, while avoiding low rated issues like foreign policy and family values. He did not attack Bush and Clinton directly, instead he criticized Washington and the falling away from traditional values, which meant Bush without having to specifically mention him. By using this approach he could utilize negative campaigning without having to tarnish himself by resorting to the mudslinging tactics he condemned.

In order to share meaning with the voters and establish his legitimacy, Perot developed the dramatic narratives of restoration, the American Dream, and being a plain speaker. However, some of his dramatic narratives were flawed by an inherent inconstancy that produced a conflicting social reality. For instance, he referred to the greatness of the United States and then urged that we once again must renew our country to make it stronger. He claimed that we lived in the greatest country in the history of man, yet he told stories of crime and corruption. He characterized the people in government and his opponents as villains who act in ways that are evil and he also stated in the same address that there were no villains.

On The Eve Of The Debates.

Going into the presidential debates, the three candidates again faced very different challenges with different campaign strategies. The media dramatic narratives characterized the debates as the last chance, the last gasp of hope for Bush to save his campaign. (CNN, October 5, 1992) However, when Bush increased his attacks on Clinton and his character, the media and the general public seemed to be actively rejecting his dramatic narratives rather than sharing them. (CNN, October 10, 1992)

The media began to share the dramatic narrative that Bush's negative campaigning was making him appear less presidential and more desperate. (CNN, October 9, 1992) Negative ads to discredit Clinton were characterized as increasingly hurting Bush more than Clinton. (CBS Evening News, October 5, 1992) Clinton had taken over Perot's most widely shared dramatic narratives among the voters increasing his support. While Bush had tried to find a dramatic narrative that shared meaning with the voters, he had yet to find one that would bring back the support he had lost.

With five weeks to Election Day, Clinton was characterized in the media as having an air of confidence. (Washington Post, New York Times, September 27, 1992) Many in the media felt that Bush had waited too long to respond to Clinton's attacks, while others felt that Clinton was still vulnerable, so October would decide the election.

It didn't.

Chapter 8
The Presidential Debates

During the general election Clinton, Bush, and Perot participated in a series of three debates. These debates provided the public an opportunity to see all three candidates together, allowing for convenient comparison of the characterization of the issues by them. In the debates, the candidates often recalled previously shared dramatic narratives by fitting them to the questions they were asked. Where this is the case, they are noted and recapped rather than repeated in detail.

The First Presidential Debate

The first debate was held at Washington University in St. Louis, Missouri on October 11, 1992. A panel of three journalists asked questions of all three candidates with the opportunity for rebuttal. There were no restrictions on the topics or subject matter of the questions.

Clinton In The First Debate.

In the first debate between the three presidential candidates, Clinton concentrated on his familiar dramatic narrative of change. He characterized his policies as a change from trickle down and from tax and spend. When elected, he would immediately present a jobs program and a plan to control health care costs. These plans would control the deficit as he had done in Arkansas. On the issue of taxes, Clinton would raise taxes on those making over $200,000 and cut taxes on middle class incomes below $52,000. This action would restore fairness to those people who saw their taxes go up during the Reagan Bush years.

In order to change government, Clinton said that Congress wanted a president who would not manipulate them by vetoing important legislation. It was the people who must have the courage to change a government that for twelve years had its chance and failed. Experience was important to Clinton, but the same old experience was not relevant in a new and changing world.

In further characterizing the need for change, Clinton described the thousands who had touched him including working people, business leaders, and even Republicans. These people had told him they wanted change. For Clinton, the debate was about the choice between "hope and fear, change or more of the same, the courage to move into a new tomorrow or to listen to the crowd who says things could be worse." (Clinton, First Presidential Debate)

To alter the Bush dramatic narrative of foreign policy to his own advantage, Clinton attempted to undermine Bush foreign policy successes by recasting real events by characterizing them using a new dramatic narrative. He characterized Bush as a president who had lost opportunities. Bush rewarded China's leaders for human rights abuses and did nothing about China's $15 billion trade surplus with the United States. Clinton would stand on the side of those kids that were carrying the Statue of Liberty. In other foreign policy matters, Clinton would not commit forces to a quagmire in Bosnia or to the tribal wars of Somalia.

In response to Bush's attacks on Clinton's credibility in protesting the Vietnam War, Clinton told Bush that it was wrong to question his patriotism. Clinton told him that his own father, Prescott Bush was right when he stood up to Joe McCarthy who had questioned the patriotism of others. Clinton honored those who had served their country. Even though he opposed the war, he loved his country and wanted to bring it together, not divide it.

When asked to define family, Clinton responded that for him it consisted of at least one parent and one child. He characterized a good family as a place of love and discipline where one learns good values. His widowed mother instilled family values in him. He had seen these same values in the people of Arkansas who, "are out there killing themselves working harder for less in... the worst economic times in 50 years." (Clinton, First Presidential Debate)

Clinton also described how he grew up in the segregated south and learned from his grandfather that all people were equal in the eyes of God. He had seen how hatred divided people, which inspired him to do all that he could to overcome divisions. Thus, he devoted his campaign to finding opportunity for all because, "We don't have a person to waste in this country." (Clinton, First Presidential Debate)

Bush In The First Debate.

In the first debate, Bush repeated many familiar dramatic narratives from his campaign by restating elements of his agenda for American renewal. Bush would meet with the new Congress to end gridlock before the special interests got to them. There were good plans out there like his plan, America 2000 for retraining and education. Stressing fairness, Bush disagreed with the notion that any tax was good because it was time that taxes were reduced.

In reply to Clinton's attacks, Bush characterized the economy as not "coming apart at the seams," but rather it was caught in a "global slowdown." It was time for a recovery because interest rates and inflation were, "the cruelest tax of all." (Bush, First Presidential Debate) He characterized the economy during the last Democratic administration as the worst in modern history, with the misery index at its highest.

In foreign policy, Bush recalled his interpretation of America keeping the peace and having won the Cold War, so now we could reduce troops in Europe because we were strong. He warned against the tendency of his opponents to pull back into isolationism and to blame foreigners for our problems. Bush had seen the burdens of war, so he did not want to cut the nation's insurance policy as there were still threats abroad.

Bush claimed that we did not need the best military in the world because we already had it. He characterized the nation and the economy as the envy of the world and recalled his progress in negotiating with Boris Yeltsen of Russia to eliminate nuclear weapons. America was more respected around the world because the concept of peace through strength had worked. Bush expressed his concern for those who might be thrown out of work due to defense cuts. To counter Clinton's criticism, Bush said that America was the first to stand up to China and to make real progress in pushing for humanitarian reforms there. Clinton was for isolationism because he did not understand the detrimental effect it would have on the nation.

In addressing the use of military force to stop regional conflicts, Bush recalled the lessons of Vietnam. Any military mission must be defined and be deployed through forging international coalitions such as the highly successful mission against Iraq. Bush was reluctant about trying to solve rivalries with force, however, he was supportive of giving humanitarian aid, which he had been doing.

Bush characterized the decline in family values as causing a decline in cities. He felt that discipline and respect for law needed to be taught. The family had to be strengthened and single mothers helped by cracking down on deadbeat dads. Bush pointed out that Arkansas was one of only two states that had no civil rights legislation in contrast with Bush's record as an outspoken advocate for civil rights. It was the Democrats who yelled before every election that the Republicans were going to cut Social Security and Medicare, but these were only scare tactics. The facts were that Bush had stood up to protect people's benefits.

Bush attacked Clinton's judgment claiming that during the Vietnam War it was wrong to demonstrate against his own country in a foreign land. He questioned how Clinton could send men and women into combat when he himself did not serve. Bush acknowledged that he had received a lot of criticism over his no new taxes pledge and characterized it as a mistake. He was the type of person who when he made a mistake, had the character to admit it.

Bush characterized Clinton's plan as going back to the Mondale Dukakis tax and spend ways because if the numbers were added up, "you end up socking it to the working man." Bush was against increasing taxes and would get the deficit down by controlling the growth of government spending. Bush said, there was a fear of Clinton in the markets and if he were elected they would drop. Bush would protect the taxpayer by vetoing spending bills because, as he often explained, "I don't think we're taxed too little, I think the government's spending too much." (Bush, First Presidential Debate)

In order to characterize himself as a candidate with experience and know-how, Bush told a series of personal experience stories. To make his case, he told of his experience in making the world safer from nuclear war, so our children could sleep better with no nuclear threat. Bush told the audience what it was like to be president, not knowing what issues would arise or what tough calls had to be made. A president could not take different positions on the same issue. A president needed foreign policy experience to handle a crisis and changing events around the world. Bush concluded by saying that he hoped that he had earned the nation's trust because the election was about trust and character.

Perot In The First Debate.

In the first debate, Perot used the dramatic narrative of being a man of the people. He told of the millions of people who "on their own" had put him on the ballot without special interest money. As he had from the beginning of his campaign, Perot claimed a populist mandate in the tradition of what, "the framers of the Constitution intended our government to be." He belonged to the people and was their servant. So, if Perot was elected, he would claim a "unique mandate."

As president, he would inform people about the issues through an "electronic town hall" in order to be sure to do what's right for the people. Envisioning the future, Perot said that on the day after Election Day he would ask the president and Congress for help to "pull together" by gathering all the good plans, which were "lying all over Washington" that never had been implemented and do something with them.

Perot claimed that he had no experience in creating trillion dollar debts, gridlock, bad schools, crime, and violence ridden cities. It was time for action because, "the party's over and it's time for the clean up crew" and Perot had the kind of experience that counted. (Perot, First Presidential Debate) Perot retold the details of his familiar dramatic narrative of the Washington mess. Using the metaphor of building a house, Perot said Washington's way of doing business was like having blueprints for a house that was never built even though you have nowhere to sleep.

Perot characterized lobbyists as villains with "thousand dollar suits and alligator shoes running up and down the halls of Congress that make policy now." (Perot, First Presidential Debate) In Washington, the president and Congress sat around blaming each other and all the while the cash register that should contain our money was empty. As part of the mess in Washington, Perot characterized the current economic policy as flawed with long term debt being financed with short term bonds that are too sensitive to market fluctuations. This policy made the economy a ticking bomb because it was totally mismanaged.

According to Perot, it was in the national interest to have manufacturing here at home because you could not convert from potato chips to airplanes in an emergency, like the industries that were converted during World War II. You can do more for the economy by making computer chips than potato chips. He also felt that we have to help Russia as an investment in the future, since this policy was "pennies on the dollar" compared to returning to the Cold War. (Perot, First Presidential Debate)

When the debate between Clinton and Bush turned to the dramatic narrative of trust focusing on Clinton's draft record and Bush's tax pledge, Perot defended Clinton and attacked Bush by pointing out that there was a big difference between making a mistake when you are young and making a mistake when you are a senior government official.

Perot said, in future conflicts we must commit the nation before committing any troops and we should not commit our sons and daughters to European problems. It was the working people who made up the all volunteer army, not the beautiful people unlike World War II when Franklin Roosevelt's sons were flying combat missions. The other countries should defend themselves, so that the money we spend defending those who have been beating us economically could be used to help our own economy.

To pay down the deficit, Perot proposed raising the gas tax. His rationale was that the price of gas was considerably higher in other industrialized countries with strong economies. The high taxes go to benefit people through the jobs created. These were things that we had to do as a result of the years of fiscal mismanagement, "it is now time to pay the fiddler" or "we will spend our children's money... taking the American Dream from them." He challenged his opponents if they did not agree with his ideas to find a better way because if they did find one he was "all ears." (Perot, First Presidential Debate)

In his version of the American Dream, Perot recast the dramatic narrative of family values. If Perot could do one thing to make the nation great he would strengthen the family in every home where every child would be loved and nurtured. Parents would be encouraged to "mold these little precious pieces of clay.. (to) live rich, full lives." He said that the country was a melting pot that had broken into pieces because everybody appeals to our differences to try to split the country into fragments. He said that we should love one another because we were in this together. He compared the nation to divided teams that fail and to united teams that win, telling the audience "if we pull together there is nothing we cannot do." (Perot, First Presidential Debate)

Using the dramatic narrative of restoration, Perot characterized the people in Washington as basically good, but they had lost their way causing our problems because the nation's founding principles had been violated by a government that had lost touch with its people. The time had come to stop talking and he would change things from business as usual because he had been fortunate enough to have lived the American Dream and wanted to restore it for them.

Little Public Response To First Debate.

After the first debate there was little change in voter preferences. Clinton led with 47% of voters, Bush had 34%, and Perot was last with 13%. The Bush characterization of Clinton's antiwar activities was not being shared as 73% of those surveyed were unaffected by them. The media characterized Bush's performance as failing to win over voters, leaving his aides disappointed. As the media reported, even his strength in foreign affairs emerged as weak when his dealing with Iraq came under attack. (Gallup Poll, October 13, 18, 1992)

The media saw Bush as resuming his campaign hoping to convince voters to take another look at his record. In the meantime, a mood of grim resignation had set in among leading Republicans and White House aides. (Los Angeles Times, October 13, 15, 1992) Conversely, the media characterized the Clinton campaign as increasing its standing and being generally pleased with their candidate's performance. (CBS Evening News, October 12, 1992)

With nothing to lose and everything to gain, Perot made the best showing leaving 47% of the viewers more impressed by him and 62% had an improved image of him, with only 5% having a more negative image. Perot was perceived as sincere because 43% felt that he had stood up for what he believed in, up from 25% before the debate. Public perception of his understanding of the issues increased from 17% to 26% and the perception of him being honest and trustworthy increased from 14% to 33%. After the debate, 32% of the viewers had more confidence in Clinton's ability to be president and 29% had a more favorable opinion of him. (Gallup Poll, October 13, 1992)

Perot was characterized in the press as being feisty, with a fondness for snappy one liners. (CNN, October 10, 1992) He played best by having strengths in many areas, while Bush appealing for a second look from disaffected voters continued to lose ground. (CBS Evening News, October 12, 1992) Public opinion of Bush and Clinton remained relatively unchanged with over half the viewers, which would suggest that most people had already shared one of the candidate's versions of social reality and were not persuaded by the other candidates.

The media began sharing a dramatic narrative about disarray in the Bush campaign and depicted an atmosphere of tension and division within the Republican Party in their effort to stay in the White House. Searching for a public gesture to demonstrate that a second term would be different, Bush threw out two old friends. (New York Times, October 13, 1992) In an attempt to demonstrate how seriously Bush was taking the state of the economy, Baker asked for top officials to submit letters of resignation dated Election Day to demonstrate to the voters that a second term would be different. (Washington Post, October 14, 18, 1992) Bush would then install a new economic team in a second term. (Washington Post, October 14, 18, 1992)

The media reported that Bush was reacting badly to his deteriorating standing in the polls. For the people who shared the media dramatic narratives, Bush would give the appearance of being desperate resulting in the undermining of his own characterizations of experience. Bush seemed to continue to expect the electorate to accept the dramatic narrative that experience mattered and that he was the most experienced of the three candidates, while simultaneously firing his own 'experienced' advisors. Removing top officials showed a lack of confidence that would share meaning with the public to undermine Bush.

This action could only further legitimize the Clinton and Perot case for change. If the administration did not effect change in four years, what evidence could they present that would indicate they could effect change during the next four? While publicly lambasting the polls, the Bush campaign seemed to be privately charting their campaign course based on them. In several dramatic narratives about the economy and even by his own admission, Bush had not only accepted Clinton's characterizations of him and the economy, he in effect admitted that Clinton was correct on these issues legitimizing Clinton's claim to office.

The Second Presidential Debate.

The second debate, which took place on October 15, 1992 in Richmond, Virginia, made history by having the unique format that employed a polling firm to select 209 audience members to ask the candidates questions.

Clinton In The Second Debate.

In the second debate, Clinton further developed his dramatic narrative of change by stressing how he would fix the economy and why it was important to do so. This time, he was more focused on himself in his answers stressing his accomplishments as governor in order to establish credibility for his programs and his legitimacy for office. In order to do this, Clinton employed several dramatic narratives about his personal experience. He told of balancing twelve budgets and cutting spending in Arkansas. He credited his success in fiscal responsibility to his ability to work with people, both Democrats and Republicans, resulting in his state ranking first in growth.

The election was about change and investing in the economy, which was why people of both parties had endorsed his program along with generals, admirals, and hundreds of business leaders. Reaffirming the dramatic narratives of putting people first and the American Dream, Clinton asked his audience for help to make America as great as it could be. He reminded them that he had entered the race so the next generation would not be worse off than their parents.

For Clinton, change included health care and he focused his attention on this issue in the second debate. He said that his interest stemmed from the fact that for him it was what the election was all about. Clinton said that this issue was the one that more people had talked to him about than any other. Some of these people had lost their jobs and businesses because of their sick children. So, on their behalf he would take on the villains of the insurance and drug companies to hold down prices while maintaining quality through managed competition.

There were some who claimed that this could not be done, but it had been done in Hawaii, where everyone was insured. To Clinton this was a "big human problem... a devastating economic problem... and I'm going to send a plan to do this within the first hundred days of my presidency." When attacked on the cost of his plan, Clinton defended it by citing the case of the savings and loan industry, which the taxpayers had to bail out because it of what he called, "The dumb way the government deregulated it." (Clinton, Second Presidential Debate)

The nation had to change its economic policies. It had to keep its economic base in order to maintain military power, so that it could continue to be a force for freedom in the world. Clinton again told the story of Bush's trip to Japan when the Prime Minister said that he felt sorry for the United States. There would be a brighter future for education with Clinton as president. Arkansas had been recognized by Time Magazine as one of two states with the most improvement in education. Clinton proposed a national program to revolutionize education by decentralizing control, giving power to better trained principals and teachers. Clinton would make schools better through involving parents beginning at the preschool level by encouraging these schools to pursue choice and accountability.

The nation's financial future would be brighter because Clinton pledged that he would reduce the deficit. Nobel Prize winners, business leaders, Republicans, and economists had approved his plan, which would grow the economy. If he could not do this, "you'll have a shot at me in four years, and you can vote me right out if you think I've done a lousy job. And, I would welcome you to do that." (Clinton, Second Presidential Debate)

When Perot said that he would take a pledge to stay on the issues and not use spin doctors or speechwriters, so "you don't have to wonder if it's me talking" because "what you see is what you get." Clinton replied, "Wait a minute. I want to say just one thing now. Ross, in fairness, the ideas I express are mine." "So, I don't want the implication to be that somehow everything we say is just cooked up and put in our head by somebody else." "I'm just as sick as you are by having to wake up and figure out how to defend myself every day. I never thought I'd ever be involved in anything like this." (Clinton, Second Presidential Debate)

Acknowledging the recent popularity of term limits for members of Congress, Clinton felt no change was needed to the current system because instituting term limits posed problems for small states and increased the influence of nonelected staff. If people really wanted a change in representation, they could simply vote for it. However, Clinton would take away the advantage of being an incumbent through campaign reform and spending limits.

Bush In The Second Debate.

In this debate, Bush contrasted his view of America with Clinton's view because it was up to the American people to choose between Clinton and raising taxes or Bush and reducing spending. Bush wanted to invest more, educate more, export more, and strengthen families. Americans faced the task of choosing someone to lead them and the free world. With a policy of peace through strength, we were responsible for toppling communism, helping the people of Somalia, and stopping the aggression of Iraq. Bush pointed out that our exports had saved us during this global slowdown, which was why he had negotiated a free trade agreement with Mexico and Canada, and why he wanted more agreements like the GATT treaty.

In education, Bush stood for choice and individual freedom, which he compared to Clinton's approach of government control. Programs in which everything was mandated and controlled from Washington did not work. Without change, we as a nation could not compete in the world. The problem with health care was characterized by Bush as stemming from lawsuits that drive up costs and make doctors afraid to perform services. Insurance must be available to all, but government must be kept out and should not set prices.

Bush called attention to many of the domestic accomplishments in which everyone could take pride, such as the home ownership initiative and economic help for cities. However, it seemed that all anyone heard were the negative things since everyone was running against the incumbent. Bush felt it was not right for others to say that he did not feel the pain of the people hurt by the recession, responding that it was not fair to say, "if you haven't had cancer... you don't know what it's like." (Bush, Second Presidential Debate)

Because Clinton had aired the first negative ads of the campaign, Bush said he had been forced to defend himself against these attacks. In response to Clinton's remark in the last debate equating Bush's questioning his patriotism with Joseph McCarthy's behavior, Bush mentioned that his father Prescott Bush always told him to "tell the truth," which was what Bush had done in public life. The trouble with Clinton was his organizing demonstrations against his country in foreign countries. Clinton also waffled on issues like NAFTA, which he first was for and then against, and then had to look at it more.

The government needed to be closer to the people, an issue that Bush agreed with Perot, and one way to accomplish this was with term limits. In response to Perot's criticism of Bush not passing reform legislation and Perot describing himself as holding hands to get things done, Bush characterized this process as more of a fight with "some pretty strong willed guys." You could not simply go to Congress and say, "I'm going to fix it," and then the problem would be solved. (Bush, Second Presidential Debate)

Bush could not see how taxes could be raised to reduce the deficit, since people were taxed too much already. Clinton talked about balancing the budget, yet Bush wanted a balanced budget amendment as well as the line item veto like the one Clinton had used in Arkansas to balance the budget, however, Congress would not give it to him.

The dramatic narrative of trust and experience characterized the differences between Bush and Clinton. To illustrate his point, in his closing remarks Bush characterized the situation of an announcer coming on the air to say that there was an international crisis. Which candidate, he asked, would you choose that has the "perseverance, the character, the integrity, the maturity to get the job done? I hope I'm that person." (Bush, Second Presidential Debate) This approach of hoping that he met the people's approval differed from his 1988 campaign when he often said that he would be president because it was his destiny.

It was what Bush did not say that perhaps became the most remembered moment of the night. Between questions, Bush stood up and looked at his watch. This simple act, that most people do without thinking about, was interpreted as indifference, apathy, boredom, or that he was hoping it was almost over.

Perot In The Second Debate.

In this debate, Perot employed his familiar dramatic narrative of the mess in Washington where people came not to serve, but to cash in. The people had no voice in what went on there. He dared the audience to just try to go up to Congress when they were in session. He told them that we had to reassert the people's ownership in government because private citizens were considered a nuisance. Public officials should have plastic surgery on their ears, so they can listen to someone besides the lobbyists who give them money. He blamed the government for terrible schools, whose policies and programs were dictated by political patronage and where the children were forgotten. It was terrible bussing little children across town to big, cost ineffective schools instead of going to small schools where everybody is somebody.

In order to develop the industries of the future, we need the best trained workers, which begins with the mother during pregnancy. With strong families, children would be loved and hugged so that they learn to think well of themselves in order to develop into a whole person. He characterized the situation as "one more time you've bought a front row box seat and got a third rate performance. This is a government that is not serving you." People who were in business would go where the labor costs were low, which was why he said, "There will be a job sucking sound going south." (Perot, Second Presidential Debate)

Perot again characterized himself as a man of the people who would address these issues without spin doctors, writers, or foreign lobbyists. He had even made the charts that he used on television himself concluding, "What you see is what you get." As president, he would go to Washington to "build some bridges" and "get everybody holding hands" to get bills passed that both parties wanted. These bills didn't pass because the people in Washington are, "bred from childhood to fight with one another rather than get results." These things were never the fault of the Democrats or Republicans, "somewhere out there there's an extraterrestrial that's doing this to us, I guess." (Perot, Second Presidential Debate)

The country needed to stop mud wrestling and solve problems in order to pass on the American Dream to our children. The national debt had become so bad that the people asked Perot to do something about it, so he left his family and business in order to run. Being lucky in his life, he was working to ensure that everyone could have the American Dream just as he did. Since leadership came from consensus, when many people were involved in solving a problem there would be those who "if they could just touch it with a screwdriver could fix it." (Perot, Second Presidential Debate)

In foreign policy, Perot illustrated how problems in our government were affecting the instability in Russia. Foreign policy was important because our support for Russia was very cost effective compared to a return to the Cold War. However, we could not afford to be the world's policeman, other countries had to pay their way. Perot felt that a country could not be a military superpower unless it was also an economic superpower. We had to rebuild the industrial base at home in order to stay a force for good throughout the world.

Perot characterized himself as a man of action and result oriented person. The people should choose him if they wanted action, not just talk. Some said that he could not take this approach with Congress, but he said that Congress and the president had to link arms and work together. Finally, he wanted the audience to remember him not as someone who created this mess, but as an ordinary citizen who paid taxes just like them. He said that he had paid over a billion dollars in taxes and for "a guy that started out with everything he owned in the trunk of his car, that ain't bad." (Perot, Second Presidential Debate)

The Perot Campaign Between The Debates.

After the second debate, Perot ran two half hour television programs titled, The Early Years and Business Success and Leadership. In these programs, Perot was interviewed about his past and how he came to be where he was today. This was his own personal story of hard work, persistence, and a bit of luck that helped him to achieve the American Dream. The purpose was to show the public the real Ross Perot by featuring him and real life experiences that illustrated the dramatic narrative of the American Dream.

The first program presented a biography of Perot describing his family, growing up, his stint in the navy, and starting a business in Dallas. Perot told about how he learned business principles from his father, whom he called his best friend.

His father was a cotton broker who built his business by being fair and treating people right. At a young age, Perot began day trading bridles, saddles, and horses, which taught him valuable lessons. At the age of seven he got a job breaking horses. He also sold seeds and cards, and delivered papers on horseback in a poor area others had abandoned.

Perot had received an appointment to the Naval Academy where he was able to meet people from all over the country. He learned leadership and the importance of standing up for one's beliefs and honor, even if it meant taking the heat for doing so. While in the navy, he met his wife on a blind date and immediately fell in love with her, marrying her four years later. One day, an IBM executive came aboard his ship and offered him a job in Dallas. So, in 1957 he and his wife moved everything they owned in the back of their '52 Plymouth and began a new life. This was a story that he often characterized as the beginning of his personal realization of the American Dream.

In the second program, Perot told about how he built a business, worked for the release of POW's, and organized the daring rescue of hostages in Iran. The history of Perot's challenges in building his company EDS was traced from its first break with Frito Lay in 1963 until he sold it to General Motors twenty four years later. Perot credited the company's success to talented people who loved to win and who had fun doing unbelievable things. Perot told the story of his lifelong commitment to help POWs and MIAs from the Vietnam War. He had helped organize relief missions to improve their treatment, and show them they had not been forgotten. When the POWs were released, they were honored by Nancy Reagan and John Wayne in San Francisco.

In December of 1978, two of Perot's employees had been taken hostage during the Iranian revolution. So, he called an old friend who assembled a rescue team of combat veterans. For the first time, Perot had asked people to risk their lives. At great personal risk, Perot went to Tehran and met with the hostages to inform them that their rescue team was in place. After he left Iran, the rescue took place and the hostages were reunited with their families in Dallas.

In his television programs, Perot presented dramatic narratives of himself as a man who would do what was necessary to help his friends. He was generous with his money, time, and talents. The point of having money was to take care of your family and to do constructive things for others. When he was asked how he saw himself, Perot said that at one time he had felt he could be the beautiful pearl in the oyster or the oyster that made the pearl. Realizing that this was not in the cards, he decided that his lot in life was to be the grain of sand that irritated the oyster to make the pearl.

In these television programs, instead of criticizing the problems he saw in the country and in Washington, he concentrated more on characterizing himself as someone who would lead, achieve, and get things done. In order to persuade voters to support him, he highlighted his business experience and being a loyal friend, concerned citizen, good Samaritan, and a man of action. Demonstrating his knowledge of business served to prove his ability to solve the nation's problems.

In his television campaign, Perot utilized many dramatic narratives designed to share meaning with the voters to legitimize his candidacy. Perot said that he was, "the only one of the candidates that had created a single job." (Perot, The Early Years) Perot utilized specific examples about his personal experience, business experience, and community involvement. They characterized him as a dedicated patriot, a loyal friend, and concerned citizen who when presented with a crisis only asked what he could do to help.

Perot picked up some support, but remained at 13% making little inroads into Clinton's 47% lead, followed by 34% for Bush. Perot supporters were more likely than the average voter to hold an unfavorable view of Bush (67%), but were more likely to be Republican (32%) than Democrat (22%). The debates seemed to have had little impact with the voters as evidenced by the lack of change among the voters in regard to sharing meaning about the issues. This was confirmed by 67% of the viewers saying that the debates would not make much difference in changing their vote. With his favorability ratings stuck below 40% for the year, Bush was now at 33% virtually ensuring his defeat. (Gallup Poll, October 11, 18, 1992)

Perot faced a serious problem as it began to appear that he could not win. Over half of his support was considered soft as 26% would consider voting for Bush and 30% would vote for Clinton. (Gallup Poll, October 18, 1992) Perhaps this threat to his candidacy spurred Perot into developing a new dramatic narrative to help shore up his support, that a vote for politics as usual was a wasted vote.

Clinton supporters were the most committed to their candidate as 63% said there was no way they would vote for another candidate. Only 57% of Bush supporters and 22% of Perot supporters were as strongly committed to their candidate. (Gallup Poll, October 18, 1992) This suggested that the Clinton version of social reality was the strongest of the three at this time, bringing to completion the conversion that had begun in April. Those people who had originally supported Perot had switched to Clinton in July and were now reluctant to return back to Perot in the same numbers because they had now come to share the Clinton version of social reality.

During this time, the media began to share dramatic narratives that characterized Clinton as being confident and demonstrating a depth of knowledge with a passion for the issues, while the Republicans stumbled through the campaign with misguided direction beset by adversity. (New York Times, October 18, 1992) Clinton criticized Bush for not telling the truth, referring to Bush's claim that Clinton would raise taxes on the middle class to pay for domestic programs. (Chicago Tribune, October 20, 1992)

The media reported that the issue of 'character' was the only one Bush seemed to have left, even though questions of character had failed to hurt Clinton. (Chicago Tribune, October 18, 1992) The White House was blaming top economic advisors for the worst economic growth since the depression. Top Bush aides and political advisors were characterized as unwilling to make tough choices to restore the economy. (New York Times, October 19, 1992) On the eve of the third debate, the media characterized this last debate as the biggest crisis of Bush's career, so he needed to score a home run with the voters. (CNN, October 17, 18, 1992)

The Third Presidential Debate.

The third and final presidential debate took place on October 19, 1992 on the campus of Michigan State University in East Lansing, Michigan.

Clinton In The Third Debate.

In the third and last debate, Clinton attacked Bush's record and defined himself as a different kind of politician. Clinton refuted the notion that the way to turn the country around was to raise taxes by punishing the middle class. He would depart from trickle down and tax and spend policies because you couldn't tax an economy that wasn't growing. Proposing a plan of investment, he would ask the wealthy to pay their share and use the money to invest in growth. After cutting costs, he would use the savings to invest in transportation, communications, and improving the environment.

Responding to those who characterized him as a tax and spend liberal who would raise taxes, Clinton said Bush had asked for larger budgets than Congress had approved, had cut taxes for the wealthy, and had vetoed tax relief for the suffering middle class. Clinton only wanted to raise taxes on "family incomes above $200,000, from 31 to 36 percent." He pledged, "I will not raise taxes on the middle class to pay for these programs. If the money did not come in there to pay for these programs, we will cut other government spending, or we will slow down the phase in of these programs. I am not going to raise taxes on the middle class to pay for these programs." (Clinton, Third Presidential Debate)

On the issue of Clinton's credibility stemming from his inconsistent responses about the Vietnam draft, Clinton came up with a new characterization of himself for this debate. He said that he had not answered these questions as well as he could have. To explain himself, he told the story of Abraham Lincoln who he claimed was against the war and who some said should not be president, nevertheless he made a pretty good president. Woodrow Wilson and Franklin Roosevelt did not "wear their country's uniform" and they still were able to lead their country in war, which he would not want to do, but was capable of doing.

Attacking Bush more than in the past debates, Clinton accused Bush of being out of touch and ignorant of the people's plight. For some time Bush had said that there was no recession. He had in effect told suffering people that doing nothing was better than compromising with Congress. Bush did not have a program on the economy or health care for three years, until it was time to run for reelection.

When Bush attacked Clinton for wavering on the issues, Clinton used this as an example of what was wrong with Bush, "People are sick and tired of either or situations" and being polarized. Instead they want a president with common sense who would do what is best for the country. (Clinton, Third Presidential Debate) Clinton again used 'read my lips' to talk about trust, making the Bush quote into a Clinton dramatic narrative of misleading the people. According to Clinton, the mistake Bush made was making the no tax pledge just to get elected despite knowing the economic realities. Instead, he should have gone before the people and told them that circumstances had changed and this was the best deal he could get.

Bush had given us trickle down economics, a failed policy that he himself had at one time called, "voodoo economics," whereas Clinton's plan had broadly based endorsement. Clinton had called for cuts in the White House staff, where Bush produced increases faster than Congress. This example characterized the point that Bush talked about cuts, but did not make them. In his dramatic narrative of Bush's biggest success in foreign policy, Clinton characterized Desert Storm as a remarkable event. The real mistake was that Bush had supported Iraq and a dictator who killed his own people.

In his closing remarks, Clinton characterized the debates as a start in giving the election back to the people. Rising unemployment and a slowing economy called for a new approach. It was time for a change, time to do better, to invest and grow rather than tax and spend. It was time to put people first, revitalize the economy, provide basic health care, and improve education. Clinton used the dramatic narrative of change to provide a vision of opportunity for people who work hard and play by the rules to be rewarded. This would not happen overnight he told the audience, but we need the courage to change.

Bush In The Third Debate.

In the third debate, Bush concentrated on his dramatic narratives of trust and experience, comparing himself and his programs to his opponents and countering Clinton's personal attacks. If Clinton was going to pay for all his proposals, Bush warned the audience to, "watch your wallet, because his figures don't add up, and he's going to sock it right to the middle class tax payer." (Bush, Third Presidential Debate) During the Reagan Bush years 15 million jobs were created in the private sector, which is better because government cannot create jobs and was already spending too much.

Bush was worried when Clinton said that he would do for the nation what he had done for Arkansas. America did not want to be at the bottom like Arkansas because we were not a nation in decline. Just because there were tough times it did not mean that we had to return to the failed, spendthrift policies of the past. Characterizing his program as stimulating investment, strengthening the family, and not relying on trickle down economics or tax and spend. Bush told his audience they must decide who would lead the recovery.

Bush then focused on Clinton's character using two main points, his draft record and his waffling on issues. Bush disagreed with Clinton about his protesting the government overseas while our soldiers were dying, which gave Bush reason to question Clinton's character and judgment. Bush said that Clinton had tried to take both sides of important issues, like he did during the Gulf War. Clinton was against the war, but he "would have voted with the majority." As president "you can't do that, and if you make a mistake you say you made a mistake." (Bush, Third Presidential Debate)

Bush spent some time defending the attacks on his record. When explaining the 1990 tax increase, he said that he had gone along with Congress to help the economy and cap spending. Since Congress appropriates the money and tells the president how to spend it, he thought he was doing what was best for the taxpayers, not for himself. Bush admitted that his signing the tax increase bill was a mistake calling it a Democratic setup that he did not want to sign.

According to Bush, the problem in dealing with spending and the deficit was that Congress needed discipline. Since it had been under the control of one party for 38 years, it was time to clean house. There had been much discussion about reform and Bush had tried repeatedly to get reform legislation passed by Congress "without loading it up with a lot of, you know, these Christmas tree ornaments they put on the legislation." One example was with a 'GI bill for kids,' which would have given money to families to choose the school that they wanted. This bill would foster competition to make schools better, but it had been blocked by Congress. Complaining that Clinton kept attacking him for vetoing bills, Bush said this was the only way to eliminate pork barrel spending to protect taxpayers.

In response to Clinton, Bush characterized his opponent's criticism of the Gulf War as hindsight. In cooperation with our Arab allies, he had tried to bring Iraq into the family of nations. When Iraq crossed the line Bush said, "This aggression will not stand," and built a historic coalition to stop it. After the war, there was no evidence that US arms or food credits had been used for weapons, so speculation to this effect was untrue revisionism.

Bush defended his accomplishments in office by characterizing himself as the kind of president people should want, one who would stand up to Congress. Looking to the last Democratic administration, Bush compared current interest and inflation rates to those in the Carter era. Bush said that the misery index was invented just for Carter and the Democrats. Most people were better off today than they were four years ago, but "all you hear about is how bad things are."

Bush called the scrutiny of Clinton's record a free ride compared to the flack that he had taken as the incumbent. In evaluating a presidential candidate people had to begin by looking at the facts. Clinton would change his position to please all groups, which Bush felt was a dangerous practice for a president. Bush told them that as president you had to make decisions even when they were not in your own interest.

Reiterating his dramatic narrative of trust, Bush emphasized that character mattered, even though Clinton did not think it did. Who would the people want in a crisis, but someone who had earned their trust and had experience from having taken the country through tough times. Some thought that foreign affairs experience was not relevant, but if a crisis arose who would lead the nation? As one who would safeguard our people and our children, Bush concluded by saying he could not do this work alone, adding, "I need your support. I ask for your vote."

Perot In The Third Debate.

In this last debate, Perot repeated his familiar dramatic narratives of the American Dream, the Washington mess, and being a candidate of the people. However, he also brought out new imaginative dramatic narratives involving hit teams, secret papers, Republican plots, and calls in the middle of the night. As for his withdrawal from the race, Perot claimed that he never quit the people and when they asked him to come back, he did.

Perot characterized Washington as a place where if you talked about something long enough you would think it had been done. The problem was that neither party had a plan that would work. This represented a departure from earlier in the debates when he had said that there were plenty of good plans around. When characterizing the mess in Washington dramatic narrative, Perot put a different spin on the tax increase than Bush had done. Perot charged that the tax increase was a trick on the American people because they had not been informed about it.

Perot declared that now was the time for somebody to begin to take responsibility in government. Bush was not taking responsibility when he vetoed the family leave bill. Perot accused Bush of letting Iraq know we would not get involved in their border dispute staking claim on the northern part of Kuwait, so when Iraq took the territory the administration 'went nuts.' There were secret papers containing instructions about Iraq given to Ambassador Gillespie that were being withheld from the public and from Congress. Since we did not accomplish our objectives after risking lives and spending a lot of money, the Gulf War had been a failure.

Perot characterized Bush and the Republicans as villains who had investigated his family, his children, and all their friends since childhood. Perot called these activities dirty tricks and a sick operation. Bush and the Republicans were making things up to avoid facing the issues. However, the most important issue for Perot was dealing with the debt and the deficit. Since the government did not work, it had to be reformed or nothing would get done.

The government was supposed to come from the people, instead it came at the people. Consequently, we need to take government away from special interests and give it back to the people. When the subject of Perot's association with General Motors was brought up, he said that the company was unwilling to recognize his warnings about problems and did not make changes when times were good, so they paid a terrible price hurting thousands of good and decent people, even entire cities.

Perot had responded to calls for help, never quitting, whenever individuals or the government had called upon him "again and again in the middle of the night" to help Americans in distress. He had continued to work on the POW project even when the Vietnamese government had, "sent people into Canada to... have me and my family killed." When he was involved with the war on drugs, he had upset big time drug dealers who sent hit teams after him. When his employees were imprisoned in Iran, he sent a team there to rescue them.

Under either party's plan, the deficit would continue to grow. To characterize the problem of government spending he used the analogy of a patient in a hospital with arterial bleeding. The first step should be to stop the bleeding. While other parties were using other people's money, Perot had put his own wallet on the table to save the American Dream for the American people and their children.

In the only direct attack on Clinton, Perot characterized Arkansas as a beautiful rural state with a population smaller than Chicago. The nation was making a mistake to cast their future on the basis of such small scale accomplishments. For Perot, Clinton using his record in Arkansas as proof that he could be president was like having run a corner store and then claiming he could run Wal-Mart. Perot again characterized the impending failure of hundreds of banks that had been kept secret from the people by Bush and Clinton, not to be made public until after the election.

Perot described foreign lobbyists who had sold out our country and were now on the staff of both campaigns telling Bush and Clinton what to do. When the election was over, they would go back to representing foreign countries. Perot did not believe that was in the American people's best interest. After his negative characterization of foreign lobbyists, Perot again shifted ground saying that, "I don't think there are any villains inside government." Instead, these were just people who did not understand business, "maybe you need somebody up there who understands when you're getting your pocket picked." He then offered to take time off from the campaign and "go to Washington, (and) hold hands." He had earlier offered his services to help resolve the issue of the enterprise zones, but nobody had called him to take up his offer.

To conclude the debate, Perot again characterized himself as being a candidate of the people, a person who had to stand up for himself. He was the chosen leader of millions of "fine, decent people who did the unthinkable" to help them take their country back. People must stop letting the media tell them who to vote for and stop letting the press say that a vote for Perot was throwing a vote away. The people would no longer tolerate gridlock, meandering, wandering, and nonperformance telling them, "Together we can get anything done." Perot looked up at the students in the audience and told them he was doing this to give them the American Dream and for the American people because he loved them. (Perot, Third Presidential Debate)

Public Reaction To The Debates.

The only candidate to benefit from the three presidential debates was Perot. Among respondents who were asked which candidate did best in the first debate, Perot did the best with 47% of the viewers, Clinton followed with 30%, and 16% for Bush. In the second debate, Clinton came in first at 58%, followed by Bush at 16%, with 15% for Perot. In the third debate, Perot came in first at 37%, and Bush and Clinton tied with 28%. Viewers' opinion of Perot's ability to deal with the deficit increased from 35% before the debate to 51% afterwards. Perot was rated highest of the three at 46% for standing up for what he believed in. (Gallup Poll, October 21, 1992)

In characterizing Clinton's character, Bush gained some support as he was seen as the most honest and trustworthy candidate with 36% to Clinton's 23% and 52% of the viewers agreed that Clinton had shown a pattern of trying to take both sides of important issues. However, when asked who had a good understanding of the issues more viewers (41%) chose Clinton. Perhaps people felt that being on both sides of the issues somehow gave him a better understanding of them.

After the debate, Bush was characterized in the media as having experienced his last chance to defeat Clinton. (Washington Post, October 20, 1992) The assertion by the media of the debates being a forum to sway public opinion stands in opposition to the findings of their own polls. The debates did not change voter support as 86% of the viewers said that the debates would not change their vote. Bush showed no change in support at 31%, Clinton lost 4% (43%), and Perot gained 6%, (18%) most likely due to some past supporters returning to him. (Gallup Poll, October 21, 25, 1992)

While the debates might change how viewers perceive the candidates including their favorability and unfavorability ratings, and how well they will handle specific issues, the evidence suggests that they have a negligible affect on how people vote, making them insignificant to the electoral process. Instead, they more likely serve as a form of entertainment where the fans root for their favorite candidate to win.

When Clinton ran for reelection in 1996, Perot also ran for a second time, however, the Commission on Presidential Debates changed the eligibility rules preventing Perot from participating in the debates with Clinton.

Candidates spend a lot of time and money on the final push to the finish line because there is a perception that voters wait until Election Day draws near to decide how to cast their vote. However, what transpired in this campaign suggests otherwise. It seems more likely that voter preference forms early in the campaign when the public first gets to know a candidate, similar to how people form first impressions of the people they meet. In the case of the 1992 presidential election, voter preferences formed early in the campaign, so by September the election was all but over.

The reason for having debates is so that the voters can see, hear, and evaluate the candidates to help them cast an informed vote. Yet, afterwards the media tells the viewers who won and who lost, what the candidates said based on their own opinions, and what the viewers should think about the candidates and the issues. Perhaps, the debates should be reevaluated as to their actual usefulness in informing the voters. They should not be viewed as a competition where one person wins and the others lose. Also, debates during the primaries between same party candidates encourages them to be negative and criticize each other providing fodder that can be used against the party nominee by their opponent in the general election undermining their chances of being elected.

Based on public response, the debates accomplished very little because by then enough voters had already made up their minds to determine the election's outcome. This is evidenced by the lack of change in the electorate after each debate and the degree to which voter's support of their candidate remained stable. Examining changes in public opinion over the course of the campaign suggests that the debates would be more useful much earlier in the campaign, when more voters are still considering their choice.

Perhaps another form of public discourse earlier in the campaign would better serve to inform the public, such as a form of town hall or free airtime for presentations, like the half hour programs Perot used so effectively.

Or, abolish the debates altogether.

Chapter 9
The Final Stretch

From the debates to Election Day, the final days of the campaign were dominated by the return of Ross Perot. In his widely viewed television campaign, Perot created the most new material of the three candidates by utilizing several new dramatic narratives. Meanwhile, playing it safe to maintain his lead in the polls, Clinton stayed the course by not changing his version of social reality significantly, instead he simply repeated and reiterated his already well developed dramatic narratives. During this time Bush continued to vary his approach as he seemed to be searching for an opening to improve his standing with the voters.

The Perot Television Campaign.

In two half hour television programs, Family and The Ross Perot Nobody Knows, Perot continued to characterize his personal life and experience in order to reestablish his legitimacy through a popular mandate based on his leadership ability. His popular support and qualifications were characterized through documentary format testimonials. Many of these stories were not told by Perot, but rather by the people who knew him. These programs presented personal stories of friends, family, business associates, and ordinary people.

Late in October, Perot aired a program featuring his family. Utilizing the dramatic narrative of family values, they recalled events in their lives that demonstrated their values, which were traditional American values. Stories of his experiences that he had used in the debates and past programs were retold, including meeting his wife, his Navy years, his children, and his awards for service to others. Participants in the program provided personal testimonials relating why the country needed a strong leader with a clear vision to face and fix our problems.

The program, The Ross Perot Nobody Knows, was narrated by Perot's special assistant who wanted to let people see the Perot she had know for twenty years. Since Perot had entered politics, the media and others had redefined him into a man she did not recognize. This program featured ordinary people telling personal stories about how Perot had touched their lives. A soldier on a mission in Iraq told the story of stepping on a mine and how Perot had helped him to recover. A woman told about seeking Perot's help in gaining the release of her husband, who was unjustly imprisoned in Mexico. When a Dallas police officer was severely injured, Perot sent his own plane so that he could have the treatment that saved his life and career. When a Guard unit was hit with a missile, Perot arranged for specialists to help them. A neighbor was injured in an auto accident and Perot sent specialists who saved him. Perot even flew back from a campaign rally to attend his wedding.

These programs did not significantly change Perot's version of social reality. He continued to use dramatic narratives about his character and abilities. However, the connection to legitimating his right to govern was indistinct. This may be why there was a growing sentiment in the media that he had little or no chance of winning in November. This likely motivated him to develop a new dramatic narrative to keep his candidacy alive that characterized a vote for Bush or Clinton as a vote for politics as usual, which was really the wasted vote. Perot added new villains to his dramatic narratives that included the press, the polls, and the political parties because they were telling people how they should vote. Perot utilized this dramatic narrative of his campaign under siege from his opponents and the media to help reconstitute his candidacy and galvanize his supporters.

Perot often used the same dramatic narratives in different television ads with himself as the central figure, the hero, who along with the American people could solve the problems facing the country. Perot sought to share meaning with the people when he said, "We, is you and me. You bet your hat we can govern, because we will be in there together." Perot often legitimized his candidacy by saying, "I'm doing this because I love you," but left the ultimate decision up to the people telling them, "The choice is yours." He often ended by saying, "It's all up to you." (Perot, Best Person, We Can Win, How to Vote, Family)

In another half hour program, Perot presented a campaign rally with ordinary people to present his message. This program featured people who had been listening to the campaign and after thinking things over, had switched from supporting Clinton or Bush and decided to vote for Perot. They explained the reasons for their decision using familiar Perot dramatic narratives of business experience, popular support, and a desire to take back their government. These people said that they were proud to vote for Perot and felt that he could win.

These personal stories were centered on the same dramatic narrative of the wasted vote. If people let the press or polls tell them how to vote and did not follow their heart, then their vote would be wasted. An election was not about voting for the winner, but about voting for what was right. If enough people felt that way, the election could turn around. By voting for his opponents, people would be voting for politics as usual. A vote for Clinton or Bush would support things as they were, things that were getting worse. This approach tied into the dramatic narrative of change since the other candidates represented politics as usual, only Perot represented real change.

In these personal stories, as in his other programs, Perot was characterized as a good and honest person who loved his country and had old fashioned values. A plain speaking man who did not have looks or a beautiful speaking voice, but who listened to the people and spoke from the heart. He said that he had used sixty million dollars of his own money, so he did not owe anything to anybody, but the people. He would often characterize his candidacy by saying, "Every step of the way, I'm Ross, and you're the boss." (Perot, Rally)

In his television programs, Perot urged the voters to purge what was evil to restore what was good. Perot and the people represented the means by which this restoration would take place. He sought to restore his legitimacy by connecting with the values of the people and denouncing his opponents who were not addressing the issues that were important to the people or the problems facing the nation.

Perot was having some success sharing meaning with the voters as 18% now supported him, but he still trailed Clinton who led with 43% and 31% for Bush. However, this was not a very significant increase considering that in September 14% of the people supported him even though he was not a candidate. (Gallup Poll, October 23, 1992) Even though his support fell and then slightly recovered, it seemed that the major accomplishment of Perot's comeback was not in gaining votes or even in increasing public concern about the issues he felt were important. His major accomplishment was reviving his public image as many of his commercials featured personal stories that seemed to share meaning with the public, because his favorability ratings increased significantly.

In a news conference late in October, Perot explained why he dropped out in July. He said that he had received reports the Republicans were planning to disrupt his daughter's wedding in the church and smear her in the tabloids with an altered photo. The day he dropped out, he said Bush called him to get his volunteers to support him and the Republicans. After the wedding and being placed on the ballot, he was urged to get back in the race. Perot also told about how, over twenty years ago, five men with guns had tried to break into his house in the middle of the night. When asked for credible proof of his accusations, Perot responded, "I don't have to prove anything to you people." (Perot, C-SPAN, October 26, 1992)

In response to these attacks, Bush called Perot's allegations crazy. This motivated Perot to use the country western song Crazy as the theme song for his campaign. Perot used it to develop a new dramatic narrative of crazy to refute and even make fun of charges that he was acting crazy. Perot said that the song's lyrics represented his love for his country. It also characterized how he felt his campaign was driving the people in Washington crazy, because they called him and the people supporting him crazy. On election eve, Perot danced with his wife and daughters to the song Crazy.

Clinton Refutes Bush Charges.

In the closing days of the campaign, Clinton used television commercials to refute Bush's claims regarding Clinton's record in Arkansas. These commercials were unique in that attack ads generally do not feature the candidates themselves. In this instance Clinton appeared, although he did not speak. Credibility was established utilizing outside forces by citing other sources such as CBS, CNN, and newspapers that had called Bush's ads misleading and wrong. Candidates often utilize sources outside themselves that the public perceives as credible so that their credibility will transfer to them.

Clinton was shown in the governor's office busily working at his desk to characterize his leadership and achievements. Arkansas led the nation in job growth and had the second lowest tax burden with the lowest government spending in the country. Arkansas could claim twelve balanced budgets, a reduction in infant mortality, the highest graduation rate in the region, and reduced crime. These statistics legitimized Clinton's record through independent outside sources. This commercial used the Washington Post to accuse Bush of lying about Clinton's record and the Oregonian to say that they no longer trusted Bush. Newspapers are often used to attack an opponent in a campaign because they give it the appearance of being objective and not coming from the candidate themselves.

Bush Attacks Clinton.

Several Bush commercials were presented in a news documentary format using a handheld camera that moved around catching ordinary people speaking candidly to criticize Clinton. These people said, "If you're going to be president, you have to be honest. Bill Clinton hasn't been telling anything honest to the American people" and he "just tells them what they want to hear." "I wouldn't trust him at all to be commander in chief." "I think that there's a pattern and I just don't trust Bill Clinton." "I don't think he's honorable." One person raised a familiar Bush criticism by saying, "You can't have a president who says one thing and does another." Exploiting the public's fear of change, another person said, "He scares me. He worries me." (Bush, Television Commercial)

These commercials featured ordinary people characterizing Clinton as untrustworthy in order to undermine Clinton's legitimacy. These comments reflected many of the Bush dramatic narratives of trust and his record to undermine the Clinton dramatic narrative of change as being safe. The people reiterated familiar dramatic narratives about Clinton. They said things like, he tells people what they want to hear. He will increase spending and the only way he can get it is to raise everybody's taxes. He raised them in Arkansas and he will raise them as president.

These commercials were presented to represent spontaneous comments from ordinary people caught on camera. However, many of them were very similar to what was said in Bush's speeches, at the convention, and in the debates. By coming from average people in everyday situations, they were designed to share meaning with the voters.

Addressing the issue of health care, a Bush commercial characterized what health care in the future under Clinton might be like. The commercial opened with a scene of a crowded doctor's waiting room. A doctor entered the room and handed a huge stack of files to a stern looking nurse who dumped them on top of an even bigger stack. A narrator proclaimed that, "Bill Clinton's health plan puts the government in control," in opposition to traditional values. The audience was drawn in as they were now at risk because Clinton's plan, "will ration health care and limit a doctor's ability to save your life." (Bush, Television Commercial)

In addition to people's lives, Clinton's plan risked already established programs and people's jobs. It would require $218 billion in Medicare and Medicaid cuts in the next five years and his plan could cost 700,000 Americans their jobs. The commercial asserted, "Government run plans have been tried in Europe, only there it's known as socialized medicine." (Bush, Television Commercial)

This indirectly referred to the rejection of socialist systems like those in Eastern Europe that had failed and were not in the American tradition. At this point, the issue of trust was recalled and the audience again was drawn into this dramatic narrative because, "You can't trust Bill Clinton's health plan. It's wrong for you, it's wrong for America." (Bush, Television Commercial) Clinton's plan was characterized with nightmarish connotations. The plan would tolerate poor quality providing no individual freedom, while instituting government dictates similar to socialist or even communist regimes. These practices were not part of the American tradition of individual freedom and competition.

In a Bush commercial that aired near the end of the campaign, a gloomy, barren, monochromatic land was shown featuring images of storm clouds and barren trees with a vulture sitting in one of them. The narrator described the Clinton record, "In his twelve years as governor, Bill Clinton has doubled his state's debt, doubled government spending, and signed the largest tax increase in his state's history." (Bush, Television Commercial) Even so, he had not helped the people of his state, which was the 45th worst in which to work and for children.

This commercial confronted issues concerning Clinton that were criticized by Bush who said that Arkansas had the worst environmental policy in the country. Even the FBI said that Arkansas had the biggest increase in serious crime. In characterizing the Clinton record to counter his dramatic narratives of change and The New Covenant, the Bush commercial served to connect Clinton's past to the future by warning, "Now Bill Clinton wants to do for America what he's done for Arkansas. America can't take that risk." (Bush, Television Commercial) To counter Clinton's claim that change was safe, Bush characterized that any change to Clinton was a serious risk for America to take.

The Final Week.

With the final showdown nearly a week away, Clinton and Perot were poised to be the big winners. Weeks earlier Clinton led the pack with 49% of the vote followed by Bush with 34%, and 10% for Perot. After the debates, Clinton fell to 43%, Bush stalled out at 31%, and Perot increased to 18%. During the final stretch of the campaign, Perot did the most of the three to improve his image. When he reentered the race in October, 60% viewed him unfavorably. That rating had dropped to 35%, with 53% viewing him as favorable. This meant that his television programs were working to improve his image with the people, but not his legitimacy to be president. (Gallup Poll, October 25, 1992)

If Perot's goal was to win the election, this approach may have been a mistake. On the other hand, if Perot wanted to restore the public's earlier favorable opinion of him, it worked. Perhaps his favorability ratings proved that his television program's primary objective was to feature his accomplishments and himself as being a good person. In contrast, earlier Perot dramatic narratives had focused on the problems in Washington and the need to solve them. Clinton had also improved his public image during the campaign. In April, only 45% felt that he had the honesty and integrity to serve as president, rising to a high of 62% in September, then falling to 52% in October. (Gallup Poll, October 25, 1992)

October provided a reversal of fortune for Perot. His favorability rating increased from 24% before the debates to 53% after. His unfavorability dropped from 65% to 35%. The most significant result of Perot reentering the campaign had been to salvage his low public approval. Bush and Clinton did not fair as well. Bush's favorability changed little from 42% to 43% and his unfavorability went from 54% to 50%. Clinton's favorability dropped from 56% to 53% and his unfavorability remained constant at 39%. (Gallup Poll, October 25, 1992)

Just before Election Day, Perot's support had stabilized at 15% and there was no longer the possibility of him getting enough votes to throw the election into the House of Representatives, unlike earlier in the campaign. Clinton's support was still the most solid with 70% of his supporters now strongly committed to him compared to 60% for Perot and 57% for Bush. With potential voters, Clinton led with 43% to Bush's 36%, with 15% for Perot. (Gallup Poll, November 1, 1992)

As the campaign entered its final week, Bush and Perot increased their attacks on the media's integrity and credibility. (CBS Evening News, October 29, 1992) Bush attacked the media's negative reporting on the economy. (NBC Nightly News, October 27, 1992) Bush began to employ the phrase "annoy the media, reelect Bush" to try to galvanize support. (NBC Nightly News, October 28, 1992) Bush also attacked Al Gore, calling him 'Mr. Ozone' and called Clinton 'Bozo,' characterizing environmental extremism and failed Democratic policies that he felt they represented. (Washington Post, October 28, 1992) The negative attacks by Bush on Clinton were characterized by the media as having little effect even though the people considered Bush to be more honest and moral. (Chicago Tribune, October 29, 1992) Bush was reported to be upset that his character and trust had been used against him. (Chicago Tribune, November 1, 1992)

In the third quarter, the nation's gross domestic product increased 2.7%, finally giving Bush some good news. (Chicago Tribune, October 28, 1992) These new figures released on the economy were good news for the country, but Clinton characterized them as not amounting to a recovery. (PBS, Nightly Business Report, October 28, 1992) However, "Bush was right, this was the beginning of the economic boom of the 1990s." (PBS, The American Experiment, May 5, 2008) While the Bush budget deal would eventually be credited for its impetus, Clinton would be the beneficiary of the economic recovery and use it to win a second term.

Bush had hoped to be helped by the recent signs of economic recovery. (National Public Radio, Morning Edition, October 29, 1992) So, he was concentrating on recent economic figures in order to galvanize support. (ABC, World News Tonight, October 28, 1992) Nevertheless, the voters apparently were still not convinced that Bush had a plan for economic recovery since consumer confidence and durable goods were down for the fourth month. (CNN, October 28, 1992) Anticipating a win, Clinton set out to lower expectations for a first term, calling some ideas unrealistic in the face of working for economic recovery and cautioning that some other promises may take longer than expected to be fulfilled. (Chicago Tribune, October 28, 1992)

Election Eve Appeals To The Voters.

On the eve of Election Day, two candidates went on network television to address the nation seizing their last opportunity to speak directly to the voters. Perot and Clinton each presented a half hour program that was broadcast on the national television networks in prime time. Bush, for some unstated reason, most likely knowing what the following day would bring, broke with tradition and did not appear.

The Perot Version of Social Reality On Election Eve.

In his address to the nation on election eve, Perot sought to undermine the legitimacy of Bush and Clinton rather than bolstering his own. He spent little time telling about himself or his plans for the country if he were to become president. Sitting behind a desk in a library like office, he created a feeling of getting down to business to characterize himself as being credible. To make his case, he used several color flip charts that he said he made himself.

In this program, Perot used two dramatic narratives. The first of these attacked Bush by using the previously developed Washington mess combining it with a direct attack on Bush's character and voodoo economic policies. The other dramatic narrative focused on Clinton, who he called the chicken man from Arkansas. Attacking Clinton's record as governor was a new approach for Perot as he had rarely criticized Clinton, instead choosing to focus his attention on Bush and Washington for most of the campaign. Now Perot said that neither candidate was up to solving the nation's problems or meeting the challenges of the future.

The first segment of the program characterized Clinton as the chicken man from Arkansas. This was a reference to the low paying jobs Clinton had claimed created economic growth in Arkansas. Since, Clinton had proposed to do for the country what he had done in Arkansas, Perot had looked at Arkansas to see what he had actually done. Using what he called his "voodoo stick," he pointed out that Arkansas had about the same population as Chicago. When the $4 billion budget of Arkansas was compared to the $1.43 trillion national budget, it was like a "corner grocery store" being compared to a "giant industrial complex." If it were a business, Arkansas would rank 248th on the Forbes 500, behind Toys R Us. Clinton was for fairness, but he had taxed the middle class while exempting the rich.

Perot described Clinton's approach as "talk is cheap, action is dear." Clinton presented solutions that sounded good, but Perot had checked what he actually accomplished because the people should be aware of the facts. After studying Arkansas, Perot could not understand how it could be a model for revitalizing America. Clinton's twelve years as governor were characterized by Perot as, "The chickens keep on clucking and the people keep on plucking." (Perot, Election Eve)

Perot pointed out that Clinton said he had improved the environment, education, and child welfare, but Arkansas ranked near or at the bottom of all fifty states in these areas. Instead of writing books, he could have gone to work and fixed these things, which should have been easy in a small state. Clinton had to be sued to remedy his disregard of abused and neglected children. Clinton had said this progress was significant, but when you are at the bottom any progress is significant, "If your net worth is a penny and you get another penny you have doubled your net worth." Perot asked his audience to think what would happen to our country with this kind of thinking in Washington. What chance did Clinton have of doing a better job in Washington than he did in Arkansas? It was the kind of state in which you could "literally just sort of grab it by the ears and fix it."

Perot said that Clinton's own hometown papers called him a "great campaigner" who "proved to be a mediocre administrator." Clinton had "mastered the art of equivocation" and was "almost inhuman in his smoother responses that sends a shiver up the spine." Clinton's tax plan had, "soaked the middle class." So, "Are there any steadfast principles, besides winning the next election, that Bill Clinton would never compromise to win popularity?" (Perot, Election Eve)

In the second half of his program, Perot concentrated on Bush and his record in Washington. Bush had created a trillion dollar debt leaving a huge burden for our children. Everyone living west of the Mississippi paid their taxes only for the interest on the debt and these payments did not get us anything in return. The problem was that no one in Washington understood business or the problems facing Americans. While Bush was vice president, deregulation had shipped jobs and industries overseas. The government had grown so large under Reagan Bush that there were now more jobs in all levels of government than in manufacturing.

Perot characterized Bush as practicing, "hands off, closed eyed, hands over the ears management." Since Bush claimed business experience in the oil industry, Perot thought that he should have employed more business principles. Having worked in an energy related field, Bush should at least know the importance of having a national energy policy. Bush's attitude was to leave things alone as if they would fix themselves, but instead they had gotten worse. If elected, Perot would fix it and rebuild the industrial base to restore 'made in the USA' as the world standard for excellence. (Perot, Election Eve)

The Clinton Version of Social Reality On Election Eve.

On the eve of Election Day, Clinton ran a thirty minute program on prime time network television. This presentation focused on Clinton's past and his record as governor. It utilized the dramatic narratives of hope, change, and putting people first that were developed during the campaign. It summarized Clinton's version of social reality at the end of the campaign. When compared to his version of social reality at the beginning of the campaign, it remained much the same.

The program opened with excerpts of the Democratic Convention showing Clinton receiving an enthusiastic reception from the delegates as he took the podium. The program told the story of Bill Clinton from Hope, Arkansas by describing his memories of growing up in a frame house with his grandmother in "a wonderful little small town. Where, you know, it seemed everybody knew everybody else." (Clinton, Election Eve) As the narrator spoke, black and white photos of the town in the fifties were shown along with video footage of Clinton in the living room of a house looking relaxed and casual without a tie.

Clinton talked about how proud he was of his grandparents. He told the story of how his grandmother had graduated from a tiny school nearby. His mother told about when he was born and how her husband, his father, had died before he was able to see his son. Wanting a better life, she went back to earn her nursing degree. Hillary told about how her husband had come from poor beginnings in spite of everyone thinking that he was born rich. His stepfather was an alcoholic, but still loved his family. Clinton told of how he got his stepfather to stop being violent toward his mother. He was a good person who loved his family, but his problem was that he didn't think enough of himself. Growing up in Hope had instilled important values in Clinton, which he shared with the people he wanted to represent. And Hope was part of the larger dramatic narrative of the American Dream that he personified.

In his office, Clinton spoke to the nation utilizing the dramatic narratives of change and the American Dream. He told the audience that he hoped the people now had a sense of his plans for the country, where he came from, and what his life's work had been about. He asked his audience, could they afford four more years of the same old thing or did they have the courage to change, to choose between fear and hope, drift and action, and the status quo and change? America was better than that. The post cold war era could be the most exciting, peaceful, and prosperous time in history. If the audience agreed, he needed their help not just on Election Day, but each day after. The job would not end, but rather would begin on that day. Clinton believed in America and if the people made him their president, he would "work his heart out" to make the American Dream real for all people. Finally, Clinton faced the cameras and said to the viewers, "I want to be your president" because he believed that "America is a nation of boundless hopes and endless dreams and the only limit to what we could do is what our leaders ask us to do and what we are willing to expect of ourselves." (Clinton, Election Eve)

Nation Encouraged By Election.

On election night it was all over and what could be considered the most bizarre presidential campaign in American history finally came to an end. Clinton won with 370 electoral votes, well over the 270 he needed. However, he did not win a majority of 50% of the popular vote, garnering only 43%. Bush came in second with 37.5% and 168 electoral votes. Perot had no electoral votes, but earned a respectable 18.9% of the vote.

With the campaign finally over, several Clinton dramatic narratives shared meaning with the electorate. In his first week as president elect, 53% of the people had more confidence in him, with 26% having less. In June, 84% had said that they were dissatisfied with the direction that the country was taking, dropping to 68% after the election. A majority (51%) of the people expected to be better off in four years, while only 31% felt they would be worse off. Clinton also fared well with the public in improving the economy at 59%, improving education 69%, increasing respect abroad 50%, reducing unemployment 58%, helping minorities 68%, and improving health care and the environment at 64%. (Gallup Poll, November 14, 1992)

Clinton faired less well with issues that had been dominated by Perot. Only 38% saw him as able to cut the deficit and 40% thought that he could keep spending in line. Despite Perot's concentration on the deficit, 49% of the people felt that creating jobs should be Clinton's first priority. Reducing the deficit rated low at 17%, but health care was even lower at 14%. Hillary's favorability had dropped from 56% to 50%, and her unfavorability increased from 25% to 29%, 41% felt she did not share their values, and 26% were worried that she would have too much influence in the new administration. (Gallup Poll, November 14, 1992)

Since the election, Clinton's favorability ratings improved to 60%, with 34% unfavorable. Clinton's ratings for honesty and integrity increased from 56% in July to 62% after the conventions and then dropped to 52% in October after the debates, reaching a post election high of 69%. Bush's ratings remained relatively unchanged with 47% favorable and 50% unfavorable. (Gallup Poll, November 14, 1992)

In 1996, Clinton would not win a majority of the votes in his reelection bid running against Bob Dole. For a second time, it would be Perot who would keep Clinton from earning a majority.

In both elections, more people had voted against Clinton than for him.

Chapter 10
From Rhetoric To Reality

A new day was about to dawn.

It would be the beginning of a new era. An era that would change the destiny of a nation and in doing so would change the world forever. On a clear winter day on the steps of the nation's capitol, the new leader stood on the edge of a new century to celebrate, "the mystery of American renewal."

In his Inaugural Address, William Jefferson Clinton called for the nation to have the courage to change as a new season of renewal had begun. While now in the depths of winter, the American people had determined the election forcing the coming of spring. As Bill Clinton took the oath of office, the ghosts of the Reagan Bush years hung deeply around the occasion. As he looked out to the crowd, he envisioned what the future would hold. The Reagan Revolution was at an end.

Now was the time for a new beginning.

The 1992 presidential election turned out to be perhaps the most significant and yet bizarre campaign in modern history. During the course of the campaign there were several pivotal events that demonstrated the use of dramatic narratives to legitimize each candidate's right to govern. These events contributed significantly to the final outcome of the election. The nature of the campaign and the resulting political culture had led to the Clinton-ization of American politics.

The election campaign began with a popular incumbent who inherited the strongest political legacy since Harry Truman succeeded Franklin Roosevelt and who appeared so unbeatable that prominent Democrats were discouraged from challenging him. However, Bill Clinton an obscure governor from a small state entered the race early with a well developed version of social reality and began to share meaning with the voters about the current state of affairs in the nation.

As the incumbent, Bush did little to develop an early version of social reality, instead he relied on previously shared dramatic narratives left over from the Reagan years, tempered by his own personal style. Only after facing a surprisingly strong opposition from within his own party did Bush do any campaigning, which was primarily reactionary responding to attacks rather than presenting any of his own initiatives. Bush did not announce his candidacy until six days before the New Hampshire primary, one month after he abruptly began campaigning. This strategy of reacting to attacks and poll data after the fact instead of developing his own version of social reality would set the norm for the campaign in which Bush would rarely, if ever lead the political debate.

Instead, it would be Clinton who would early on set the agenda for the campaign. When besieged with scandal and personal attacks, he would stay the course by repeatedly returning to his original version of social reality. This strategy of creating and inculcating action based dramatic narratives to share meaning with the voters most likely saved his campaign, especially when his credibility was low and later when Bush attacked his legitimacy.

On the other hand, Bush developed no coherent version of social reality of his own at the beginning of the campaign, instead he waited until September. This lack of focus and constant changes led to the perception that his campaign was in disarray and that he had no real plan for the nation. This perception would prove to be a liability that was picked up by the media and the public haunting him throughout the campaign.

After the New Hampshire primary, Perot changed the political landscape by speculating that he might run for president. Perot demonstrated the power of how a candidate can share meaning with the public by employing several familiar dramatic narratives while having few, if any, real positions on the issues. These dramatic narratives shared meaning with the voters enabling him to eventually lead both Bush and Clinton in the polls.

It would ultimately be Perot who would sway the outcome of the campaign through the use of dramatic narratives and strategic timing. After creating one of the most successful independent campaigns in history, Perot would drop out of the race on the day of Clinton's acceptance speech at the Democratic National Convention handing Clinton an unprecedented post convention bounce in the polls. This move catapulted Clinton into first place for the first time in the race, a place he would hold for the rest of the campaign. Bush would never recover, even the Republican National Convention could not give him the rebound he needed.

In September, Bush launched his version of social reality when he began campaigning, blaming his slow start on trying to conduct the nation's business while being unfairly victimized by Clinton. By then public support had shifted to Clinton and had solidified enough so that Bush's initiative had little effect, making the race all but over. In October, Perot reentered the race armed with new stories of deceit and political intrigue accusing the Republican's of forcing him out of the race. Being an official candidate allowed Perot to buy television time to speak directly to the people and conduct one of the most bizarre political campaigns in American history.

Despite all his campaigning, Perot was not able to recapture the ground swell of support he had initially enjoyed. As the campaign moved into the debates, public support had solidified and the high hopes that the debates would reverse Bush's political fortunes were never realized. Perot was the biggest benefactor significantly improving his public image, while Clinton and Bush remained virtually the same. Despite trying various strategies, in the campaign's closing weeks neither Bush nor Perot were able to make a significant enough gain against Clinton, leading to a Clinton victory. Given the margins between Bush and Clinton over the course of the campaign, had Bush developed a coherent version of social reality at the same time as Clinton, or had Buchanan and Perot not entered the race, their political fortunes most likely would have been reversed. As it was, this was not to be.

The significance of this campaign lies in how a widely popular incumbent could fall so far so fast to be defeated by a relatively obscure newcomer plagued by serious ethical problems and character flaws that had ended other political careers. It also demonstrates how a political novice with no party support could capture the imagination of the nation to sway the election's outcome. Insight into how this happened can be found in how each candidate constructed their respective version of social reality.

The Nature of Social Reality.

In order to get elected, candidates must create and share their version of social reality with the voters. Social reality is how people make sense of the world around them. Life can be chaotic, things can happen for no apparent reason. Social reality is how we organize and make sense of our perceptions and expectations including what we see, hear, feel, and experience. Social reality is important to us because it determines how we interpret our perceptions and what we do about them, so it can have tangible consequences. Candidates can utilize this process by characterizing events in a manner that helps them get elected.

A candidate's version of social reality is usually comprised of selected portions of the larger societal social reality. It gives a particular interpretation of events with the purpose of legitimizing the candidate and undermining their opponent. It has to be compatible with the larger societal view of social reality in order to be accepted by the public. If not, a candidate may be perceived as too extreme or out of touch with the people. These specialized versions of social reality can fall into generally accepted categories that often have a specific name like conservative, moderate, or liberal, but can be given their own set of unique characteristics.

The Clinton Version of Social Reality.

The Clinton version of social reality centered on the characterization of the government as being corrupt and the nation as coming apart at the seams. Clinton's characterizations of the problems in government were widely shared as evidenced by the rise of the angry voter. Since Bush had inherited the Reagan legacy, Clinton needed to characterize Reagan as having hurt the nation, which meant characterizing the decade of the eighties as a time of greed and corruption. Instead of being the restorers of American greatness, Reagan and Bush became its destroyers in Clinton's vision. In essence, Clinton was running not only against Bush, but against the legacy of Ronald Reagan.

Since Clinton began campaigning, Bush's approval rating as president had steadily declined as a growing number of people were becoming dissatisfied with the job he was doing as president. The vilification of Bush and the government in Washington was a very effective dramatic narrative that was widely shared with the public and in the media. In order to get people to change it had to be made attractive to them, so Clinton had to increase dissatisfaction and uncertainty in the current government, while reducing uncertainty about himself.

If the level of public uncertainty about Clinton was higher than Bush, he would likely lose. If it was higher about Bush, Clinton would benefit. So, Clinton's characterization of his vision of the future not only had to be perceived as being better than the present, it also had to be perceived as safe and nonthreatening to reassure the voters that Clinton's leadership was not risky. To do this, Clinton employed dramatic narratives of himself as a new kind of politician who had the ability to solve their problems and public skepticism of him began to fade.

In order to reduce uncertainty, Clinton's version of change included a change in national leadership, a change in the Democratic Party, and a change in the nation. Change became a matter not only of changing the direction of the country through a new administration, but also of bringing about a change in social reality. In order to present himself as a new breed of politician and an agent of change, Clinton distanced himself from the dramatic narratives of the past that could hurt the public's faith in his legitimacy for office.

Calling himself a new type of Democrat, he characterized himself as a new, young, moderate leader who rejected old style Democratic labels like tax and spend big government liberal. If a program was given a new name like The New Covenant, and if it sounded new to the people, it would not conjure up past negative dramatic narratives. Clinton's new dramatic narratives served to remove past negative connotations that the voters might react against. So, when Bush called him a tax and spend liberal, Clinton simply rejected the label allowing him to also attack tax and spend policies as a failure. In doing so, Clinton was able to selectively take credit for government successes, while demonstrating that he had experienced the evils of government, so he could claim a common experience with the people.

The Bush Version of Social Reality.

The Bush version of social reality was the least distinct or well defined of the three candidates. It was also the one that changed the most throughout the campaign giving the perception that he had no plan and his campaign was in disarray. During the primaries, Bush appeared to have been caught without a plan when he was attacked by Buchanan as being too moderate and not concentrating on the problems at home. When he took the approach of remaining presidential, he was attacked for being out of touch with the people.

Since Bush had held back from campaigning for so long, he had let Clinton define him and set the agenda for the campaign. When he finally entered the campaign, how he began campaigning made him appear reactionary and in trouble. Bush lacked his own agenda and seemed to be motivated by the accusations of others. When Bush moved to the right in response to Buchanan and to shore up conservative support, Clinton became more conservative and claimed the middle ground. As a result, the media characterized Bush as weak and extremist.

Many of the dramatic narratives Buchanan used against Bush in the primaries that shared meaning with the voters were later picked up by Clinton. Coming from a member of his own party, Buchanan's attacks had the effect of establishing and legitimizing many of the dramatic narratives that other candidates later used to undermine Bush's record as president. This made a previously strong president appear to be a weak candidate unfit for a second term as he was under siege from a faction in his own party, which should have been supporting him. Bush had the burden of being attacked by every candidate in the race, some of whom only attacked him and no other candidate.

However, Bush chose a different target to legitimize his past performance as president by characterizing Congress as villains who had blocked his programs and hurt the American people. By campaigning against Congress, Bush was the only candidate to run against an opponent who was not an individual person or actually a candidate running for office in the campaign. This was a dramatic narrative that the public found difficult to share meaning with because in any drama, like a book or movie, the hero fights an individual who is cast as the villain, not a group of undefined people who are not individually mentioned.

Throughout the primary campaign, Bush presented an indistinct characterization of himself, who he was, and what he stood for. In early descriptions of world events, Bush did not even include himself in his own dramatic narratives. While he had the blessings of his party and the sanctifying agent of incumbency, he did not effectively utilize a populist mandate nor did he cite spiritual or traditional forces to legitimize his claim to office. This strategy was not effective because his lack of any version of social reality and his reactive responses fueled media characterizations of him being weak and his campaign being disorganized without a message. These characterizations, combined with Clinton's attacks, hurt his approval ratings as president.

During the Republican National Convention, the dramatic narrative of family values became the core of the Bush campaign. Foreign policy and family values were widely characterized by Bush and shared with the people who saw him as the best candidate to handle these issues. The problem was that these issues were not important to most people, consistently ranking at the bottom in the polls. It was the economy that was the most important issue with the people, but Bush waited until September to present any plan to address it.

The Bush version of social reality had convinced voters that he had the experience to handle foreign policy, but failed to convince them that this mattered. The dramatic narrative of family values was received negatively in the media and was not shared with the people as a significant issue in the campaign. Perhaps, it was Clinton's negative characterizations of Bush that counteracted that message.

By his own admission, it was not until after the convention that Bush began to actively campaign. Upset with his opponents' criticism, which he characterized as unrelenting and personal, Bush described how he had tried to concentrate on running the country and waiting to run until the election was fully underway. By then enough people had made up their mind making the race all but over and Election Day all but a formality.

Not until late in the campaign did Bush raise the issue of Clinton's character and judgment in order to undermine Clinton's legitimacy to be president. Even though Clinton was plagued by serious doubts over his credibility for most of the campaign, as the race progressed and Bush increased his attacks, the perception of Clinton's character actually improved in the public eye. Since Bush employed many dramatic narratives about his own experience, Clinton's delegitimizing dramas about Bush lowered the public's approval of his job as president.

Incumbency was implied, if not stressed in the issue of who would best handle a crisis, as was raised by Bush. This approach promoted Bush's experience and exposed Clinton's weaknesses by exploiting the people's fear of the uncertainty of change. If Clinton was elected, who knew what might happen, but by voting for the incumbent Bush, the people knew what to expect. Bush seemed to think the implication was clear and the people would get it. They would make the right decision to stay with an experienced incumbent because he was already president, rather than elect an untrustworthy, unknown, and inexperienced candidate. This was a very risky strategy, because they didn't get it, and elected Clinton instead.

As the campaign progressed, while other candidates were calling to change the mess in Washington, Bush could not call for change or criticize the failures of the government. This made his position untenable as his ratings in the polls declined, so Bush shifted ground and tried to characterize himself as the agent of change. This was an impossible dramatic narrative to share meaning with the voters because Bush had been a part of the government for the last twelve years, so he could not easily distance himself from it and the state of the country.

When Bush called for change, it was likely perceived as an admission of the failure of his policies. To overcome this problem, he characterized the villain and his primary opponent as Congress, rather than Clinton or Perot. In effect, Bush had made a tactical miscalculation and in essence validated Clinton's claim that America was in decline, so change was really necessary. Since Bush had held back from campaigning for so long, he had let Clinton define him and set the agenda for the campaign.

The Perot Version of Social Reality.

In order to legitimize his candidacy, Perot needed to make a convincing case for change so that voters would be persuaded to transfer their allegiance from past Republican and Democratic versions of social reality to vote against Bush without switching to Clinton. In order to do this, Perot employed two persuasive dramatic narratives. First, he made the case of an intolerable situation in Washington in which the administration was ruining the country and hurting the people. However, he ran the risk of persuading voters to leave Bush, but not convince them to support him, so they would end up supporting Clinton instead.

Second, after he had demonstrated the need to be involved in the campaign, he presented a solution by characterizing himself as the man of the people who could get the job done. In order to persuade the electorate of the need for change, Washington was characterized as unresponsive to the people while refusing to address important issues. This dramatic narrative called attention to the problems that must be addressed and solved. This was the motivation for Perot's claim to office. It was the motivation for everything he did in the campaign and the basis of his version of social reality.

The task for Perot was to establish his legitimacy and to distinguish himself from the other two candidates as the only person who could solve the nation's problems. He accomplished this when he presented his vision of a better future, even though it was unclear what sort of future he sought to create. In order to do this, he developed the dramatic narrative of being a man of the people and cast himself as the logical candidate to provide the solution. He was cast as the hero, fighting for the people against the villainous Bush to clean up the mess in Washington. The proof of his ability to govern was based on his dramatic narratives of being a success in business, a wonderful father and family man, a citizen devoted to his country, and a 'can-do' type of person who could get the job done no matter what the odds. The primary legitimizing agent for Perot came from his grassroots campaign because he could claim that he had been sanctified by the people who had asked him to run.

After a strong showing in 1992, Perot qualified for federal campaign funds for the 1996 presidential campaign. So in 1995, he formed the Reform Party and former Colorado governor Dick Lamm was slated to be the party's candidate for president. However, the Federal Election Commission would only give the funds to Perot since he had run as an independent, so he became a presidential candidate for a second time in 1996. Even though he was not permitted to participate in the presidential debates this time around, he was able to keep Clinton from winning a majority of the votes cast. In 2000, the Reform Party ran Pat Buchanan as its candidate for president, so the FEC awarded him $12.6 million in campaign funds. He only received 449,225 votes, or 0.4%, so the Reform Party lost funding for 2004 and Buchanan returned to the Republicans.

The Fracturing of Social Reality

When a group's social reality is challenged either externally or internally, it may change to accommodate the new circumstances or it can fracture resulting in the creation of two competing versions of social reality. Both of these events occurred in this campaign. When it came under pressure, the Democrat's version of social reality changed to accommodate Clinton's characterization of himself as a new kind of Democrat. When he moved to the center, the left wing did not splinter off, attack him, or support another candidate, they supported him to win the election.

In the case of the Republicans, the opposite seems to have occurred. Buchanan splintered the Republican version of social reality early on by publicly concentrating on conservative issues creating dissatisfaction with Bush supporters that fractured party support. This pushed Bush to the right allowing Clinton to take the middle ground when Bush should have cast himself as a moderate. Many of Bush's supporters likely became dissatisfied with him and switched to Clinton, or sat out the election. This was the beginning of the end for Bush.

When a political party has a faction that wants candidates who fit their ideology or they won't support them, it virtually ensures their defeat. It's better to win with a candidate of your own party who has widespread appeal and shares some of your values than to stick to your ideology and lose to a candidate who shares few or none of them. Ideology conflicts can be resolved once in office, rather than in public during the election alienating voters and making the party appear divided.

While ideology is important to communicate what a party or candidate stands for, it can potentially alienate more voters than it attracts. Parties can get into fights over ideology that splits the party motivating people to vote against them and vote for their opponent. What is more effective is winning elections first, and then governing. If you lose, you can't govern or implement your policies. Once you win, ideology and policy can be worked out in the process of governing keeping it separate from campaigning.

To be successful, political parties need to put finding a candidate who can win over finding the perfect candidate who appeals to a specific faction and their ideology, because no candidate can appeal to everyone. It is better for a party to support an imperfect candidate and win than to holdout for ideology and loose.

After all, if you are hungry, isn't it better to get half a loaf of bread than no loaf at all?

Chapter 11
Creating The Right To Govern

The 1992 presidential election demonstrated the importance of a candidate creating their version of social reality and skillfully communicating it to the voters to legitimize their right to govern. This process was shown to be more important to a candidate's political fortunes than their positions on issues, popularity, credibility, or even past experience.

For instance, Bush had the most experience and the highest initial popularity of all the candidates, but the lack of a coherent or articulate version of social reality that shared meaning with the voters sharply reduced his legitimacy to govern. Clinton was an unknown candidate inexperienced in national politics or foreign affairs, who overcame scandal by crafting dramatic narratives as part of a panoramic version of social reality and then repeating them until they became widely shared with the public. Initially, Perot had virtually no issue positions, yet he crafted a coherent version of social reality and for a time led in the polls. This demonstrates the importance of utilizing a clear version of social reality made up of artistically crafted dramatic narratives that share meaning with the voters.

When candidates characterize themselves and events in their version of social reality to legitimize their right to govern, they seek to reduce uncertainty about themselves to persuade the public that they are the best person to serve in office. They also try to undermine their opponent's legitimacy by increasing uncertainty about them in the minds of the voters. This can be accomplished through the process of shared meaning. Candidates use negative dramatic narratives about their opponent to try to separate the voters from their existing version of social reality, so that they will no longer support the other candidate.

This can leave a void that voters look to have filled, opening the way for the other candidate to replace the old version with their new version of social reality. For instance, Clinton, with Perot's help, vilified the government as corrupt and repugnant to motivate people who had held the Reagan Bush version of social reality to reject it. Then, Clinton could replace it with his version. Bush lost vital support because he did not initially defend or support his version of social reality.

A candidate must seek legitimacy by creating a connection with commonly recognized and established sources of credibility for their candidacy through party endorsements, at political conventions, in primaries, and through incumbency. The sharing of communal values can be accomplished through populist mandates that demonstrate the people's support. This is most commonly accomplished by citing past elections and being reelected to office as proof that a candidate represents the people and has their support.

Social reality is a powerful legitimizing force because it can help candidates explain who they are, what they stand for, and why they are running for office. Candidates tend to characterize themselves as personifying deeply held and well established values and beliefs that they hold in common with the people they want to represent. This helps them to share meaning with the voters by connecting their political principles to the traditional values of the past and to unify the audience behind those values. This serves to reduce uncertainty about themselves, so that voters can feel comfortable voting for them.

Conversely, candidates might attack an opponent by showing how the political principles of their opponent are alien or repugnant to the traditional values of the people. They do this to create uncertainty about an opponent in the minds of the voters to help to defeat them. Voters are more likely to be motivated to vote against someone with a high degree of uncertainty than for someone with a low degree of uncertainty because uncertainty can make people uncomfortable. When people are uncomfortable they are more likely to do something about it, like voting. The more intense the feelings, the more motivated they can become. So, if you want to motivate people to do something, make them angry or fearful. This is why negative campaigning can be so effective.

Shared Meaning and Dramatic Narratives.

In order to legitimize their right to govern, a candidate must create their version of social reality. Then, they must make a connection with the voters, usually through the media, and communicate their message to them so that they will understand it. This is commonly done through the use of dramatic narratives, which are a persuasive telling of events often based on a few facts or events that are characterized in a manner that is neither factual nor fictional, but somewhere in between. This makes them more interesting or dramatic, so that the public will pay attention to them. They often include characterizations about the candidate, their opponent, and the circumstances in the country.

As part of a campaign, candidates create and communicate many dramatic narratives. When the public hears or sees these dramatic narratives, a connection is made and the candidate and the voter share meaning because they both understand what these dramatic narratives mean. There are several well established dramatic narratives that candidates utilize because people are already familiar with them making them easier to understand.

The process of shared meaning is essential to a campaign because it is how a candidate motivates voters not only to vote, but also to support them by campaigning, donating money, or volunteering for them. By sharing meaning, ideas that exist in a person's or candidate's mind can motivate behavior creating actual physical reality. Sharing meaning is a powerful process because it has the potential to change perceptions and expectations, as well as motivate behavior.

It could be said that rhetorical forms fall into two categories, fact and fiction. There is the inherent assumption that if a candidate is not telling the truth they are lying. So, if fact comprises those things that are verifiably true, and fiction is an imaginative creation developed through invention that does not represent actual reality, candidates who share meaning through dramatic narratives utilize neither fact nor fiction. Instead, they take an inherent reality, like the economy or health care, select a few pertinent items and present a dramatic narrative that is their characterization interpreted to fit into their version of social reality. This maneuvering between fact and fiction falls within the realm of dramatic narratives.

In dramatic narratives, real world events are explained to create and sustain shared meaning with the public and to support a candidate's version of social reality. Much of political social reality is constructed through dramatic narratives that are presented to help legitimize a candidate or to undermine their opponent. How else could the euphoria following the success of the Gulf War be called a failure? The event itself did not change, only people's perception of it changed. Being able to exploit and adapt existing social reality and commonly shared meanings is essential to legitimating a candidate's right to govern.

Candidates often exploit well established dramatic narratives that have been well defined within society like restoration, rebirth, and the American Dream. This helps to make a candidate's version of social reality more easily understood since these dramatic narratives are ones that the electorate already knows. Candidates need to create dramatic narratives that tie into the social reality of the larger society. They accomplish this by affirming common values and beliefs connecting their version to those of their audience.

Over the course of the 1992 presidential election there were several dramatic narratives employed by all three candidates that were similar in nature. These narratives were repeated throughout the campaign demonstrating that they shared meaning with the voters regardless of which candidate they supported.

These dramatic narratives were shared by all three candidates.

1. The American Dream. The American Dream is an old and powerful dramatic narrative that characterizes America as the land of opportunity where anyone can realize his or her potential. It originates from the Declaration of Independence that proclaims all men are created equal and have the right to the pursuit of happiness. The American Dream is about everyone having the opportunity to be successful and prosper from their own work.

America is a place where everyone is equal regardless of who they are or where they came from. It is about an upwardly mobile society where the next generation will be better off than the last. It is the hope of parents that their children will have it better than they did. It can also include benefits like getting a college education, having a good job, or home ownership.

The American Dream dramatic narrative is used by candidates because it is familiar to practically everyone, including people all over the world. It is so powerful that it motivated millions of people to leave their homes and seek a better life in America.

The American Dream was perhaps the most commonly utilized dramatic narrative employed to support the candidates and was used extensively by all three in the campaign. It was frequently used as a legitimizing agent for Clinton's candidacy. Clinton often claimed that he ran for president in order to restore the American Dream for our children because he could no longer stand by and witness the next generation become the first to be worse off than their parents. This dramatic narrative was primarily action driven as it was Clinton's actions and achievements that were characterized as enabling the realization of the American Dream.

In order to fulfill the promise of the American Dream, Clinton called for a new type of leadership to reinvent government, so it could meet the challenges the nation faced. The American Dream had been destroyed by the people in Washington, by a government that had lost touch with the people and their values. Clinton drew the people into his dramatic narrative when he said that the people needed the courage to reject the failed policies of the past and embrace his vision of the future, so together they could restore the American Dream. The characterization of hope was Clinton's personal realization of the American Dream, which made it an extension of this dramatic narrative. Hope served as a reference to Clinton having grown up in humble beginnings in a small town called Hope, Arkansas and rising to achievement, recognition, and success through hard work.

Clinton characterized himself as the personification of the American Dream and he understood the people since he was one of them. This made him uniquely qualified to help them obtain and keep their own version of the American Dream. During the campaign, Clinton often said that no matter how far he went, he would think of the small town were he came from called Hope. Connecting this dramatic narrative of his hometown to the nation, Clinton said that he still believed in the promise of America and in the promise of a place called Hope. It was this dramatic narrative of typical small town Americana that served as the basis for his definition of the American Dream because it shared meaning with many people.

Perot employed a similar version of the American Dream dramatic narrative during his campaign. In his version, Perot set himself up as an example of someone who had the good fortune to live and benefit from the American Dream and so he wanted to pass it on to our children and to their children. The focus of his version was on future generations and not so much on the present or past. In using the dramatic narrative of the mess in Washington, Perot supported his contention that the American Dream was under siege. The national debt had motivated him to enter the race because he saw no other candidate addressing this issue. It was the growing debt and the unwillingness of the folks in Washington to do anything about it that mortgaged our children's future and threatened the American Dream.

Bush employed the American Dream dramatic narrative when he told the story of how he and Barbara went to Texas in another era to begin a new life. This story was often used by Bush to represent his personal participation in the American Dream. He told about his early days in Texas starting a business. This was experience that he had drawn upon to help solve the problems of the country. However, now Bush saw the American Dream as under attack by a villainous government that destroyed individual freedoms. Fundamental American values were being eroded by an obstructionist Congress that was out of control and no longer representing the people.

In Bush's view, the American Dream was threatened by tax and spend liberals like Clinton. So, the nation needed Bush to protect the people from Clinton and a Congress that destroyed individual freedom and raised taxes. His vision of the American Dream was based on empowering all people to make their own choices and to reach their potential by offering economic opportunity. For Bush, the American Dream was a place where people found a better life for themselves and their children. It was the American Dream that had made America the most dynamic society in the world.

2. Rebirth. The rebirth dramatic narrative focuses on a person who experiences a defining moment that dramatically changes the direction of his or her life. The presidential candidates employed this dramatic narrative to describe a pivotal moment in their own life that brought them into public service or to run for office. The circumstances of the moment of rebirth are often told in detail and characterized in a dramatic style.

Throughout the campaign, Clinton characterized the defining moment in his life as when he realized his destiny was in public service. The story usually began with him growing up poor in Hope and how as a young man he met President John Kennedy in the Rose Garden at the White House. He thought what a wonderful country America was because he had the opportunity to meet the president of the United States. This event was characterized as the defining moment in his life, a symbolic passing of the torch between generations that led him into public service, to become governor, and to seek the presidency.

Perot's rebirth narrative was a subtler one. When Perot announced he was reentering the race in October, he characterized it in terms of a rebirth. Shortly before reentering, Perot had finally been placed on the ballot in all fifty states, so he felt he had an obligation to the people to run. It was at this time that he had been sanctified by the people because they had drafted him as their choice for president. Even though he had already been in the race, his reentry was the closest to a rebirth experience within the dramatic narratives he used in his campaign.

Bush utilized two different versions of the rebirth dramatic narrative in his campaign, although they were not as well defined as his opponents' versions. Bush described his experience as a decorated pilot in World War II when he was shot down and rescued by a submarine at sea as a defining moment in his life. The other dramatic narrative characterized how he and Barbara drove to Texas after the war to begin a new life. In Texas he raised a family and started a business that taught him valuable lessons he carried into public life. Later, he would run in his first election launching a life of public service. Although these experiences were frequently described throughout the campaign, how they motivated him to pursue a life of public service and run for president was indistinctly conveyed.

3. Restoration. There are times when people feel that in order to move forward to a better future, they need to go back to the past in order to restore something good that has been lost. The restoration dramatic narrative begins in the past when times were good and people were virtuous. Then there comes a time of troubles that brings on the problems that exist today. They may feel that their problems are due to the people losing their way or that their leaders have become corrupted, so things can be resolved by returning to the values of the past.

Restoration is also an old and familiar dramatic narrative in religious doctrine. It is based on the Garden of Eden, which was an idyllic paradise that was lost when Adam and Eve succumbed to temptation and were expelled to live a life of hardship. So, at various times in history, when people suffered a time of hardship they interpreted it as a falling away from their true values. Even today, when people face a time of troubles there arises a movement to change the corrupt present by returning to the ideals of the past. By restoring the ideals and values of the past, they will resolve their problems to improve their present condition.

A variation of restoration is the founding. In many groups there is a founding dramatic narrative that tells the story of how an organization, a people, or a nation came into existence. It includes dramatic narratives about how and why it was formed and the notable people in its history. The founding is important because it is more than just a recounting of the past, it tells what a group of people stands for, what kind of people belong to it, and how they are expected to behave. For example, the American founding dramatic narrative tells how America was founded, the qualities of the people who founded it, and what it means to be an American. When groups, organizations, or nations find themselves in difficult times, they might utilize restoration as a means of returning to the values and principles of its founding and its founders to restore what made it great. Restoration could be characterized as a means of 'societal rebooting.'

In an election campaign, candidates utilize the dramatic narrative of restoration as a means of legitimizing their candidacy and undermining their opponent. A challenger may characterize the incumbent or the party in power as corrupt, having fallen away from the values of the people. If the challenger is elected, they will restore the government to the values that made it great before the current regime was elected. In this manner, a challenger seeks to drive a wedge between their opponent and the voters by asserting that their opponent has strayed, been corrupted, or is no longer consistent with the values of the people and so must be replaced.

During the 1992 campaign, each candidate utilized the founding dramatic narrative, which is a variation of restoration. Restoration relies on basic principles of freedom and equality set forth in the founding of America and personified by its current and past leaders. The candidates share communal values that they personify by calling for restoration of the principles and values that America was founded upon that made it great. Change can be used as a variation of restoration because it is necessary to change who the people elect to office in order to restore the original ideals set out by the founders.

Clinton employed the restoration dramatic narrative in his version of social reality as an action based dramatic narrative centered around himself as the agent of change who would restore the government to the people based on the traditions and values established at the founding of our nation. He characterized the present government as corrupt and having no vision, leadership, or strategy. It was a government that practiced divisiveness, so it was in need of reform. The country needed a president with a new approach to resolving the economic problems facing the country. The New Covenant was the motivation for Clinton's restoration dramatic narrative because it referred to restoring the solemn bond between the people and the government. It was founded on the most sacred principles of the nation and would restore the values that had been lost.

Clinton included the voters in this restoration narrative when he characterized the election as a crusade to put people first and to restore the forgotten middle class in order to build a new economic order. It was Clinton who would restore America to its former greatness by creating jobs and rewarding hardworking families abandoned by Washington. As a part of his program, he would restore fairness to the tax system, legal system, and health care system. In revolutionizing government, he was the agent of change who would restore the government to the people.

Throughout the campaign, Clinton frequently called for change in order to restore America. For him, change represented three elements: a change in himself from old style Democratic politicians, a change in the Democratic Party that rejected the failed policies of the past, and a change in government to put people first. In order to restore the nation, people must have the courage to change. It is through change that restoration would be realized so the people could have a better future. It was through change that the principles and values of the past would be restored to the government, to the people, and to the nation.

In Perot's case, restoration was a call back to the people's values drawing upon their traditions. The government was full of corruption and disarray because the folks in Washington had forgotten the people who sent them there. Utilizing several references to the falling away from traditional values, Perot implied much about the current state of the country and the failure of the other candidates to help the people. Thus, Perot created a reason for him to restore the government by acknowledging the public's growing disillusion with the other candidates in order to legitimize his own candidacy.

In establishing his campaign's legitimacy, Perot developed many dramatic narratives that utilized restoration to convince voters to support him. It was the people's role to restore the government to correct the evil without impairing what was good. Perot justified his running based on the restoration of basic values in government by addressing the issues that were important to the people. Perot and the people represented the means by which this restoration would take place. He connected with his audience using restoration by evoking communal values that epitomized the people's principles, linking their values with his own.

Bush alluded to restoration when he told of returning to the work he started twelve years ago. This dramatic narrative suggested that somehow he had been driven off course by Congress and that he now must return to an earlier mission. He hinted at restoration when he said that government was too big and cost too much. However, he did not create a strong alternate vision of what America would look like after it had been restored under his leadership. When he mentioned foreign affairs, Bush did cite the restoration of freedom and democracy around the world and alluded to the need to restore individual freedom from government at home. Here, he was the central hero who would restore the government. With the people's help and with the new Congress, Bush would restore the government to basic decency that would empower the people.

4. A Vision of a Better Future. During the campaign, each of the candidates created a vision of the future that would be better than the present. In order to legitimize their right to govern, each of the candidates had to create and communicate their own clear, unified vision of the future. This vision served to represent the candidates' purpose for seeking office and specified what they hoped to accomplish if they won. If a candidate cannot clearly articulate a vision of the future that they want to create, the public is more likely to question why they are running for office. The creation and sharing meaning about a vision of the future is important because it serves to reduce uncertainty about a candidate in the minds of the public.

Candidates can accomplish this task in one of two ways. The first is to characterize the present in terms of past successes and accomplishments. A vision of the future is based on the ability of a candidate to replicate past successes. Bush developed his vision of a better future based on a positive image of America. In order to accomplish this, he characterized legislative changes that he and the people had accomplished together.

The second way was employed by Clinton and Perot. It makes the future appear better by downgrading the present. They characterized the present conditions as intolerable with the people suffering and the country falling apart. The purpose is to degrade the present to make the vision of the future as attractive as possible. This was perhaps why Clinton recast the eighties as a decade of greed and government irresponsibility, whether it had any basis in fact or not.

Once the people had been made aware of how bad things really were, they would welcome a change. This process can be analogous to the evangelical process of a religious conversion. People are persuaded into changing their old views of social reality by casting them as repugnant, motivating them to question and eventually abandon them. This can leave a void that creates an opportunity to present a new and improved social reality that can replace the old one.

Legitimization.

An election campaign can be seen as a series of attempts to legitimize a candidate's right to govern and to undermine their opponent's legitimacy in order to be elected to office. In this regard, agreement between one candidate and their opponent can serve to either delegitimize the candidate who agrees by downgrading them to the same level as the opponent they seek to undermine, or it can bolster their opponent's position by elevating them to the same level as the candidate who agrees with them. In either case, agreement often serves to undermine a candidate who finds an area of agreement. This happened when Bush accepted the dramatic narrative of change.

If the objective is to delegitimize an opponent in the minds of the voters, what would motivate candidates to find areas of agreement? During the campaign, there were areas where all three candidates agreed, which they used to legitimize their right to govern by establishing several sanctifying agents. Political fortunes seem to be derived from what sanctifying agents each candidate selected to support their political legitimacy to convince the people to vote for them. The success of these depends on what events are selected, how they are characterized, and what dramatic narratives are shared with the public.

In developing their version of social reality, these sanctifying agents were employed by the candidates to legitimize their right to govern.

1. The People. Candidates frequently legitimize their right to govern by evoking the will of the people. There can be a public aversion to those who seek office for their own designs. So, a candidate must seek office because they are following the will of the people or for the good of the people, often through self sacrifice, but not to further their own goals or ambitions.

The candidates in the 1992 presidential campaign called upon the people by referring to serving in office, winning past elections, being supported by ordinary people, grassroots organizations, and other such populist mandates. Candidates must find and communicate a compelling reason to draw support from the people. The people are always the hero in a candidate's dramatic narratives. They are never criticized, no matter what the state of the nation or economy. The nation's problems are never the fault of the people, even though they elected the folks who made the mess in government in the first place.

The candidates find the people not only an important sanctifying agent to legitimize their campaign, but also an agent of action in their dramatic narratives as it is the will of the people that will prevail. The candidates often said that the people have the choice to elect the kind of government they want, yet the government they elect needs to be changed every election. All three candidates used ordinary people as a form of proxy to attack their opponents in ways that they could not do without running the risk of damaging their public persona.

Candidates need to be seen interacting with the people, from individuals to large crowds. Clinton used television commercials showing him at campaign rallies surrounded by enthusiastic crowds. Perot used individual testimonies to show support. Showing a candidate with the people, especially in television ads and news reports, serves to legitimize them with the voters as a sanctifying agent. Meeting with ordinary people shows that they are open and approachable, even if they really are not. Showing a candidate in front of large groups of people demonstrates that the people actively support a candidate and provides a critical visual element to share meaning with the voters. This is why old fashioned events like political rallies and shaking people's hands are still an important mainstay of election campaigns, even in a mass media age.

It is not enough to be chosen by the people, a candidate also has to be one of them. During the campaign, the candidates went to great lengths to demonstrate how extraordinarily ordinary they really were. As a candidate seeks to create a public persona the voters can empathize with, they come to emulate them in various ways. Candidates must demonstrate that they have the average person's tastes so they participate in ordinary activities, while trying not to look overly intelligent or talented. They must represent the average person's values and beliefs. If the people are convinced a candidate is like them, they will be more likely to empathize with them and support the candidate because people tend to like people who they perceive are similar to themselves. This serves to reduce uncertainty about a candidate and what they might do in office. If the people do not perceive a candidate as someone like themselves, they can be perceived as out of touch or elitist. A candidate's version of social reality must be relatively stable to reduce uncertainty, while being flexible enough to account for change. Having shared meaning based on the people allows for new dramatic narratives and a version of social reality that can adapt to changing circumstances.

In order to legitimize his candidacy, Clinton called upon the people themselves. In claiming a populist mandate, he would establish an administration that would come directly from the people and be in their best interest. In characterizing the purpose of his running for president, Clinton employed two dramatic narratives with similar messages focusing on different segments of the population. These were putting people first and remembering the forgotten middle class. The dramatic narrative of remembering the forgotten middle class was very similar to putting people first, it just focused on a more specific group. In these dramatic narratives, Clinton was characterized as the hero of the people, a man who would make people his priority when elected. The people were good, decent, and hard-working, but had been abandoned by their government, a government that had helped villains who did not share the values of most Americans. Government should serve the people, rather than the people serve government.

In this respect, Clinton would make the people the focus of government. He often said that he knew the people's troubles, that he too had friends lose their jobs and homes. There were people in trouble whom he knew by name. This added to the dramatic narrative of a leader close to the people who knew firsthand their problems, could feel their pain, and who shared their hopes and dreams. Clinton used these narratives to share meaning with people who felt that they had been abandoned by government, so Clinton would return fairness to government by rewarding people who worked hard and played by the rules.

Whenever confronted by a crisis stemming from criticisms or scandal during the campaign, Clinton used the people as a means of damage control to deflect criticism. The Clinton version of social reality was primarily action oriented in that many of its dramatic narratives shared meanings revolving around taking action on the people's behalf by putting people first, restoring the middle class, or responding to the need for change. In order to deflect Bush's criticism of his lack of experience in foreign affairs, Clinton employed a variation of putting people first to circumvent this issue. Clinton connected foreign policy to domestic policy to counter the Bush claim that his leadership abroad would create success at home. When Bush attacked Clinton, Clinton often responded by reversing the causality. For instance, instead of using success abroad to help at home, the nation needed to be strong at home so it could be a world leader.

Even as unforeseen events like scandals and revelations about his past presented themselves, Clinton returned to familiar shared meanings with the public in order to defend himself against attacks and galvanize his support. Clinton utilized commonly shared meanings by characterizing these attacks as attacks on the American people themselves. He depicted these events as preventing him from solving their problems. This approach may have contributed to attracting supporters to defend him because they did not center on him, but rather on the people.

Throughout the campaign Bush made little claim to any kind of populist mandate based on the support of the people. Having run for Congress and certainly as being a part of the Reagan Bush landslides of 1980 and 1984, Bush had significant electoral success, yet there was relatively little use of these past events to demonstrate any support from the people. He was rarely shown with average people or in front of a large campaign rally, as were the other candidates. Bush made no significant claims that the people had legitimized his right to govern. This omission is all the more striking since Bush had enjoyed an unprecedented high level of support and approval in the polls that his campaign virtually ignored. The only recognition by Bush was the acknowledgment that the people wanted change, so Bush tried to characterize himself as the agent of change, with little success.

Political candidates typically utilize popular mandates by reminding the people of their past elections and service in public office, thereby legitimizing their right to govern. Perot was the only candidate who could not claim such a mandate, so he had to develop another sanctioning agent to fulfill this need. As a result, Perot took a decidedly different approach by creating the shared meaning of the accidental or reluctant candidate chosen by the people to run. In doing so, Perot created a public persona of a man of the people who was drafted in a grass-roots movement.

Initially, Perot said that he would run only if the people wanted him to run. In the early primaries Perot characterized his movement not as a campaign, but rather as a petition drive. His organization was characterized as all volunteer in order to further this populist image, even though he financed it himself. Perot withdrew from the race for the good of the people, saying that a three way race would not serve the people's interests when the Democratic Party was now addressing important issues. When Perot returned to the race, he again called on the people by claiming that the other candidates were not addressing the issues that were important to the people, but rather they were trivializing the election. Saying that the people had spoken, Perot had reentered the race after his name had been placed on the ballot in all fifty states. These dramatic narratives criticized his opponents and bolstered his legitimacy. The heroes in his dramatic narratives were the hardworking volunteers, and those in the military who had served their country and were now forgotten. He emphasized that he was the servant of the people referring to himself by saying, "I'm Ross, but you're the boss."

2. External Forces. In legitimizing their right to govern, candidates often call on forces outside themselves. These are meant to show the voters that the candidate has wide spread support. This can be very effective because people are often swayed by the opinions of others in choosing a candidate. People have predispositions based on their version of social reality that can be as important or in some circumstances even more important than the actual candidates themselves. People often vote for labels like party affiliations, ideology, or policies that can make the personal attributes of a candidate virtually inconsequential. This was evidenced by the fact that the voters supported and elected Clinton despite the ongoing issues of character that plagued his campaign.

Throughout the campaign, Clinton utilized The New Covenant to share meaning with the voters. The New Covenant was unique to Clinton and was not used by the other candidates. This dramatic narrative contained sacred and religious overtones that called on spiritual forces outside Clinton himself. The New Covenant was defined by Clinton as the solemn bond between a leader and the people founded on the most sacred principles of the nation. This served as a reference to his commitment to the people and his vision of government. It centered on Clinton as the main actor who would return the government to the people by restoring the bond between himself as president and the people. In order to restore the bond there needed to be a change in how government conducted business, as well as a change of administration. Change fits in with the dramatic narrative of restoration because it allows the government to be restored without altering or destroying its structure. Employing the restoration dramatic narrative recalled past traditions and values upon which America was founded, and change represented having faith in a better future.

Bush seemed to rely primarily on his party's endorsement as a sanctifying agent. During the Republican National Convention, many prominent Republicans spoke of their support for him, but this approach was not effectively utilized after the convention. Having been president, Bush could have utilized the support of other people including government and business leaders, like Clinton did. Bush sought to share meaning with the voters using the dramatic narrative of family values. This was based on his belief in the family as constituting our nation's most important institution. Bush characterized the two parties' differing visions of the family as a cultural divide. Bush also had the external sanctioning agent of his incumbency. Much has been made of the political advantages an incumbent candidate has over their challengers. Certainly, the fact that a candidate had been wearing the mantle of the presidency for four years and the vice presidency for eight years, should legitimize their right to govern. However, this means of legitimating his right to govern was never effectively utilized.

Perot did not have the support of traditional political external forces like covenants, party conventions, past elections, or incumbency. Instead, he called upon the grassroots support of the people as his sanctifying agent. Many of his television programs were based on external forces from a wide variety of people. Many of the traditions and values Perot sought to uphold were ones that he shared with the people who supported him. So, he called on external sanctifying forces like the traditional values of the people and the American Dream.

3. Inner Forces. In legitimizing their right to govern, candidates often call on forces from within themselves. These can include the inner qualities of character, trustworthiness, experience, and the ability to get things done. They do this to show the voters that they are the best candidate for office. While there were some qualities they had in common, the ones that were considered important by the voters varied based on how they were characterized in dramatic narratives. For instance, people thought honesty mattered for Bush, but not for Clinton. This was evidenced by voters not trusting Clinton, while feeling that he had the best plan.

The Clinton version of social reality served to legitimize his right to govern by characterizing him as an experienced leader who had a plan to improve the government in Washington and rejuvenate the state of the nation for the people. In order to accomplish this, Clinton was characterized as a competent, effective governor. His accomplishments were characterized as having demonstrated effective leadership. Many experts like Nobel Prizewinners, economists, business leaders, Republicans, and even the author of Perot's economic plan endorsed his candidacy.

Clinton utilized the power of the rebirth dramatic narrative by employing stories of how he came to a life of public service. He often told the story of when, as a young man, he went to Washington D.C. to meet President Kennedy. When he returned, he wanted to go into a life of public service. This experience was characterized throughout the campaign as the defining moment that shaped his life. Clinton implied that he could do for the nation what he had done for Arkansas. He was often depicted as a hardworking and thoughtful leader who was genuinely interested in people and could get things done. In Clinton's version of social reality, his characterization of change was presented as safe and not threatening to reduce uncertainty about him.

At first Bush sought to legitimize his right to govern by characterizing himself as an experienced world leader. After the convention, he sought to share meaning through his program, An Agenda for American Renewal. This program reiterated his accomplishments in the past to demonstrate that he could meet the challenges of the future. In order to share meaning with the voters and undermine Clinton's legitimacy, Bush used the personal qualities of trust and experience to contrast himself with his opponent. When Bush talked about them, he was providing a reference for two dramatic narratives, one featuring his own accomplishments and experience, and the other contrasting Clinton's lack of qualities to be president. Bush shared meaning about his experience by reflecting on his accomplishments of the past to legitimize his claim to a second term.

When developing a right to govern, candidates often recall their record and experience to show that they can do the job in office. In this respect Bush called on his foreign policy experience and Clinton his record in Arkansas. Bush called into question Clinton's judgment and character to increase uncertainty about his ability to lead the nation and to make the difficult decisions that a president has to make. Clinton's lack of foreign policy experience would result in Clinton not being able to handle a crisis or to lead the military into conflict. This issue was important considering that Clinton did not serve his country, but instead protested the war while abroad, which Bush felt was wrong. In contrast, Bush had served his country and had demonstrated the ability to handle a crisis.

In order to set himself apart from his opponents, Perot claimed no experience in creating the current problems. He characterized himself, not as a person who was wise in the sophisticated ways of government, but as a person who had learned about things by doing. He was a candidate who did not have political analysts to tell him what to say or how to say it. He called upon his personal experiences to make himself seem likable and effective. Throughout the campaign he used his own brand of wit and homespun phrases. This characterized him as someone the average person could identify with. Perot often cited his experience in business as a person who worked hard and came from humble beginnings to achieve great success.

4. Unexpected forces. While candidates and their campaign organizations plan how they create and communicate dramatic narratives to form their version of social reality, there are times when circumstances create them on their own. There are also times when candidates connect with dramatic narratives that already exist in society. These can help as well as hinder their candidacy. Because many of these dramatic narratives were not directly originated by the campaigns, they were not described in earlier chapters.

One element that can have an impact on a candidate's success is how they use music to inspire and motivate people. Music is a well established means of sharing meaning with people to motivate behavior because it makes an emotional connection with them. Many of the winning candidates have had campaign theme songs that tied into the larger social reality. Reagan used "God Bless The USA" by Lee Greenwood. Clinton used "Don't Stop" by Fleetwood Mac, which was not only a dramatic narrative to share meaning with the voters to tell them what his campaign was about, it also signaled a generational shift in presidential politics. Since the public has a wide variety of tastes in music, it is helpful to consider just what a song might communicate and who will share the meaning. Clinton's choice connected with his supporters. In contrast, Perot used the country western song "Crazy" because the media and his opponents had called him crazy due to his actions. Throughout the campaign, Bush made no significant use of music.

Candidates share meaning with the voters through the colors and logos they utilize to represent their campaign. The most common and effective are red, white, and blue, often using variations of the American flag as a logo because this appeals to the people's values and traditions, fulfilling their expectations. Some candidates may use other colors to stand out from the crowd of candidates like yellow, green, or purple. However, colors and logos that diverge too much from those in the larger societal social reality are generally not as effective.

As much as political campaigns try to control events, they can be subject to unexpected forces. This can give them a high degree of uncertainty making them unpredictable. There can be a turn of events that creates shared meaning with the media and the public. Hillary made perhaps her most well known remark in response to a reporter's questions when she said, " I suppose I could have stayed home and baked cookies and had teas, but what I decided to do was to fulfill my profession which I entered before my husband was in public life." (March 16, 1992)

One of the most widely shared quotes was when Clinton said, "I feel your pain." This took place when he was interrupted by an AIDS activist at a campaign rally. While this phrase came to characterize his empathy for people, at the time Clinton was reported in the media as being angry. He said, "If I were dying of ambition, I wouldn't have stood up here and put up with all this crap I've put up with for the last six months." "You do not have the right to treat any human being, including me, with no respect because of what you're worried about." "I have treated you and all the people who've interrupted my rally with a hell of a lot more respect than you've treated me, and it's time you started thinking about that. I feel your pain, I feel your pain, but if you want to attack me personally you're no better than Jerry Brown and all the rest of these people who say whatever sounds good at the moment." " If you don't agree with me, go support somebody else for president but quit talking to me like that." (Campaign Rally, Laura Belle Nightclub, New York, NY, March 27, 1992)

While candidates work hard to develop their public identity and shape voters' perceptions, there comes along a shared meaning that preexists in the public mind to create an emotional response, so that they may not even be aware of it. This can happen when candidates unintentionally share meaning with unintended consequences. These instances can be too specific or contingent on individual circumstances to analyze in any general sense. However, there is one that has reoccurred in several election campaigns potentially affecting their outcome. This is what could be characterized as the Dick Grayson effect.

There has been much debate over the degree to which a vice presidential candidate affects a presidential candidate's legitimacy. Since the two candidates are going to spend a lot of time together, it is natural for the public to form perceptions and make comparisons between them. One potential perception is based on Dick Grayson, the fictional name for the comic book character Robin, of Batman and Robin. When seen together, the two candidates can have a resemblance to the actors from the 1960's television program. A vice presidential candidate, a side kick of sorts, who shows comparatively youthful vigor can be perceived by some as immaturity or lack of fitness for office, which can affect people's perception.

Picture in your mind George Bush and Dan Quayle, their gestures and speaking styles. Then picture Batman and Robin. Consider other candidates like John Kerry and John Edwards, Bob Dole and Jack Kemp, or Mitt Romney and Paul Ryan. Perhaps even John McCain and Sarah Palin. Preexisting dramatic narratives can affect media characterizations and public perception of candidates influencing how people vote without their necessarily being aware of them. It is significant that these candidates failed in their bid for office. Additionally, McCain was characterized by the media as a womanizer with an eye for attractive women, who married a model and beauty queen. So, did he select Palin so he could be seen and photographed campaigning with two attractive women, Palin and his wife? (The Times, June 17, 2008, Daily Mail, June 7, 2008, LA Times, July 11, 2008)

5. Negative Campaigning. In every election campaign there is the issue of negative campaigning and who slings the first handful of mud. In the 1992 presidential campaign, there is no doubt that Clinton was the first to negative campaign. He was the first to do it in his early primary speeches beginning with his announcement to run in which he chastised the corrupt values in Washington. He also ran the first negative television commercials of the general election attacking the Bush economic record.

Despite the criticism over negative campaigning, it is a very effective tool for a candidate to utilize. Just as literary forms like novels and movies use heroes and villains engaged in conflict to connect with an audience, political dramatic narratives also utilize heroes to save the people from villains out to harm them. Candidates utilize dramatic narratives to make voters fearful or angry of their opponent by characterizing them as a villain who is destroying the country and everything the people hold dear. This can motivate people to withdraw their support of their opponent and vote against them. Voters are more likely to support a candidate who is cast as the hero who will save them from a terrible fate or impending crisis. Throughout the campaign voter response to negative campaigning suggests that they actually encourage candidates to do it.

Negative campaigning serves to delegitimize an opponent by increasing the voters' perception of uncertainty about them. The more voters are uncertain about a candidate and what they will do, the more likely they are to be motivated to vote against them by voting for their opponent. If an incumbent is a well meaning person whose ideas aren't too bad just different, why vote to unseat them? If two candidates are well meaning, but have different ideas, people can be less motivated to even vote at all. The lack of voter turnout may be more due to the perception that electing either candidate will result in the same outcome, rather than due to voter apathy.

The accusation of negative campaigning can be used effectively to neutralize an opponent. If a candidate complains that their opponent is using unfair tactics or dirty tricks it can create a chilling effect motivating them to reduce or stop their negative ads, particularly if they are working and are sharing meaning with the voters. This can be an effective diversionary tactic to draw public attention away from their own negative ads. Clinton used this tactic effectively by accusing Bush and the Republicans of dirty tricks and being unfair, while running negative ads of his own.

A candidate could interpret the intensity of an opponent's negative campaigning as a measure of how well their own dramatic narratives are being shared. A candidate is more likely to run negative ads against an opponent they perceive as a threat to their candidacy. Complaining about a candidate's negative campaigning can be a form of negative campaigning in and of itself. However, it is not negative campaigning to point out an opponent's shortcomings, failures, and weaknesses. This is part of the process of legitimizing a candidate and testing their fitness for office. However, there is an ethical line that should not be crossed between what is considered political and what is personal.

6. Persuasive Ability. From his announcement speech to election eve, the Clinton version of social reality was the most fully developed and complete of any of the candidates. Clinton was the only candidate to use all available means of persuasion to create his legitimacy to govern. He used massive amounts of repetition and reiteration to hammer home his message. In order to persuade people to vote

for him, Clinton had to demonstrate that change was essential. He did this by constructing a version of social reality characterizing Bush as corrupt and repugnant to persuade people to abandon their previously held beliefs. He then constructed an attractive social reality to persuade them to support him. The Clinton dramatic narrative of change proved to be so persuasive it was used by Perot and even adopted later by Bush.

In order to persuade the people to vote for him, Bush tried to use the dramatic narratives of trust and experience, which Clinton was fairly successful in undermining. Perot was initially successful in persuading people that he knew how to get things done, so he could solve the nation's problems. However, he undermined his own persuasive ability by dropping out of the race. When he did return, his dramatic narratives about himself were effective in restoring some of the public's support, but it was not enough to win

Social Reality and Society.

In any society there is a larger overriding social reality that is shared by the people into which a candidate can fit their own version of social reality. This includes an overriding set of dramatic narratives that forms a nation's social reality. All three candidates utilized this social reality in order to create their own dramatic narratives, so that they could more easily share meaning with the voters. The nature of social reality and dramatic narratives utilized in political campaigns can have larger ramifications for society.

People create dramatic narratives that tell the public what is valued, what is important, and how to make sense of events. How a society interprets social reality through shared meaning can determine how successful it can become. The creation of dramatic narratives can determine the success or failure of many endeavors like businesses, products, advertising, music, television, and movies.

The media is the primary means by which we communicate dramatic narratives in society including entertainment, news, and politics. This is important because it tells us about how we perceive ourselves and what we value. For instance, if people are constantly told that the economy is in trouble, they may come to believe it whether or not it is actually true. Instead of people perceiving reality as it is, their shared meanings can motivate behavior to make their perception a reality. How we as a society come to perceive things like right and wrong is often socially constructed.

If enough people come to think something is right, does that make it right?

Chapter 12
Capitol Hillary

Considering his own statements and actions, there is a substantial amount of evidence that George Bush did not want to seek nor serve a second term as president. From the very beginning, Bush seemed reluctant to campaign and when he did, there was little drive shown to win. For instance, during the New Hampshire primary, Bush did not begin to campaign until his public image was tarnished by a challenge from Pat Buchanan.

Typically, a candidate will formally announce that they are running for office in a place of significance to them and their candidacy, and then begin campaigning. In Bush's case, he did not announce that he would run for reelection until February 12th, only six days before the February 18th New Hampshire primary.

Since Bush had been defending himself against Buchanan since January 16th, it was inconceivable that he would campaign for so long before formally announcing that he was running for president. In contrast, Bill Clinton announced his candidacy on October 3, 1991 and campaigned for four months before New Hampshire.

During the primaries, Bush only responded to criticism and did not develop any kind of coherent campaign until September 10th. By Bush's own admission, he spent the primaries in the White House, conducting the nation's business. Suffering relentless personal attacks, he waited until after the summer convention to address them.

If Bush was waiting until after the GOP Convention in August to begin to campaign, he waited an additional critical three weeks until he announced his plan for the nation in September. In contrast, Clinton went directly from the Democratic National Convention in July to the campaign trail and was campaigning during the Republican National Convention.

It was not until September 10th, that Bush announced his campaign plan called An Agenda for American Renewal. Since the Republican Convention ended August 20th, why did he wait so long to begin campaigning?

By waiting until September, Clinton gained an insurmountable advantage that Bush could not overcome. During the time Bush was not campaigning, Clinton was able to redefine Bush and set the agenda for the rest of the campaign. By the time Bush entered the race, public opinion about him and the issues had largely been formed.

When Bush did enter the race, there was little focus to his campaign. As time went by, the focus of his campaign kept changing. First it was family values, then it was change, and then it was experience and trust. His campaign commercials asked people who they would trust in a crisis and who had the experience to run the country, yet they failed to clearly assert that Bush was that person. Clinton and Perot set up similar dramatic narratives of action, but they placed themselves in the center of their own dramas as the obvious choice to be the agent of change.

Bush's campaign style and rhetoric was much weaker in 1992 than during the 1988 campaign. In 1988, he made definite statements like, "I will be president it is my destiny" and the famous "read my lips, no new taxes." In 1992, Bush would say that he hoped he had passed the muster of the people and they would support him. He would end speeches and the debates by saying, "I hope you will let me continue to be your president."

This was a decidedly different message and delivery style. When compared to 1988, in 1992 Bush appeared to be going through the motions as if he had to be convinced it was his duty to run for reelection, rather than being motivated by his own initiative.

During the general election, Bush made many mistakes that proved to be detrimental to his campaign. By admitting he had made a mistake by breaking his tax pledge, he damaged his own credibility undermining his legitimacy to be president. When he said that he had mismanaged the economy and asked for the resignation of his economic advisors to demonstrate a second term would be different, he proved Clinton's assertion that his domestic policy had been a failure.

When he used family values, Bush let Clinton define what he meant by it. And when Bush adopted the issue of change, he undermined his own legitimacy because if change was needed, what had he been doing for the last four years?

There can be an aversion to candidates who seek political power, but they must clearly say that they want to be elected to office because all too often it is only implied. Bush seemed to avoid saying that he wanted to be reelected, while Clinton frequently asked the people to elect him president. Political parties and campaign donors should require candidates to be able to clearly articulate their version of social reality utilizing dramatic narratives that will share meaning with the voters before getting their support.

No candidate should run out of convenience, duty, to help their resume, to get a book deal, to increase their speaking fees, to get attention, to further a cause, to bolster or repair their public image, because it's their turn, because they are the incumbent, or to fulfill other people's expectations. A candidate should run because they want the job and will campaign to the best of their ability to get it. As Clinton often put it he would, "work his heart out."

Many people who were instrumental in the two Reagan and first Bush victories were conspicuous by their absence. Some were reported in the media to have been waiting to be called to help, but were never asked. Bush did not effectively utilize people like Ed Rollins, Peggy Noonan, or Ronald Reagan. Reagan did not defend attacks on his legacy or appear in campaign ads. Even the Bush campaign's most valuable campaigner, First Lady Barbara Bush was reported in the media to have wanted to stay in the White House and not campaign, leading to speculation that she was tired of politics.

Years later, Mrs. Bush would say in an interview, "I love Bill Clinton." "I think he (Bill) thinks of George a little bit like the father he didn't have." (C-SPAN, Daily Mail, January 22, 2014) She told about how, "Bill visits us every summer." She also said in an interview that the Clintons had saved them from having to endure what would have been the worst four years of their life.

These statements raise the question, if she is so comfortable with Clinton given what he said about her husband during the campaign, what were her true feelings about serving a second term? While some negativity has come to be expected in election campaigns, there were instances when Clinton got personal saying things like Bush had abandoned families, lied to the people, and would do anything to get elected because he was "personally untrustworthy."

If ever a party missed an opportunity it was the Republicans in 1992. There was little success in explaining Bush's accomplishments or his reasons for vetoing key legislation. During the campaign, Bush ran against Congress, yet Congressional leaders and many members from both parties did not seem to publicly support either candidate, giving the impression of wanting to sacrifice the election.

With a new president in office, some in Congress could raise taxes and pass programs they may have wanted, but could not publicly support. This raises the question, some members of Congress publicly state they are against raising taxes and want to lower them, but do they acquiesce to other members because they really want to raise taxes to increase revenues, but then don't have to deal with the repercussions? Consider that after the election, Congress blocked Clinton's economic stimulus package, but allowed tax increases to pass.

During the campaign, Bush spent a great deal of time criticizing Congress calling them obstructionist because he felt personally betrayed by them. However, he did not effectively utilize the House post office or banking scandals to criticize them. Bush often said that he had to put up with excessive pork and "Christmas tree ornaments" Congress had added to bills in order to get the programs Bush wanted. However, no one in Congress answered his accusations, instead Congressional leaders and high profile Democrats hid out during the campaign. They were conspicuous by their absence from the Democratic National Convention and did not campaign for Clinton, even though he had their support.

Bush often referred to political tradeoffs with an obstructionist Congress. It was in one of these tradeoffs, the 1990 Budget Deal, when Bush agreed to raise some taxes in exchange for spending cuts from Congress to reduce the deficit and balance the budget. Bush often said that he had given his hand in friendship to Congress and they "had bitten it."

This would explain his anger with Congress during the campaign and why he made a nonperson entity that was not in the race such a prominent villain in his dramatic narratives. Given that Clinton used Bush raising taxes as a major issue, it is understandable that Bush later accused Congress of being in "cahoots" with Clinton.

One way legislation could be used to undermine the legitimacy of an incumbent president could be illustrated by the tax compromise of 1990. In passing a combination of spending cuts and tax hikes, the Democratically controlled Congress had fashioned a bill that could potentially hurt Bush no matter what he did.

If he did not sign it, he could be accused of vetoing spending caps as proof that he was not willing to hold down government spending making the deficit worse and mortgaging our children's future. If Bush signed the bill, he could be characterized as being deceitful for breaking his "read my lips, no new taxes" pledge, which would damage Bush's legitimacy.

Bush signing the bill into law was Clinton's most frequently used argument to convince voters that Bush was unfit for office and to legitimize Clinton's candidacy. As president, Bush could have gone to the American people to explain the tax bill before he signed it.

Unfortunately, he seemed reluctant to explain or defend any of his decisions or actions assuming the people would just 'get it.' With little information provided by Bush, the condition was right to characterize the nation's problems as being caused by him, making the passage of this bill a no win situation for Bush because he had been backed into a corner.

During the campaign it was common for Bush's charges against Clinton to be covered in a news report that would be followed by Clinton's response. Conversely, a Bush rebuttal of a Clinton accusation was much less often the case. The slow responses to Clinton's attacks by Bush gave the appearance of weakness and an admission of guilt.

In October, Bush aired a commercial that showed specific examples of how much people's taxes would increase if Clinton was elected. Within a day, Clinton responded with an ad of his own that showed the Bush ad pointing out where it was wrong. A similar incident had occurred in September when Bush unveiled his plan for America. A video with Clinton's response was aired immediately after Bush's announcement was aired on C-SPAN.

It is helpful for a candidate to have a rapid response team to reply to their opponent's charges and assertions. However, Clinton often responded to Bush so fast it raises the question of how this was accomplished.

The on again, off again, candidacy of Ross Perot was yet another factor that worked against Bush. Perot's actions appeared to be erratic and unpredictable on the surface, but consider what he actually accomplished. While Perot occasionally mentioned his concerns with Clinton, the brunt of his attacks were concentrated on the problems in Washington, which meant Bush. In one of his television programs, Perot said that his problem with the people in Washington was that they had abandoned military personnel during the Vietnam War.

Perot had well known differences with Bush over how this issue was handled. Perot thought the government should demand that they all be accounted for and shouldn't leave even one person behind. He had helped many POWs and their families. For instance, he was reported to have paid the medical bills for John McCain's first wife when she was injured in a car accident while he was a POW in Vietnam. (New York Times, February 27, 2000)

If timing is everything in politics, when Perot dropped out of the race he chose the best moment to maximize the benefit to Clinton and inflict maximum damage to Bush. Before Perot entered the race, the majority of the voters supported Bush. After Perot entered the race and began criticizing Bush, many voters changed their support until the majority was against Bush. Perot did this by creating a version of social reality remarkably close to Clinton's version.

So, when Perot dropped out, his supporters switched to Clinton two to one over Bush. It was at this time, for the first time in the campaign, that a majority of the people supported Clinton instead of Bush. Up until then, Clinton had been in third place trailing both Bush and Perot. This was a major shift in voter preferences that Bush would never be able to overcome.

Whether he intended to or not, Perot had in effect handed Clinton the election. While Perot had given Clinton the support he needed to win, it was up to Clinton to maintain that support. Clinton was in a position to benefit from Perot's withdrawal because he had created a version of social reality that would attract and keep Perot supporters, so they would not vote for Bush.

Perot had one of the most successful independent candidacies in history, and for a time eclipsed both Clinton and Bush in the polls. Riding a wave of popular support, Perot unexpectedly dropped out of the race. When he withdrew, he said it was because his opinion of Clinton and the Democratic Party had improved. They were renewed and were now addressing the issues.

When he reentered the race, he changed his mind saying that the candidates were not addressing the problems the people wanted solved. This raises questions as to what motivated these seemingly bizarre actions that defied any conventional approach to political campaigns.

fter his withdrawal from the race, Perot faced growing criticism in the media while his approval ratings fell in the polls. It may have been this damage to his public image that prompted him to return to the campaign.

Before his withdrawal, Perot's messages dealt with the problems in Washington. After his return, most of his television time was devoted to presenting personal accolades from people who knew him and telling the nation what kind of person he really was. By his own definition Perot was results oriented, a get things done kind of person. His strongest claim to be president was that he could make things happen because he had the experience to get results.

It can be insightful to evaluate Perot's candidacy based on his own criteria in terms of what he actually accomplished. He frequently said that he was a person who could get things done. So what did he do? In evaluating the results of his efforts, Perot did not win the election nor did he significantly increase public concern about the issues he said were important. What he did accomplish was to improve his approval ratings and his standing with the public.

By the end of the campaign, he had less people voting for him then he would of had in July, but he maintained a large number who felt he was a person who stood up for what he believed. Judging by his actions and his statements, as the election progressed it seemed that Perot never actually wanted to be elected president. He often said that only a crazy person would want the job.

Perhaps he himself summed up the motivation for his actions best when he said he had given up trying to be the pearl in the oyster or the oyster that created the pearl, instead his fate was being the grain of sand that irritated the oyster to make the pearl.

From Campaigning To Governing.

From the moment Clinton assumed the mantel of the Presidency, he needed to forge a new social reality. As a candidate, he campaigned to increase uncertainty in the minds of the voters to motivate them to vote for him, so he could win the election. This meant that his old version of social reality had to be divisive, critical, and negative, at least in part, because people are more likely to be motivated to vote by feelings of discontent, uncertainty, anger, or fear.

In order to govern as president, Clinton must reduce uncertainty by being inclusive because now he represents all Americans, not just those who supported him. He must make the transition from campaigning to governing. A transition other presidents had made.

After an election, a president, or any other elected official, must forge a new version of social reality that is inclusive of all the people, especially those who voted against them. This new social reality serves to bring people together to reduce uncertainty, so the public can have confidence in their leaders and the government. This helps a candidate make the transformation from a candidate to become a leader. Failure to do so can result in political divisions not healing.

This transformation is the process of political development that will further a politician's career. It begins with a candidate who must create uncertainty about their opponent by being divisive and negative. After they are elected, they need to make the transformation to become a leader. This involves working with people including members of the other party.

They must exhibit leadership qualities, which includes being able to build consensus to get things done. After serving in office for many years, they may be considered a statesman, which is a politician who puts the good of the nation and the people above political considerations, even above their own interests.

For a candidate who ran on change, Clinton appeared reluctant to change after being elected. Instead of legitimizing his presidency by governing, Clinton continued to utilize campaign style dramatic narratives that had brought him electoral success to support his version of social reality.

Continuing to utilize campaign techniques as a means of governing after an election can serve to maintain a version of social reality that may exclude some of the electorate maintaining the divisiveness of the campaign, inhibiting the larger social reality from unifying the nation.

This marked the beginning of the never ending campaign and the culture of divisiveness that is prevalent in politics and society today. Continuing to govern by campaigning likely contributed to the Republican resurgence of 1994.

Governing and campaigning are different processes. Campaigning is about galvanizing support, so people are motivated to go out and vote for a candidate and support their campaign. This often entails being divisive, negative, and casting the opponent as a villain, so that people will be motivated to vote against them.

Governing is a different process than campaigning. Governing is about unity, creating consensus, and considering the greater good. It is about being gracious, consolatory, and working together with people including those who disagree with you or who are on the opposite side of the political fence.

Bush used governing as a means of campaigning by saying that he was running the nation's business as justification for not getting out of the White House to campaign. As a result, he was characterized as having experience, but lacked a plan for the nation.

Clinton was an effective campaigner, but used campaign techniques to govern that carried the divisiveness of the campaign into his administration. Each of the candidates seemed to have a different approach when it came to campaigning as well as governing, with varying degrees of success. So,

Campaign like a Democrat, govern like a Republican.

Capitol Hillary.

Eight years later...\

So, what does a former president and his wife do after leaving office? Where do they live after having lived in the White House? Most presidential couples have done something similar, except the Clintons did something that no other presidential couple in recent times has ever done.

Truman was born in Missouri and returned to his home in Independence after leaving the presidency to live in the Wallace home he and his wife Bess had shared for years with her mother.

Eisenhower retired to Gettysburg, Pennsylvania near his ancestral home of York. Johnson was born in Stonewall, Texas, so after leaving office he went home to his ranch in Stonewall. Nixon was born in Yorba Linda, California and retired in San Clemente, California.

Carter was born in Plains, Georgia and returned there after his presidency. Reagan was born in Tampico, Illinois, but spent most of his life in California as an actor and governor. After leaving office he moved to Bel Air, California, spending time at his ranch near Santa Barbara.

George H. W. Bush was born in Milton, Massachusetts and moved to Texas representing it in Congress before being elected president. After leaving the White House, he retired to Houston and Kennebunkport, Maine. George W. Bush was born in New Haven, Connecticut and moved to Texas becoming governor. After leaving office he moved to Dallas.

Only Gerald Ford did something different. He was born in Omaha, Nebraska, grew up in Grand Rapids, Michigan, and represented them in Congress. He moved to Denver, Colorado after leaving office.

After leaving the Presidency and moving out of the White House, the Clinton's did not go back to their home as did other presidential couples. They went to New York and Hillary went on to Capitol Hill. Instead of representing the citizens of her home state of Arkansas, who had helped her husband win the White House and her become First Lady, Hillary represented New York in the US Senate, a state with which she had no discernible connection or history.

Since then,

After many years and many elections, politicians utilize many of the same dramatic narratives and people still vote for them. This brings up several questions.People consistently express their discontent with the government and its failure to get things done, yet they keep reelecting the same people. Why do the voters keep accepting explanations like, "If you like your health insurance you can keep it," (Used over 37 times between June 6, 2009 and March 19, 2010) or, "I did not have sexual relations with that woman." (January 26, 1998) Or "weapons of mass destruction." (October 16, 2002.)

Perhaps, it's because people vote for labels or ideology rather than the person and their qualifications. Perhaps, they vote for the benefits candidates promise them. Perhaps, it's time for the people to hold politicians to a higher standard.

Perhaps, people should stop blaming their elected leaders and take responsibility for voting them into office in the first place. Perhaps, voters should stop being motivated by party affiliation, ideology, and negative campaigning. Candidates will stop the negativity and divisiveness when people stop responding to it. Voters need to learn about the issues and the candidates' positions for themselves, so that they can cast an informed vote and not rely on the opinions of others.

Perhaps the process of choosing candidates bears examination. Based on the evidence of their overall effectiveness, the current primary system should be abolished and replaced with a national primary system, because it is inherently undemocratic for the same small group of voters to determine who the vast majority can vote for in every presidential election.

The current system allows third party and independent candidates to circumvent the primaries and go directly to the general election, so they are not subjected to the same review and scrutiny that the two major party candidates must undergo.This can potentially undermine the legitimacy of the electoral process when third parties prevent the winner from getting a majority of the votes cast. They should have to participate in the primaries and meet a minimum threshold in order to proceed to the general election.

In examining the 1992 presidential campaign and its outcome, Clinton was the beneficiary of a series of events. It began with Buchanan challenging Bush from within his own party. Buchanan's attacks shared meaning with the voters and were later used effectively by Clinton and Perot against Bush.

Buchanan forced Bush to become more conservative making him appear extreme. This allowed Clinton to claim the middle ground as a moderate. Perot attacking Bush likely did the most damage to Bush and his withdrawing from the race when he did catapulted Clinton into the lead for the first time in the campaign.

So, what if events had played out differently? It is likely that if it were not for Buchanan and Perot, Bush could have won a second term and the Reagan Revolution would have continued. Given the pattern of history, it is likely that a Democrat would have followed a second Bush term in 1996.

But who would it have been? It is not likely it would have been Clinton, because political parties don't readily give losing candidates a second chance to run. The last time that happened was with Nixon who lost in 1960 and would have to wait eight years until 1968 before running again to win.

If just a few things had been different, it is plausible that there would have been no Clinton Presidency. So, Hillary would not have been First Lady, which she used to legitimize her running for the Senate and going to Capitol Hill, and then to run for the presidency.

So, if there had been no Clinton Presidency, how would American politics be different today?

A Unified American Social Reality.

The importance of creating and maintaining social reality extends beyond political campaigns to maintaining the very survival of a nation itself. The creation of a unified social reality has been used throughout history for nation building and sustaining. The United States came together as a society with a common social reality of being uniquely American, based on the principles set out by its founders.

As history unfolded, many dramatic narratives were added to the larger American social reality based on their collective shared meanings like the Declaration of Independence, the American Revolution, the Great Awakening, westward expansion and Manifest Destiny, the Civil War, the Great Depression, World War I and II, the New Deal, the Cold War, and the war on terror, as well as others.

The fracturing of a unified social reality can be seen in other nations like Canada, Spain, and The United Kingdom. These are nations where different social realities manifested themselves in separatist movements, such as Quebec, Scotland, and the Basque region. In these instances, the nation remained intact, but political concessions often had to be made to keep it together.

In some cases, nations have even broken up including Yugoslavia, Czechoslovakia, and the USSR. In the breakup of the Soviet Union, the people of the former Soviet states such as Latvia, Lithuania, and Estonia did not seem to share a common social reality with Russia, so when given the opportunity they succeeded. In Germany, unification was possible despite enormous economic and political costs because there was a historically unified social reality.

If America becomes a nation of two or more competing social realities with no unified American social reality, they might find a political voice that could lead to separatist movements or potentially divide the nation. Such a division did take place at one time resulting in the Civil War. The lack of any such legitimate political movements signifies that there still is an American social reality, battered though it may be.

However, the increasing polarization of political ideology has become manifested in not only political systems that become increasingly unable to function, but in our communities. This is evidenced by the shrinking number of battleground or swing states and districts in elections.

When social reality fractures what can be done to restore it? If one version of social reality breaks down, what will take its place? A new social reality can grow naturally from dramatic narratives that share meaning with people throughout society or it can be created intentionally by groups or individuals.

A fractured social reality can be restored if the people want it. A leader, like the president or presidential candidates can help to forge a social reality that values unity and working together for the good of all people and the nation. It has happened in the past, so it can happen again.

For society to function effectively, there must be a common social reality that the people and their leaders support and reaffirm.

ABC News Poll, January 28, 1992.
ABC World News Tonight, [Television]. January 15, 1992.
ABC World News Tonight, [Television]. March 6, 1992.
ABC World News Tonight, [Television]. August 26, 1992.
ABC World News Tonight, [Television]. October 28, 1992.
ABC News, This Week, [Television]. August 23, 1992.
Bond, R., [Speech]. Republican National Convention, Houston, TX, August 17, 1992.
Bradley, B., [Speech]. Democratic National Convention, New York, NY, July 13, 1992.
Brown, R., [Speech]. Democratic National Convention, New York, NY, July 13, 1992.
Buchanan, P., [Speech]. Republican National Convention, Houston, TX, August 17, 1992.
Buchanan, P., [Television]. Television Commercials, (1992).
Bush, B., [Television]. Interview, C-SPAN, January 22, 2014.
Bush, G., [Booklet]. Agenda for American Renewal and Accomplishments Through Leadership. 1992.
Bush, G., [Television]. Network Address, September 12, 1992.
Bush, G., [Press Releases]. Backgrounder, July to August, 1992.
Bush, G., [Press Release]. Briefing Paper, August 15, 1992.
Bush, G., [Press Releases]. Bush Fact Sheets, April to August, 1992.
Bush, G., [Press Releases]. Bush On The Issues, January to February, 1992.
Bush, G., [Press Release]. Talking Points, August 14, 1992.
Bush, G., [Speech]. Inaugural Address, Washington, DC, January 20, 1989.
Bush, G., [Speech]. Announcement Speech, J.W. Marriott Hotel, Washington, DC, February 12, 1992.
Bush, G., [Speech]. Acceptance Speech, Republican National Convention, Houston, TX, August 20, 1992.
Bush, G., [Speech]. AT&T Corporate Headquarters, Basking Ridge, New Jersey, September 18, 1992.
Bush, G., [Speech]. Burrill Lumber, Medford, Oregon, September 14, 1992
Bush, G., [Speech]. Detroit Economic Club, Detroit MI, September 10, 1992.
Bush, G., [Speech]. National Guard Association, Salt Lake City, UT, September 15, 1992.
Bush, G., [Speech]. New Hampshire State Legislature, Concord, NH, February 12, 1992.
Bush, G., [Speech]. Republican National Committee, Gala Lunch, Houston, TX, August 21, 1992.
Bush, G., [Speech]. Small Business Legislative Council, February 5, 1992)
Bush, G., [Speech]. Tulsa, OK, September 22, 1992.
Bush, G., [Television]. Television Commercials, 1992.
CBS Evening News, [Television]. January 3, 1992.
CBS Evening News, [Television]. March 4, 1992.
CBS This Morning, [Television]. August 4, 1992.
CBS Evening News, [Television]. August 13, 1992.
CBS Evening News, [Television]. August 17, 1992.
CBS Evening News, [Television]. September 21, 1992.
CBS Evening News, [Television]. October 5, 1992.
CBS Evening News, [Television]. October 12, 1992.
CBS Evening News, [Television]. October 29, 1992.
Chicago Tribune, August 6, 1992.
Chicago Tribune, August 24, 1992.
Chicago Tribune, August 30, 1992.
Chicago Tribune, September 1, 1992.
Chicago Tribune, September 6, 1992.
Chicago Tribune, September 13, 1992.
Chicago Tribune, September 21, 1992.
Chicago Tribune, September 22. 1992.
Chicago Tribune, October 2, 1992.
Chicago Tribune, October 18, 1992.
Chicago Tribune, October 20, 1992.
Chicago Tribune, October 28, 1992.
Chicago Tribune, October 29, 1992.
Chicago Tribune, November 1, 1992.
Clinton, B., [Speech]. Announcement Speech, Little Rock, AR, October 3, 1991.
Clinton, B., [Speech]. Inaugural Address, Washington, DC, January 20, 1993.
Clinton, B., [Booklet]. Putting People First How We Can All Change America. (New York, NY: Times Books 1992).
Clinton, B., [Booklet]. Putting People First; A National Economic Strategy for America. (1992).
Clinton, B., [Booklet]. A Plan for America's Future, (1992).
Clinton, B., [Television]. Election Eve Telecast, November 1, 1992.
Clinton, B., [Press Release]. The Arkansas Record, February 1, 1992.
Clinton, B., [Press Release]. Creating Jobs, September 16, 1992.
Clinton, B., [Press Release]. Four Hundred CEO's Endorse Clinton, September 21, 1992.
Clinton, B., [Press Release]. Health Care Plan, September 24, 1992.
Clinton, B., [Speech]. Acceptance Speech, Democratic National Convention, New York, NY, July 16,1992.

Clinton, B., [Speech]. A New Covenant for American Security, Georgetown Univ., Washington DC, Dec 12, 1991.
Clinton, B., [Speech]. A New Covenant for Economic Change, Georgetown Univ., Washington DC, Nov 20, 1991.
Clinton, B., [Speech]. A New Covenant; Responsibility and Rebuilding the American Community, Georgetown University, Washington DC, October 23, 1991.
Clinton, B., [Speech]. American Federation of State, County, Municipal Employees, Las Vegas, NV, June 17, 1992.
Clinton, B., [Speech]. Campaign Rally, March 27, 1992.
Clinton, B., [Speech]. Cleveland City Club, Cleveland, OH, May 21, 1992.
Clinton, B., [Speech]. Democratic Leadership Council, New Orleans, LA, May 2, 1992.
Clinton, B., [Speech]. Drexel University, Philadelphia, PA, April 22, 1992.
Clinton, B., [Speech]. East Los Angeles College, Los Angeles, CA, May 14, 1992.
Clinton, B., [Speech]. Economic Club of Detroit, Detroit, MI, August 22, 1992.
Clinton, B., [Speech]. Foreign Policy Association, New York, NY, April 1, 1992.
Clinton, B., [Speech]. Los Angeles World Affairs Council, Los Angeles, CA, August 13, 1992.
Clinton, B., [Speech]. National Association of Manufactures, Washington DC, June 24, 1992.
Clinton, B., [Speech]. National Educational Association, Washington DC, July 7, 1992.
Clinton, B., [Speech]. University of Notre Dame, South Bend, IN, September 11, 1992.
Clinton, B., [Television]. Television Commercials, (1992).
Clinton, B. and H., [Television]. Sixty Minutes Interview, January 26, 1992.
CNN Newsmaker, [Television]. January 18, 1992.
CNN Headline News, [Television]. March 5, 1992.
CNN Headline News, [Television]. July 14, 1992.
CNN Headline News, [Television]. July 16, 1992.
CNN Headline News, [Television]. August 17, 1992.
CNN Headline News, [Television]. August 18, 1992.
CNN Headline News, [Television]. August 22, 1992.
CNN Headline News, [Television]. August 23, 1992.
CNN Headline News, [Television]. August 24, 1992.
CNN Headline News, [Television]. August 25, 1992.
CNN Headline News, [Television]. August 26, 1992.
CNN Headline News, [Television]. August 27, 1992.
CNN Headline News, [Television]. September 18, 1992.
CNN Headline News, [Television]. September 28, 1992.
CNN Headline News, [Television]. October 2, 1992.
CNN Headline News, [Television]. October 2, 1992.
CNN Headline News, [Television]. October 5, 1992.
CNN Headline News, [Television]. October 9. 1992.
CNN Headline News, [Television]. October 10, 1992.
CNN Headline News, [Television]. October 17, 1992.
CNN Headline News, [Television]. October 18, 1992.
CNN Headline News, [Television]. October 27, 1992.
CNN Headline News, [Television]. October 28, 1992.
CNN, The World Today, [Television]. September 20, 1992.
CNN/USA Today Poll, September 4, 1992.
Cuomo, Mario, [Speech]. Nomination Speech, Democratic National Convention, New York, NY, July 15, 1992.
Cuomo, Mario, [Speech]. University of Notre Dame, South Bend, IN, 1984.
Daily Mail, UK, January 22, 2014
Democratic Debate, [Television]. WMUR, Manchester, NH, January 19, 1992.
Democratic Debate, [Television]. WETA, Washington, DC, January 31, 1992.
Democratic Debate, [Television]. KUSA, Denver, CO, February 29, 1992.
Democratic Debate, [Television]. MPT, College Park, MD, March 1, 1992.
Democratic Debate, [Television]. WLS, Chicago IL, March 15, 1992.
Democratic Debate, [Television]. WNBC, New York, NY, April 5, 1992.
Democratic National Convention, [Official Program]. New York NY, July 13-16, 1992.
Democratic National Committee, [Press Release]. July 1, 1992.
Democratic Party Platform, [Booklet]. July 13, 1992.
The Gallup Poll, January 3, 1992.
The Gallup Poll, January 6, 1992.
The Gallup Poll, January 9, 1992.
The Gallup Poll, January 12, 1992.
The Gallup Poll, January 26, 1992.
The Gallup Poll, February 2, 1992.
The Gallup Poll, February 5, 1992.
The Gallup Poll, February 16, 1992.
The Gallup Poll, February 23, 1992.
The Gallup Poll, March 1, 1992.

The Gallup Poll, March 3, 1992.
The Gallup Poll, March 10, 1992.
The Gallup Poll, March 15, 1992.
The Gallup Poll, March 25, 1992.
The Gallup Poll, April 5, 1992.
The Gallup Poll, April 12, 1992.
The Gallup Poll, April 15, 1992.
The Gallup Poll, April 26, 1992.
The Gallup Poll, May 3, 1992.
The Gallup Poll, May 12, 1992.
The Gallup Poll, May 24, 1992.
The Gallup Poll, June 7, 1992.
The Gallup Poll, June 10, 1992.
The Gallup Poll, June 21, 1992.
The Gallup Poll, July 2, 1992.
The Gallup Poll, July 15, 1992.
The Gallup Poll, July 22, 1992.
The Gallup Poll, July 26, 1992.
The Gallup Poll, August 4, 1992.
The Gallup Poll, August 9, 1992.
The Gallup Poll, August 16, 1992.
The Gallup Poll, August 25, 1992.
The Gallup Poll, September 5, 1992.
The Gallup Poll, September 13, 1992.
The Gallup Poll, September 19, 1992.
The Gallup Poll, September 23, 1992.
The Gallup Poll, September 27, 1992.
The Gallup Poll, October 4, 1992.
The Gallup Poll, October 11, 1991.
The Gallup Poll, October 13, 1992.
The Gallup Poll, October 18, 1992.
The Gallup Poll, October 21, 1992.
The Gallup Poll, October 25, 1992.
The Gallup Poll, November 1, 1992.
The Gallup Poll, November 2, 1992.
The Gallup Poll, November 14, 1992.
The Gallup Poll, November 21, 1992.
The Gallup Poll, December 23, 1992.
Gallup/CNN/USA Today Poll, February 9, 1992.
Gingrich, N., [Speech]. Republican National Convention, Houston, TX, August 18, 1992.
Gore, A., [Speech]. Acceptance Speech, Democratic National Convention, New York, NY, July 16, 1992.
Houston Post, August 28, 1992.
Houston Post, September 12, 1992.
Jordan, B., [Speech]. Democratic National Convention, New York, NY, July 13, 1992.
Los Angeles Times, August 28, 1992.
Los Angeles Times, September 8, 1992.
Los Angeles Times, September 10, 1992.
Los Angeles Times, September 17, 1992.
Los Angeles Times, September 25, 1992.
Los Angeles Times, September 28, 1992.
Los Angeles Times, October 9, 1992.
Los Angeles Times, October 11, 1992.
Los Angeles Times, October 13, 1992.
Los Angeles Times, October 15, 1992.
Miller, Z., [Speech]. Democratic National Convention, New York, NY, July 13, 1992.
NBC Nightly News, [Television]. July 14, 1992.
NBC Nightly News, [Television]. August 22, 1992.
NBC Nightly News, [Television]. October 27, 1992.
NBC Nightly News, [Television]. October 28, 1992.
New York Times, January 14, 1992.
New York Times, January 24, 1992.
New York Times, January 27, 1992.
New York Times, January 28, 1992.
New York Times, January 29, 1992.
New York Times, January 30, 1992.

New York Times, February 19, 1992.
New York Times, March 30, 1992.
New York Times, April 25, 1992.
New York Times, April 30, 1992.
New York Times, July 10, 1992.
New York Times, July 11, 1992.
New York Times, July 12, 1992.
New York Times, July 13, 1992.
New York Times, July 16, 1992.
New York Times, July 17, 1992.
New York Times, July 23, 1992.
New York Times, August 10, 1992.
New York Times, August 12, 1992.
New York Times, August 16, 1992.
New York Times, August 17, 1992.
New York Times, August 18, 1992.
New York Times, August 21, 1992.
New York Times, August 22, 1992.
New York Times, August 28, 1992.
New York Times, August 29, 1992.
New York Times, August 30, 1992.
New York Times, September 10, 1992.
New York Times, September 12, 1992.
New York Times, September 17, 1992.
New York Times, September 19, 1992.
New York Times, September 21, 1992.
New York Times, September 27, 1992.
New York Times, October 1, 1992.
New York Times, October 2, 1992.
New York Times, October 3, 1992.
New York Times, October 13, 1992.
New York Times, October 18, 1992.
New York Times, October 19, 1992.
New York Times, October 24, 1992.
New York Times, October 26, 1992.
New York Times, February 27, 2000
New York Times/CBS Poll, January 10, 1992.
New York Times/CBS Poll, February 22, 1992.
New York Times/CBS Poll, April 25, 1992.
New York Times/CBS Poll, April 30, 1992.
New York Times/CBS Poll, October 6, 1992.
NPR, All Things Considered, [Radio]. August 18, 1992.
NPR, All Things Considered, [Radio]. September 23, 1992.
NPR, Morning Edition, [Radio]. October 29, 1992.
NPR, Morning Edition, [radio]. September 7, 1992.
PBS, The American Experience, [Television]. May 5, 2008.
PBS, Nightly Business Report, [Television]. October 28, 1992.
PBS, Washington Week, [Television]. January 3, 1992.
PBS, Washington Week, [Television]. March 6, 1992.
Perot, R., [Television]. CNN, Live with Larry King, February 20, 1992.
Perot, R., [News Conference]. C-SPAN, October 26. 1992
Perot, R., [Speech]. National Press Club, Washington DC, March 18,1992.
Perot, R., [Speech]. Announcement to re-enter race, Dallas, TX, October 1, 1991.
Perot, R., [Television]. Best Person, October, 1992.
Perot, R., [Television]. Business Success, October, 1992.
Perot, R., [Television]. Family, October, 1992.
Perot, R., [Television]. How to Build a Business, October, 1992.
Perot, R., [Television]. How to Vote, October, 1992.
Perot, R., [Television]. Last Week, October, 1992.
Perot, R., [Television]. Our Children, October, 1992.
Perot, R., [Television]. Pouring Money, October, 1992.
Perot, R., [Television]. Purple Heart, October, 1992.
Perot, R., [Television]. Rally, October, 1992.
Perot, R., [Television]. Red Flag, October, 1992.
Perot, R., [Television]. The Early Years, October, 1992.

Perot, R., [Television]. The Ross Perot Nobody Knows, October, 1992.
Perot, R., [Television]. The Storm, October, 1992.
Perot, R., [Television]. Time, October, 1992.
Perot, R., [Television]. Trickle Down, October, 1992.
Perot, R., [Television]. Unfinished Business, October, 1992.
Perot, R., [Television]. Washington Mess, October, 1992.
Perot, R., [Television]. We Can Win, October, 1992.
Perot, R., [Television]. Election Eve telecast, November 2, 1992.
Presidential Debate, Washington University, St. Louis, Missouri, October 11, 1992.
Presidential Debate, Richmond, Virginia, October 15, 1992.
Presidential Debate, Michigan State University, East Lansing, Michigan, October 19, 1992.
Quayle, D., [Speech] The Commonwealth Club of California, May 19, 1992.
Quayle, D., Acceptance [Speech]. Republican National Convention, Houston, TX, August 20, 1992.
Quayle, M., [Speech]. Republican National Convention, Houston, TX, August 19, 1992.
Reagan, R., [Speech]. Inaugural Address, Washington, DC, January 20, 1981.
Reagan, R., [Speech]. Republican National Convention, Houston, TX, August 17, 1992.
Republican National Convention, [Official Program]. Houston TX, August 17-20, 1992.
Republican National Committee, [Press Release]. Convention Themes in Houston, August 6, 1992.
Republican Party, Platform, [Booklet]. August 13, 1992.
Tsongas, P., [Speech]. Democratic National Convention, New York, NY, July 13, 1992.
University of Michigan, American National Election Study.
Washington Post, January 2, 1992.
Washington Post, January 3, 1992.
Washington Post, January 16, 1992.
Washington Post, February 19, 1992.
Washington Post, February 20, 1992.
Washington Post, March 12, 1992.
Washington Post, March 20, 1992.
Washington Post, July 12, 1992.
Washington Post, August 20, 1992.
Washington Post, August 23, 1992.
Washington Post, August 24, 1992.
Washington Post, September 8, 1992.
Washington Post, September 10, 1992.
Washington Post, September 23, 1992.
Washington Post, September 27, 1992.
Washington Post, September 30, 1992.
Washington Post, October 2, 1992.
Washington Post, October 3, 1992.
Washington Post, October 10, 1992.
Washington Post, October 14, 1992.
Washington Post, October 18, 1992.
Washington Post, October 20, 1992.
Washington Post, October 28, 1992.

HH
Heather Hill

www.ingramcontent.com/pod-product-compliance
Lightning Source LLC
Chambersburg PA
CBHW020611270326
41927CB00005B/275